BARNYARDS and
BIRKENSTOCKS

BARNYARDS and
BIRKENSTOCKS

Why Farmers and Environmentalists Need Each Other

DON STUART

Washington State University Press
Pullman, Washington

Washington State University Press
PO Box 645910
Pullman, Washington 99164-5910
Phone: 800-354-7360
Fax: 509-335-8568
Email: wsupress@wsu.edu
Website: wsupress.wsu.edu

Library of Congress Cataloging-in-Publication Data

Stuart, Donald D., 1943-
  Barnyards and Birkenstocks : why farmers and environmentalists need each other / Don Stuart.
    p. cm.
  Includes bibliographical references and index.
  ISBN 978-0-87422-322-4 (alk. paper)
1. Environmental protection—United States. 2. Agriculture—Environmental aspects—United States. 3. Farmers 4. Environmentalists. 5 Agriculture and state—United States. 6. United States—Environmental conditions—Political aspects. I. Title.
  GE197.S778 2014
  333.760973--dc23

                                                                                                    2014017376

Fine Quality Books from the Pacific Northwest

*For Charlotte, whose ideas made this book
and whose love made it possible.*

Contents

Acronyms	viii
Introduction: The Cherry Valley Dairy	1
1. The Farm–Environmental Paradox	7
2. Farmland—Why We Lose It and Where It Goes	15
3. Agriculture's Environmental Risks	29
4. Opportunities Lost When Farms Disappear	49
5. Voluntary Incentives—Pro and Con	61
6. Regulations—Pro and Con	77
7. Choosing Between Incentives and Regulations	99
8. Taxes and Government Spending	115
9. Environmental Markets	127
10. Local Food, Consumer Influence, and Farmer Privacy	145
11. Choosing Between Zoning and Conservation Easements	163
12. Climate Change	185
13. Livestock, the Public Lands, and the Environment	195
14. The Federal Farm Bill	211
15. Tools for Dialogue—the Common Ground	225
16. Two Visions for the Future of Agriculture and the Environment	235
Notes	243
About the Author	274
Index	275

Acronyms

ACEP—Agricultural Conservation Easement Program

AFBF—American Farm Bureau Federation

AFT—American Farmland Trust

ARC—Agricultural Risk Coverage program

AUM—animal unit month

BAT—best available technology

BLM—Bureau of Land Management

BPT—best practicable technology

CAA—Clean Air Act

CAO—Critical Areas Ordinances

CEAP—Conservation Effects Assessment Project (CEAP)

COCS— Cost of Community Services

CRM—coordinated resource management

CREP—Conservation Reserve Enhancement Program

CRP—Conservation Reserve Program

CSA— consumer supported agriculture

CSP—Conservation Stewardship Program

CWA—Clean Water Act

DOE—Department of Ecology

EPA—Environmental Protection Agency (also USEPA)

EQIP—Environmental Quality Incentives Program

FACT—Wisconsin Farming and Conservation Together

FDA—Food and Drug Administration

FEMA—Federal Emergency Management Agency

FQPA—Food Quality Protection Act

FRPP—Farm and Ranchlands Protection Program

FSA—Farm Service Agency

IPM—integrated pest management

MAEAP—Michigan Agriculture Environmental Assurance Program

NPDES—National Pollution Discharge Elimination System

NRCS—Natural Resources Conservation Service

PDR—purchase of development rights

PLC—Price Loss Coverage program

SCS—Soil Conservation Service

SEPA—State Environmental Policy Act

TDR—transfer of development rights

TMDL—total maximum daily load

USDA—U.S. Department of Agriculture

USEPA—U.S. Environmental Protection Agency

USFS—U.S. Forest Service

USFWS—U.S. Fish & Wildlife Service

WHIP—Wildlife Habitat Incentives Program

WRP—Wetlands Reserve Program

WTO— World Trade Organization

The Cherry Valley Dairy

ERIC NELSON did everything right.

A successful career in government made him manager of agriculture programs for King County, Washington. His job was to help local farmers survive and prosper in one of the busiest, most rapidly growing counties in the nation.

But Eric was also a third-generation dairy farmer and his agricultural roots were calling. In mid-life, he gave up his career in the city to buy a dairy at the rural-urban edge, about forty-five minutes outside Seattle. He wanted this two-hundred-cow dairy farm to become a laboratory where he could put into practice everything he'd learned (and preached) about farming on the urban edge.

So he went for it.

Eric opened a farm market in his historic barn beside the Cherry Valley Road. He created a petting barn where visitors could bring their children to see the calves and perhaps buy one to raise themselves on their small rural properties further up the road. He offered punch cards to kids from the elementary school across the street who came in to buy apples, chocolate milk, or ice cream bars. When a card was full, he made a donation to the PTA. He sold his milk direct to Beecher's Cheese, a local artisan cheese company that had a new facility at Pike Place Market, the historic farmers market and tourist destination in the heart of downtown Seattle.

The Cherry Valley Dairy acquired a loyal direct-market clientele. Eric was recognized in the press as one of a new breed of progressive farmers building better local food systems for urban communities.

Eric's farm had been protected from development by a King County agricultural easement. So he didn't have to pay as much for the property as he would have had the land been eligible for residential subdivision. And he knew the county was committed to the success of farming on this site.

Eric wanted his customers to feel good about buying from him, and he believed in responsible citizenship. So he was committed, from the start, to managing his dairy so it would be friendly to the environment.

King County is at the heart of the Pacific Northwest's economic prosperity. It includes the City of Seattle and several thriving suburban cities that surround it. It is a major West Coast port, the home of Microsoft, the birthplace of Boeing. And like many American urban centers, it is growing. With two million people, King County contains a third of the population of the state of Washington. More than half the entire state's population is found in King and its two neighboring counties, Snohomish to the north and Pierce to the south.

The area immediately around the dairy is rural. But it isn't far from all that economic activity and growth. It lies right at the edge of the "rural-becoming-suburban" town of Duvall, Washington. Much of the farm's pasture is on flat, low-lying, flood-prone land near the Snoqualmie River. The dairy barn, farmhouse, and other structures are on slightly higher ground at the foot of a hill which rises just to the south. Further up that hill there are hundreds of homes that are a part of Duvall. Those homes are also part of the extended sprawl of greater urban Seattle, to which many of their owners commute to shop, do business, and work at places like Microsoft, Boeing, Amazon, Nordstrom, and T-Mobile.

Over the years, the growing residential development above Eric's farm has steadily increased the surface water runoff from all the new roads, roofs, and driveways. That runoff flows down the hillside, across Cherry Valley Road, and onto the farm. It carries with it the pollutants and sediment from all those new back yards and hardened surfaces.

Drainage of Eric's farm fields has historically required ditches to help remove surface water and keep the land dry enough to be farmed and grazed. Over the years those ditches became more important as the runoff from above increased. But the ditches needed maintenance. When the water coming down the hillside reached the low, flat land on Eric's farm, it slowed down and dropped most of its sediment load—filling up his ditches. As the uphill community grew, the ditches needed cleaning more and more frequently.

Unfortunately, cleaning mud out of ditches can damage salmon habitat, and endangered salmon are a big problem in the Pacific Northwest, a problem that worsens as the region grows. Water, muddied by dredging a ditch, can carry silt downstream and plug up the clean gravel beds needed by spawning fish. And it can spread accumulated pollution. These days, before farmers can clean ditches like the ones on the Cherry Valley Dairy, they must obtain a permit. These ditches are, after all, a kind of stream. They are either fish habitat themselves, or they are connected to it.

Permits usually require that the landowner carefully remove and relocate any fish, then temporarily divert or otherwise dewater the ditch before doing any work—a costly proposition. They often also require that the owner mitigate for any impacts of maintaining the ditch by planting trees and shrubs along its banks and by creating riparian buffers that are helpful for fish. This, too, can be costly. The buffer mitigation might destroy an access road that borders the ditch. Or it might require converting valuable working fields from growing marketable crops or pasturing livestock to, instead, providing unpaid-for habitat for salmon. Meeting all these requirements can easily run to many times the expense of the actual dredging. Getting the permits takes time. The farmer may need to begin applying for the next permit not long after completing the work under the one that preceded it. This becomes an ongoing expense for a dairy farmer already working hard to make a living in the face of highly uncertain milk prices.

As I said earlier, Eric tried to do things right. He thoroughly familiarized himself with this permitting process. He became a commissioner with his drainage district, a local government that helps landowners keep their property dry. He was elected to the board of supervisors of the King Conservation District, another local government that helps farmers improve their environmental performance. As a former King County employee, he understood the regulatory system and the politics that drove it.

But all that expertise didn't make meeting its demands any less of a challenge.

Over the years, Eric and his farmer-colleagues struggled with the logic and the social fairness of these permits. They asked themselves: Who is really to blame for this situation and who should be responsible for fixing it?

Certainly it was Eric who needed to clean out those drainage ditches in order to continue growing hay and grazing livestock. He made his living selling the milk he produced on this farm. Some of that sediment was caused by his activities. The presence of his cows, and of his ditches, definitely affected salmon habitat in the area. Clearly, some of the responsibility was his.

On the other hand, most of that silt did not come from Eric's farm. In fact, those healthy grass-pasture farm fields actually filter and remove much of the silt and pollution that comes down off the hill behind. If this farm had not been protected by an agricultural easement and had instead been developed into residential housing like the properties uphill, most of that surface water would now be in underground drainage pipes and out of sight. There wouldn't be any opportunities to create buffers or plant shrubs and trees along open ditches. All of the silt and pollution, and more, would be headed straight downstream with nothing to stop it. So it is a very good thing for the fish that this farm still exists. Its disappearance would be another in a long succession of small fish-habitat tragedies for the region.

Moreover, Eric's farm was there long before any of those houses were built on the hill above. When this farm was first homesteaded, there weren't many salmon problems, other, perhaps, than overabundance. In those days, the hillside may have been forest, as was most of King County. Small amounts of silt from occasional ditch-cleaning would have been quite insignificant.

But today, given all the other impacts on salmon—mostly caused by increasing economic activity throughout King and its adjacent counties— extra silt in the last remaining salmon spawning beds is a matter of real concern.

It is doubtful that the homeowners on the hill knew anything about Eric's problem. Most likely, the City of Duvall complied with all current laws when they permitted development of those homes. King County, not known for a relaxed attitude on environmental standards, no doubt did its best in establishing requirements for development throughout the county. The other towns up and down the Snoqualmie-Snohomish watershed probably did their best as well. The local environmental community has fought for years to protect those fish, seeking meaningful constraints on the new construction and varied business enterprises that affect the fish. Eric's ditch cleaning requirements were, no doubt, among their successes.

Clearly, all those laws and development requirements have not been good enough. The cumulative impact of the human activities in the region is just too great. The fish are still at risk, the runs still in decline, and Eric's farm is still under pressure.

One might ask why this dairy should even be located on that floodplain. Maybe it could be at the top of the hill instead of all those houses. It could, that is, were it not for the fact that the land at the top of that hill, even with no houses, would probably sell for upwards of $50,000 per acre—at least ten to twenty times what any dairy in the country could afford to pay for pasture or hay land. Since Eric's flood plain would be very costly to develop, it also contains the only land a farmer can afford to own and the only undeveloped land left where farming is possible. The existence of this undeveloped land, in this location, is why this farm is still in agriculture. Cherry Valley Dairy, like a great many other farms, is located in an environmentally sensitive place for the simple reason that this is the only place left for a farm to be.

Fair or not, Eric was the person who needed those ditch-cleaning permits. So he was the one from whom the public agencies were able (and needed) to extract fish mitigation conditions.

In 2011, Eric finally gave up the farm and returned to a job in the city. He now consults with local agencies and organizations to help save farms. His attitude toward his recent farming experiment is philosophical. Asked about it, he'll smile and say: "Well, I gave it my best shot."

There were other factors that contributed to Eric's decision to let go of his dream. And ditch maintenance is but one of many environmental challenges he and other farmers across our country face every single day. Most of these environmental problems are every bit as complicated as Eric's ditches. True responsibility for them is just as obscure. As we consider who is at fault for the ditch maintenance troubles on this historic local dairy farm, as we struggle to assign social responsibility and decide who should bear the burdens of fixing these and other environmental problems in agriculture, it isn't hard to see how people might have very different points of view.

Eric Nelson and friends, near Duvall, Washington. *Courtesy of Eric Nelson*

CHAPTER 1

The Farm–Environmental Paradox

Farmers and environmentalists need each other.

This may seem surprising since there is so much they disagree about. They fight over nearly every environmental issue we face: pollution, climate change, zoning, wildlife habitat, water rights, public lands.

Farming has extensive impacts on the environment, both good and bad. So farmers and environmentalists will always be inextricably bound together. Unfortunately, they have very different cultures, politics, and worldviews. Both would be far better off if they worked together—a farmer-environmentalist coalition would have immense political clout. But instead of cooperating, they are usually at odds. And their continuing fight has created a stalemate that damages American agriculture and cripples badly needed protections for the environment.

After working professionally with both farmers and environmentalists for many years, and after seeing scores of situations much like the one outlined in the introduction to this book, I've come to appreciate and respect the perspectives of each side and to find it painful to watch their conflict. Important public policy decisions driven by their disagreements are made every day in courtrooms, local government council chambers, state legislatures, and Congress. Their struggle has become a deepening tragedy affecting everyone.

On those occasions when they do agree, the gains are remarkable. But most of the time they fight. When they fight, they both lose, and so do the rest of us.

I believe the only way these two groups will ever come to terms is if each begins to see their issues through the eyes of the other. This book was written to provide that alternative insight, to demonstrate why their conflict is harming all of us, and to show how we can end it.

The Environmental Impact of Our Agricultural Landscape

Farmers and ranchers own and manage over half of the total United States land base, including some of our most environmentally sensitive areas. And farming transforms these landscapes. Native trees and vegetation must be removed to make way for crops. Excess water is drained. Dikes are built to control flooding. Energy is used. The soil is tilled. Fertilizer is added. Weeds are removed. Insects and other "pests" are controlled, often with chemical pesticides. The very contours of the natural landscape are changed. Native wildlife habitat is displaced when large areas are cultivated in a single plant type or grazed by livestock. Fresh water is diverted for irrigation.

Every one of these activities affects the environment. The impacts of all of them together can be profound. Much of this is the inevitable price of growing food for a massive global population. But how our farms are managed can make a very big difference.

While working farms can harm the environment, their continued existence can also help. When farms disappear, they are seldom replaced by native forest. Quite often they are developed. Unlike most developed lands, working farms filter surface and ground water and can improve water quality. They provide habitat and migration corridors for wildlife. They reduce atmospheric carbon, recharge our aquifers, and detain surface water to prevent flooding. They also create a barrier against inefficient and environmentally harmful urban sprawl. And they provide these services while still producing the food we humans need to exist.

So long as these farmlands continue in agriculture, they also offer some of our most affordable opportunities to upgrade society's environmental performance. For example, keeping farm fields in cover vegetation during the off season or limiting tillage can filter and remove impurities from polluted surface water. Restoring field edges to native shrubs or cultivating an off-season feed crop can create new habitat or resting and feeding places for birds and can aid the migration of other wildlife. The strategic application of chemical fertilizers, careful management of rangeland grazing, or recycling livestock waste to generate energy can reduce greenhouse gas emissions or sequester carbon. By conserving and leasing out excess water rights, farmers can help enhance the flows of over-appropriated streams and rivers. Keeping farmland in cultivation and out of development can improve the function of nearby critical environmental areas like wetlands and riparian zones along the edges of streams and rivers. These benefits can be accomplished at a much lower cost than one would need to pay for the same environmental improvements in any urban or developed landscape. And they can be much less costly than purchasing farmland outright for conversion to pure environmental use.

The need for cost-effective environmental gains of this kind has never been greater. And it will increase in the years ahead as rising populations, urban growth, land development, and other future economic activities (including farming) continue to degrade environmental quality. The public inclination to protect the environment is also likely to increase.

Where else might one look for similar opportunities for improvement? Our nation's public lands are already largely committed to the preservation of natural conditions, so opportunities for substantial environmental "lift" on those lands seem scant. Our urban and suburban areas are already committed to development. So, while we may seek to limit the worst of the harm we cause with new development, we would hardly look inside the city for inexpensive places to mitigate for the damage that inevitably results from it.

The question for both farmers and environmentalists is not whether we will see new environmental laws affecting agriculture, but what form those laws will take. Will those new laws prevent environmental degradation while also taking advantage of the amazing opportunities to dramatically enhance farmers' contributions to environmental quality? Or will we seek rigorous regulations and, where we can, completely convert our farms to pure environmental uses and out of agriculture entirely?

The outcomes will depend on whether farmers and environmentalists come to see each other's points of view and begin to work together. Or whether they continue to feud.

A Model for Change

Securing a future that includes both prosperous agriculture and a healthy environment will require powerful tools that can be decisive on a nationwide scale. Happily, there are such tools. Unhappily, none of them will be easy to secure:

1. *Regulation:* Agriculture needs an effective, clear, and stable regulatory framework for healthy farming practices. This framework must establish a minimum level of acceptable performance, protect the public interest, and be predictably, affordably, and consistently enforced. The rules must be strategic, fair, and sensitive to social and economic cost and constrained to address only those behaviors and activities that truly require regulating.

2. *Consumer marketplace:* We must leverage consumer concerns about the environment by creating new product and industry-wide certifications in the food processing and distribution sectors. This will simplify consumer choices and empower them to influence improved environmental performance by farm producers. But it will also require the creation of standards on which we can broadly agree.

3. *Incentives:* Our farm–environmental incentive programs must be much better funded at a level commensurate with the need. They must also be scrupulously strategic, cost effective, and used in a way that is fair to the tax-paying public as well as to farmers.

4. *Conservation economics:* Environmental incentive funds will go further and we will need less regulation if we take full advantage of the farm business benefits that can result from good environmental stewardship in agriculture. Both incentives and regulations can leverage and draw upon these built-in benefits. Specific examples are provided throughout this book.

5. *Environmental markets:* We must create sound environmental markets that tap funding from development to provide mitigation and offsets that can make up for the unavoidable damage it causes. We must use those funds to purchase inexpensive new environmental services from farmers while helping them practice agriculture profitably.

6. *Zoning:* We need effective land use laws that protect farms from sprawl and fragmentation but do so in a stable and predictable way so property owners can buy, hold, and manage their land without facing sudden changes in the underlying rules affecting its use, value, and ownership.

7. *Purchased development rights:* We need adequately funded programs that purchase development rights from farmers on our best farmlands. This will allow them to cash out the non-agricultural value of their land. And it will make continued use of the land for growing food and providing environmental services profitable and therefore sustainable.

8. *Economic viability:* Farmers are better able to stay on the land, and to afford environmental stewardship, if their farms are profitable. We must help by providing business, marketing, and economic development assistance to farmers seeking to remain in agriculture.

Each of these tools represents a promising part of the solution. Each has its strengths. But each also has its limits. None of them, alone, will be enough. We need all of them, together, if we are to deal with the massive, nationwide scope of the problems we face.

Polarized Solutions

If you look closely, these tools actually reflect just two basic points of view about how to solve these problems: we either compel people to behave as we feel they should, or we ask and incentivize them to do so.

Naturally, there is a fundamental difference of perspectives on these two approaches. That difference lies at the heart of the farmer–environmentalist dispute. It has polarized and isolated each side from the other and made each inflexible in their views on preferred solutions. People on both sides have come to feel certain they know which of these is best and often they feel theirs is the only answer.

All this "certainty" about the solutions can produce self-reinforcing, circular logic. When the proposed solutions to a problem seem onerous, it's easy to believe that no real problem exists. If there is no problem, the motives of those claiming that there is seem suspect. If you mistrust someone's motives, you're not likely to put much faith in what they're proposing.

But the problems are real. Both sides have legitimate concerns. Both have solutions that work and that are essential to the ultimate fix. We need the optimal use of all these tools if we are to succeed. The tragic reality is that ending the conflict between farmers and environmentalists turns out to be a lynchpin for creating the universal positive support and critical political mass required to get any of these solutions adequately adopted.

The Farm–Environmental Paradox

These circumstances have created a paradox both for environmentalists and for farmers.

Environmentalists tend to prefer regulation as a means to deal with environmental issues in agriculture. There are definitely times when regulation can work quite nicely, and occasions when it is the only workable answer. But it has its limits. The potential for overregulation in agriculture is very real. In addition, the diversity of agriculture, the vast numbers of farmers, and the complexity of their various circumstances all make it challenging, as well as socially and fiscally costly, to regulate this industry.

This poses a paradox for environmentalists. Of course, the loss of our farms could cost us jobs, worsen rural poverty, reduce availability of food, and could potentially make the United States as dependent on foreign food as we have become for oil. But even if we are prepared to accept these risks, there are also environmental downsides to excessive regulation. We could lose all those environmental services our farms provide. We could end up with a hopelessly fragmented rural landscape. In some places, we could see smaller farms replaced by larger corporate operations. In others, we could see farms replaced by environmentally damaging houses, factories, and shopping malls. We could discover that without the help of farmers the costs of making up for the inevitable environmental impacts of our nation's growth and prosperity are simply too high. Too much regulation of agriculture could actually turn out to be a big environmental mistake.

Farmers face their own paradox. Like other businesspeople, most farmers much prefer to deal with environmental issues through voluntary incentives funded by government and working through the marketplace. Existing government incentives programs can be quite effective, but there has never been enough public funding to make these programs work as they should. So incentive programs have come to lack credibility with many environmentalists. Without political support from environmentalists, there will never be enough funding to make these programs truly effective at the necessary scale, and they will never have the chance to become more credible. Farmers are also a steadily diminishing political minority in the United States and one that is badly misunderstood by the public. Their fight against the regulations favored by environmentalists alienates the environmental support they need to secure funding for the incentives they must have to avoid the need for those selfsame regulations. It sometimes alienates support from the broader urban public as well.

The Need for Balance and the Challenge of Fairness

The obvious answer, of course, is a balanced mix of reasonable regulations and soundly funded incentives—a mix of all of the tools listed above. That sounds like something farmers and environmentalists ought to be able to settle through negotiation and cooperation. Unfortunately it hasn't worked that way.

A major reason it has not lies in how hard it is to assign responsibility for environmental problems. Our nation's growing, vigorous, and diverse population generates conflicting social values: economic prosperity versus a healthy environment, for example. Finding equitable balance between those conflicting values is extremely challenging. Since we typically lack an agreed-upon rationale, let alone a process, for resolving these kinds of conflicts, we are forced to decide them in the political arena. Whether farmers or environmentalists win or lose is nearly always decided in Congress, at a state legislature, or before a local county or township council.

In these settings, the stakes are high. The decision-makers are often poorly informed. Science, logic, and fairness are far less important than is public perception and political clout. There are few rules. Decisions can go one way one day and the other the next. Outcomes are often all-or-nothing.

Given this setting for making decisions, of course they fight!

Why They Need Each Other

That farmers and environmentalists are destined to deal with one another does not, of course, mean they must be locked in combat. The reasons they should work together may not be intuitive, but they are straightforward nonetheless. Farmers need environmentalists and environmentalists need farmers for the same two reasons:

First, neither one is going to go away.

The need and public demand for environmental protection will continue and grow in the years ahead. And people will continue to eat. Both farmers and environmentalists are essential. Neither seems likely to be beaten into submission by the other any time soon. Each will retain substantial social and political influence in the years ahead.

Second, each is necessary to the success of the other.

A farming-friendly environmental community could help enhance the view of farmers as stewards of the land, engendering deep consumer, public, and political support. Environmentalists could help farmers secure funding for environmental incentives. They could help them get economic development assistance that keeps them profitable and on the land. They could motivate consumers to pay a premium for environmentally responsible, and American, farm products. If environmentalists demand excessive regulation or if they push for full restoration of farms to natural forests, wetlands, floodplains, and habitat, they could drive our farmers out of business. But they might also be willing to back away from the more painful farmer regulation if they could get good results by other means.

Conversely, an environmentally-friendly agriculture industry might voluntarily correct (or agree to regulation of) some of its current environmental issues. It might encourage the use of the many environmental measures that can also be helpful for farming. It might self-regulate in closely-knit farming communities, thereby easing the challenge of environmental enforcement. It might also offer dramatic new and inexpensive opportunities for restoration and other affirmative environmental improvements that are essentially impossible to regulate into existence. Famers could prevent adoption of important environmental policy and do a lot of damage. Or they could help environmentalists find reasonable and responsible solutions that might actually gain the political traction needed to get adopted.

Both farming and the environment are currently at risk. Each is in a position to do the other a lot of good. Each could help the other while advancing its own interests.

So an alliance between farmers and environmentalists could achieve political miracles for both. Of course, for such an alliance to emerge, each side must come to recognize their own need for the other's help. And each must feel sure that their counterparts fully understand that this interdependence is mutual.

Among the obstacles to farmer–environmental cooperation is the sense that these parties are so very far apart there is no way to bridge the immense gap between them. It turns out, however, that they do often cooperate, and much of the time helping the environment on a working farm also helps the farm business. Throughout this book there are stories about projects like this. They are described in sections entitled "Conservation Economics." These stories are from my home state of Washington, but they are indistinguishable from thousands of similar projects happening daily in local communities throughout the United States.[1] Our farm–environmental problems are, unfortunately, too great for us to hope that they could all be solved so painlessly. But projects like this are common, and they help close the gap between farmers and environmentalists.

It is also good news that the circumstances which have driven our farmers and environmentalists into their current politically-charged corners are entirely of our own making. We can undo what we have done. Farmers and environmentalists, rural and urban residents, conservatives and liberals alike, all of us in fact, need to challenge our comfortable (even if deeply held) assumptions about how the world works. Once we accept the complexity of our problems and the very real challenges we face in solving them, we can start reversing the deadlock that has put us here.

At the close of each chapter in this book, there are sections separately addressed to each of the two sides in this dialogue. These sections ask each to rethink their logic on key misconceptions about farming, the environment, or the political realities that surround them. Despite their headings, whether you are a farmer, an environmentalist, or a concerned citizen, these sections are for you. We all need to understand the conflicting points of view that are driving this deadlock if we are to find ways to deal with it.

CHAPTER 2

Farmland—
Why We Lose It and Where It Goes

Half of the total land area of the United States is in agriculture.[1] Most of that land, nearly a billion acres, is privately owned by perhaps 1 percent to 2 percent of the U.S. population.[2] How, when, or if those few farmers decide to sell their farmland has a profound impact on the environment.

Those billion acres also feed the nation. They generate close to $300 billion in annual sales, making agriculture one of our leading industries.[3] Yet the people who own those lands are not particularly wealthy.[4] And their ownership of all that acreage is not a luxury. That land is in business—the business of growing food and fiber. Its future use hangs on the business success of the farmers who now own it. When one of the nation's 2.2 million farm businesses fails or its owner decides to quit, the business assets are sold. Most of the business asset value will be in land.[5] And, just as one would expect for any other market sale, this land invariably goes to the highest bidder.

In much of the United States, especially in our more populous regions, the highest bidder will almost always be someone whose planned use for the property is more intensive than was the agriculture it will replace—uses like residential or recreational housing, warehouses, retail sales, manufacturing, and office space. Those buyers can easily outbid a farmer. In those areas where there is little development pressure, the buyer may be a farmer, but it is likely to be a large corporate operation that is in a financial position to expand.

Why does this happen? And what is its impact on the profitability and environmental sustainability of agriculture?

Farm Value versus Market Value

Farming requires comparatively large amounts of land for each dollar of economic value generated. So there are often a great many other more intensive, so-called "higher and better" uses,[6] that will generate much more annual revenue per acre and that will, therefore, support paying a much higher purchase price than can agriculture. For properties at or near the urban edge, these other uses may include commercial and industrial development. Or

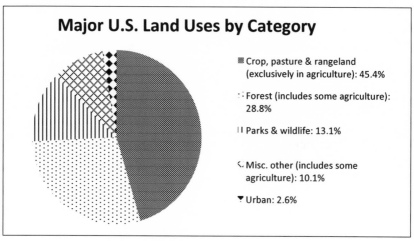

Major U.S. Land Uses by Category

▩ Crop, pasture & rangeland
(exclusively in agriculture): 45.4%

∷ Forest (includes some agriculture):
28.8%

Ⅱ Parks & wildlife: 13.1%

ᔕ Misc. other (includes some
agriculture): 10.1%

▼ Urban: 2.6%

2.1 Major U.S. Land Uses by Category[7] (USDA Economic Research Service, May 2006)

the land might be suitable for apartments or single family dwellings. Further from town, there will be commuters willing to drive a bit for a more "rural" experience, for a larger lot, or just to pay a little less for a home site.

Even well beyond usual commuter distances, far from cities and deep in traditional farm country, non-farm buyers will often be able to pay much higher prices for recreational or second homes, for retirement properties, for resort developments, for industrial sites, for homes from which they will telecommute, or for many other non-agricultural uses.

At today's prices, a residential developer in a large American city might be quite happy to pay $200,000, $300,000, or more for a usable, 50' x 100' residential building lot (much more for properties with multifamily, commercial or industrial possibilities, or with other amenities). In areas within commute distance from urban centers (a distance that continues to grow) market value can have much less to do with size than with whether a single family residence can be built there. Residential developers commonly pay nearly the same for forty acres well out in farm country or for five acres in a semi-rural area as they might pay for a small lot inside the city.

This is still much more than a farmer can pay. So the reason farmland falls out of working agriculture is quite simple. Farm businesses can't compete at these prices.

The ownership of land has a carrying cost. This is measured by how much could be earned by the money that is invested in it if that same money were instead placed in an equally secure alternative investment.

To illustrate, suppose Farmer Jones owns one hundred acres of cropland with a market value of, say, $3,000 per acre, or $300,000 total. He could, if he wished, sell the land and invest the $300,000 in bonds or mutual funds that might, hypothetically, earn a 6 percent annual return. That would produce an income of $18,000 per year, without him having to spend another dime in expenses or lift a finger in labor to earn it. For there to be any logic in his keeping $300,000 invested in his farmland, Jones has to be earning enough from growing crops to cover the $18,000 annual "investment carrying cost," along with his other expenses (hired labor, seed, fertilizer, fuel, equipment, interest on loans, etc.), and to earn himself a reasonable income from his own labor as well. If he can't make that happen, he may hang on for a while. But sooner or later he will be out of the farming business and the land will sell.

When farmers compete with one another for the purchase of farmland, what they must consider is the net productivity of the land versus the carrying cost of the investment required to own it. No rational farm businessperson can pay more for land than its value as a productive farm business asset if the purpose is to keep that land in agriculture over the long term.[8] Someone making that same calculation for a non-farm use for that land will obviously make a different choice.

Unfortunately, the same $300,000 sum that would be needed to buy a nice urban residential building lot might also be quite competitive in a bid for Farmer Jones's one hundred acre farm parcel—$3,000 per acre is a pretty typical farm business value for good, irrigated crop land in farm country. That $300,000 could also potentially outbid a farmer on 1,000 acres of non-irrigated grain crop land. Or it might buy as much as 3,500 acres of lightly vegetated rangeland.

There can be water availability, access, or other issues that might discourage the outright development of some of these properties. But even so, given their limited farm-business values it is obvious why they can be a tempting buy for people accustomed to paying urban prices. And given the comparably higher intensity uses to which these lands will be converted, it is also clear why they will often be priced well above what a farmer can afford to pay, especially if the buyer can further subdivide and resell them.

Farmers on the urban edge may try to cope with this economic pressure by increasing the intensity of their farming use, hence the rising popularity of direct-market farming. This helps, but it is not a long-term fix. Even if they double or treble the per-acre value they can justify through income from their farming business, their residential, commercial, and non-farm industrial land competitors are often quite able to pay ten or twenty times as much. On average, our nation's farms generate only about $322 per acre in annual gross sales revenue.[9] Compare that with the gross rental revenue one might anticipate from almost any other land use and it becomes quite clear why farmland is so vulnerable to conversion.

Moreover, this problem is not confined to the urban edge. Even at great distances from urban areas, far beyond any practical commute to a major city, non-farm buyers still wreak price-havoc in farm communities. Despite the recent successes of small-acreage, direct-market farmers in urban edge areas, the profitable size for a commercial, wholesale farming operation is quite large. (These represent 99 percent of the nation's farms.) For a wholesale commercial potato farm to generate a family income might today require room for perhaps three 160-acre irrigation circles, or about 500 acres. A non-irrigated wheat farm might require more like 5,000 acres to support a family. A cattle ranch might require access to closer to 15,000 acres.

When non-farm buyers begin opportunistically purchasing modest parcels in various locations throughout a rural agricultural landscape, the result is fragmentation of the farm land base. This can soon make it impossible for a capable and ambitious farmer to find a farm parcel (or parcels) of a sufficiently large size, contiguous to (or even sufficiently near) another farm, let alone at an affordable price, that they can assemble enough land to make up a workable family farm.[10]

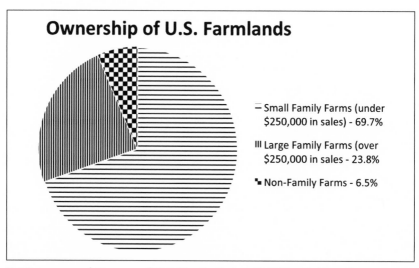

Ownership of U.S. Farmlands

= Small Family Farms (under $250,000 in sales) - 69.7%

||| Large Family Farms (over $250,000 in sales - 23.8%

▪ Non-Family Farms - 6.5%

2.2 Structure and Finances of U.S. Family Farms: 2005 Family Farm Report, Robert Hoppe and David Banker (USDA Economic Research Service, May 2006)

While farmers are competing with the rest of us for land, they also face a bitterly challenging global marketplace for the farm products they must sell to afford that land. U.S. farms are not nearly as large as many of us have come to believe; the average farm size is currently a modest 418 acres.[11] Nor are they nearly so "corporate."[12] The U.S. Department of Agriculture (USDA) estimates that about 91 percent of U.S. farms are small family operations with less than $250,000 in gross annual sales and that may or may not be actually earning a profit.[13]

These small family farms own just under 70 percent of the nation's agricultural land.[14]

The Challenge for Farm Business Investment

Beyond the long-term profitability of the farm business, farmers whose land has acquired a market value that exceeds its value as a productive farm business asset find themselves in a difficult position for another reason as well. Certainly nobody is unhappy to learn that their land has increased in value.[15] But the knowledge that, when the farm next sells, no farmer is going to be able to buy it for what it is worth can have a big impact on the business decisions that must be made by its owner today.

As with most business owners, farmers need to constantly invest in improvements that will make their business grow and succeed. For farmers, these are often investments in fixtures to the land: improvements like new worker housing, a new or improved barn or work building, livestock fencing, a new irrigation system, or improved drainage.[16] A dairy farmer may need a new feed lot, a milking parlor, a larger livestock waste lagoon, or a waste handling system. A hop farmer may need a hop kiln. A grain farmer might want an additional storage silo. Or any crop farmer may want to invest in carefully conserving and enriching the topsoil, knowing that one day that healthy soil will produce a better crop.

Normally these would all be logical investments to consider. In each case they might be expected, over time, to add to the farm's income. Take that new irrigation system, for example. That will save on the cost of water and perhaps on energy. It will save on fertilizer and chemicals—these can be applied much more efficiently through the irrigation system. It will save on labor. It will probably produce a healthier, more uniformly desirable, and marketable crop. And it will reduce runoff and associated soil loss (as well as reducing pollution in a nearby stream). It will be a big investment, but it may be a very good one and one that, under ordinary conditions, any good business person would need to have in mind.

But none of these investments will pay off overnight. That irrigation system, for example, will someday pay for itself and start generating a positive return, but that could easily take ten years, maybe more. If the current owner is the age of an average farmer, he or she is at least fifty-seven years old,[17] not that far away from retirement. It may not be long before this farm is up for sale.

If this farm has a market value that is higher than its farm business value, it will have become clear to its owner that, when it next sells, it will not be selling to another farmer. A farmer won't be able to afford it. If it were to be purchased by a farmer, a nice new irrigation system, barn, fence, or grain silo would clearly add value that could be reflected in a higher purchase price. Instead, we know this land is going to sell to a non-farmer, perhaps to a developer. And that non-farm buyer is going to have absolutely no interest in any of those farm business improvements. If anything, "improvements" like this will detract from the farm's value. That irrigation system, for example, will just represent something more that must be removed before development can begin. Or think how that potential developer-buyer might react to a dairy farmer's nice new $80,000 manure lagoon?

Knowing this, if you were the owner of this farm, how would you feel about making these investments? You now find yourself, in effect, operating two enterprises: a farm business and a land investment business. And those two enterprises have inconsistent needs. What you might invest in to help the one will quite likely detract from the value of the other.

That a great many American farmers are placed in exactly this position ought to be deeply troubling to anyone concerned for the competitive health and future economic sustainability of our nation's agriculture industry.

Movement toward Corporate Agriculture

As we shall see later, American agriculture is less "corporate" than we might think. But large agribusinesses do control a substantial share of farm production.[18] These large corporate operations are likely to use the more "industrial" farming practices that have come in for criticism in recent years.[19] But they can also sometimes be in a better position to deal with regulatory issues than their smaller, family-farm brethren. And they are in a better position to have some limited control over the prices they are paid in the global marketplace.

In those areas of the country where there may be less development pressure, farm failure probably also results in accelerating the movement of land out of family farming and into more corporate and industrial agriculture.

How Land-cost Stability Improved Water Quality

Larry Cochran in fields near Colfax, Washington. *Photo by Charles Gurche, courtesy of American Farmland Trust*

Larry Cochran is a third generation dry-land wheat farmer in the Palouse area near Colfax, Washington. Fortunately, Larry's farm is far enough away from any cities that the market value of his land is about the same as its agricultural business value. So Larry hasn't faced tempting offers from developers. Should they ever need to sell, he and his family know that the buyer will be another farmer who will appreciate its productive farm business value.

Soil loss is a serious issue in the hilly Palouse. Sediments wash into nearby rivers, causing pollution, or are carried across the landscape by the wind. Larry remembers his grandfather taking great pains to protect the soil. He limited tillage and grew a cover crop in the off-season. He captured moving soil sediment and returned it to thinning hilltops. He kept a few cattle to enrich the soil. Larry's father taught him these practices and Larry is passing along this same ethic to his son.

This multigenerational investment in soil conservation is paying off for the family business; their land is much more productive than neighboring properties where these practices have been neglected. And conservation stewardship on Larry's farm has also protected local waterways for three generations now—going on a fourth. But that investment was only rational because Larry's grandfather, his father, and now Larry have known for sure that this land will always stay in agriculture.[20]

For Environmentalists Only

[FARMERS, DO NOT READ!]

Who Needs All That Farmland?

With half the nation's land in agriculture, an environmentalist might be thinking: "Maybe we just don't need that much farmland. So what if some farms go out of business? Maybe that's just as well; if you can't be both a successful farm business and environmentally responsible, maybe you shouldn't be in business anyway. With fewer farms, we'd have less farm-generated pollution. We could convert some of that land back into trees, wetlands, floodplains, and a more diverse and natural landscape."

Let's explore this line of thinking. If we make farming less profitable (perhaps through increased regulation, perhaps by allowing land costs to rise), and if this drives many of our farmers out of business, what are the implications?

We need to start by acknowledging that this would have economic impacts, human costs, losses to rural communities, reduced access to local food, and increased American dependence on overseas food supplies.[21] Even if we feel we can live with those non-environmental consequences, does allowing (or precipitating) the loss of American farms actually make some kind of sense as a purely environmental matter?

Let's first consider those areas of the country where land prices are primarily influenced by urban development pressure. (While this situation does not exist in all of the country, it does exist in a sizeable percentage of it.[22]) Where the market value of farmland is higher than its agricultural value, the lack of farmer-buyers would presumably have little or no impact on the price of the land. Of course, driving farmers out of business would probably accelerate the rate at which our farmlands go on the market for sale. A temporary increase in the supply of developable land might briefly reduce prices. But unless the environmental community suddenly comes into a great deal of money with which to buy up that land, the net effect still seems more likely to be a simple increase in the rate of conversion of farmland into more intensive non-farm uses which are much less friendly to the environment.

The consequences we'd see would certainly include fragmentation of the land base into much smaller parcel sizes. Construction of roads and structures would increase impervious surfaces, which intensify flooding and slow the recharge of our aquifers. There would be more nonpoint pollution—pollution that originates in small amounts from many, diverse, widely separated sources that are difficult to identify and monitor—and we would be unable to adequately regulate or to cost-effectively recapture and treat that pollution, especially in areas outside the urban core. Fish and wildlife habitat would be lost and migration corridors would be blocked. Riparian and other natural buffers would disappear. Carbon sequestering vegetation would be destroyed. And we would see increased food and commuter transportation impacts on energy and climate.

None of this is an environmental improvement over open, undeveloped, working farmlands.

Of course we would all like to see improved management on those farmlands. But if those lands become fragmented or developed we lose any opportunity we might have had to improve that management.

Even in deeply rural areas, with little urban pressure, land is still worth a lot of money. When it is purchased for conversion to environmental uses, it is at a substantial cost. That usually happens only on those rare occasions when a lot of cash is available from government, private mitigation, or wealthy charitable sources. Yes, if we first damaged our farm economy, the cost of deep-rural farmland might be reduced. But even if it was, where will the money come from to buy it for the environment? And as it fragments, the market value is actually likely to soon rise.

Conversely, if you leave the farm in place, operating, profitable, and earning its way, but alter its management so the worst environmental harms disappear and its environmental benefits are maximized, the total public and economic cost is much lower. Maybe purchasing and fully restoring some key critical areas on our nation's farms will sometimes turn out to be necessary. But for the rest, why would we want to buy the whole farm when only a few of its natural productive benefits are actually needed? Why would we want to undertake the expense of owning and maintaining "natural" land (at a cost that is often underestimated)?[23] It can be much cheaper to leave that ongoing maintenance to a private landowner, one who can pay a part of those costs out of the revenues from agricultural sales.

Unless we have the money on hand to buy out our nation's farms and restore them to native conditions, a policy that bankrupts our farmers and drives them off the land doesn't make any environmental sense.

Who's to Blame?

Urbanites often complain about farmers who sell out for development. But it doesn't make much sense to blame the farmer. In some cases, farmers have accumulated value in their land, and may own it outright. But in many others, that land may have been deeply mortgaged—for its original purchase, for cash to cover other business investments, to buffer losses in bad years, and very often to cover ongoing operating expenses. Even where a farmer will receive significant cash equity upon selling out, that value is likely the product of a lifetime—or perhaps generations—of personal or family labor and investment. This may be the principal asset upon the value of which its owner hopes to retire. The farmer may also have family whose needs and wishes must be considered.

Who, among those of us who live in the city, would readily and happily sell our home, on the eve of our retirement, for less than it is worth, as a charitable gesture to a needy family or so someone could have the house who was preferred by the community but who couldn't afford to pay full price? Even if we wanted to do that, as a few of us might, the vast majority of us simply cannot.

Blaming the farmer for how the world works makes no sense.

In fact, the farmer is the very last person to truly want to see his or her farm converted to development. Farmers typically spend their entire lives and careers working a single piece of land. They have learned everything there is to know about its soils, contours, pest problems, crop potential, climate, drainage, and other issues and opportunities. They know the best strategies for making that farm flourish and pay. They have invested heavily in its barns, fences, soils, equipment, and housing. They may have been raised there and raised their children there as well. So they have also committed a lot of thought and effort to making it a safe and desirable place to live. This is, for them, a life's work or perhaps the work of several generations. Of the many farmers I've met and with whom I've discussed these issues over the years, there has not been a single one who said they would prefer that their farm be someday converted out of farming and into development.

When farmers sell their land to a developer, they do so because they have no other realistic choice. Society has wired up our political, legal, and economic rules such that they effectively compel these sales. If we don't like it, that is what we need to do something about.

For Farmers Only

[ENVIRONMENTALISTS, DO NOT READ!]

The Private and the Public Interests in Farmland Loss

As a farmer, you may feel that the sale and purchase of farmland is a private matter, one that is nobody's business but the buyer and the seller. Let's agree that it definitely is not the farmer's fault when farmland ends up converted to a non-farm purpose. But it is also not just the farmer's business. Farmland loss has an impact on the entire community, rural and urban residents alike.

For example, among those affected by the development of farmland are other farmers. A healthy local farm economy depends on the local businesses that support it. In many farm communities, farmers even exchange their land with one another from year to year for the most efficient planting of rotation crops which will maximize fertility and minimize pest losses. As each farm disappears and its land falls to other uses, local support businesses (equipment dealers, seed suppliers, food processors, farm credit providers, farm service professionals, etc.) also disappear—making it ever harder for the remaining farmers to survive. Those rotational exchanges become impossible. Non-farmers moving into a farm landscape create problems for the remaining farmers—problems like increased non-farm traffic, pressure on land prices, neighborhood dogs, theft and vandalism, and nuisance complaints over noise, smells, and agricultural chemicals.[24]

Moreover, as each farm is developed, the environmental benefits it has been providing disappear. As the landscape is broken up into smaller and smaller parcels with more and more owners, the likelihood increases that all the remaining landowners in that community (farmer and otherwise) will end up facing heightened environmental regulation.

As a farm landscape fragments, incentive-based solutions to environmental problems also become less workable. Where the land in a community is split up and held by thousands of landowners rather than a few dozen or a few hundred, it becomes difficult to treat each property as unique and to offer individualized incentives for its improved management. The in-person technical assistance and on-site professional program management that voluntary incentives require can quickly become unrealistically costly.

Nearby urban communities also suffer consequences as the environment suffers and mitigation requirements increase for local developers and businesses. There are non-environmental consequences as well. Public services (police, fire protection, utilities, schools, transportation, etc.) cost more to provide to sprawling development. Local food disappears. Food-related employment diminishes. There is less diversity and stability in the economy and a diminished quality of life for everyone.

So everyone in these communities (both the farmer and the non-farmer) has an interest in finding fair and reasonable ways to avoid those outcomes. Farmland loss is everybody's business, not just the farmers who sell and the developers who buy.

Leaving It to the Marketplace

Many farmers also argue that the solution to farmland loss is to simply remove "unnatural" government constraints that prevent farms from becoming more profitable. Farmers are entrepreneurs. They believe strongly in the power of a free market economy. So it is understandable that a farmer would be convinced that we could rely on the marketplace to correct the differential in land-purchasing power between farms and other land uses.

The argument is that we should end artificial land use and environmental regulations that drive up the costs of farm production, damage farm profitability, and make it more difficult for farmers to afford land. Without "artificial" land use controls, farmland would become increasingly scarce (as it sold for other uses), food would then become more expensive, and higher food prices would make the surviving farmers more profitable and able to compete for land. The market would solve this problem.

This line of thinking is appealing, not just because it seems consistent with the logic of a free market, but also because the alternatives are so difficult to accept. If sprawl, farmland fragmentation, and unprofitable farms are somehow inherent in our economic and political system, the solutions seem both undesirable and out of reach. The only answers that remain probably involve more government, more land use zoning and regulation, and more taxes to pay for purchasing development rights on farmlands. These aren't outcomes that appeal to most farmers. It is much more pleasing and empowering to believe that the answer is simpler—just take off the restraints and allow a free unfettered marketplace.

Certainly increasing our farm businesses' ability to afford land will help. Greater profits would definitely help farmers pay the higher land investment carrying costs discussed earlier in this chapter.

But let's also be realistic. Consider broadly how a farmer actually uses land. Take a single square foot of flat, fertile, easily buildable land and plant a seed there. Then water, protect, fertilize, tend, and otherwise invest in that seed for six months until it has grown into a healthy plant and produces a marketable crop. Then harvest and sell that plant for anything from a few cents to a couple of dollars—gross. And then either leave that land fallow or grow a nonprofitable cover crop there for the next six months, maybe even for another year.

Now compare that activity with what an industrial plant, a warehouse, an office building, or a retail store might earn, over an entire year, on that same square foot of ground. Compare it with what people pay for a year to rent or to buy a square foot of residential property. Consider, as mentioned above, that average annual farm-gate sales in the United States are currently at around $322 per acre—gross (that's under a penny per square foot). It seems pretty clear that even if we could remove all government regulation of our farms, by the time higher food prices addressed this problem, we'd all be starving or facing a massive global social, political, and economic collapse.

A farmer friend of mine puts it this way: "Maybe there's someplace where increased farm profitability might make it possible for farmers to compete with developers for land. But in my community, I don't see that happening in my lifetime."

We will come back later, in some detail, to the pros and cons of purchase of development rights (PDR) and zoning programs for agriculture and to the public fairness issues with both. Certainly we need to increase the profitability of agriculture. But, for now, let's just acknowledge that the preservation of our farmland is going to take a great deal more than just increasing farm profitability. It seems highly unlikely that farming will, any time soon, become sufficiently lucrative, on its own, that it will be able to beat out other more land-intensive business activities in the competition for land.

If something is going to be done about that, it may need to be something that isn't easy to accomplish, that requires the help of government, and that simply cannot be done by individual farmers on their own.

CHAPTER 3

Agriculture's Environmental Risks

Chapter 2 showed how and why farmland is often lost to development. But what about the farms that stay in business? Our farms provide abundant social, economic, and material benefits, of course. Food, for example! But it would still be irresponsible if we saved farmland for agriculture but then sat back and watched those farms get managed in a way that gravely harmed the environment.

The impacts of agriculture on the nation's landscape are certainly less concentrated than those of urban development. But they cover a lot of territory, a fact that is clearly visible to anyone who crosses the country by air. The risks they pose are intensified by the fact that those farms are often located on our most vulnerable lands: in fertile flood plains along the edges of rivers and streams, on sensitive and naturally arid landscapes, on highly-erodible hillsides, on the sites of former forests, or on former natural wetlands and adjacent to current ones. Along with occupying half the nation's land, these farms consume some 80 percent of our fresh water.[1] So looking down at those thousands of square miles of grazing and cultivation from the air, it is easy to imagine how a lot of harm could be done if they are not carefully managed.

Let's see if we can understand and assess those risks.

The Diversity of Agricultural Land Uses

First of all, we need to appreciate that all farms are not the same. Each of the different kinds of farming has its own risks and issues. And each individual farm, within a farming type, is also quite unique. Each presents a different kind of challenge as we consider how best to address those issues. A few statistics can highlight these differences.

Livestock pasture and rangeland account for about two-thirds of the 922 million acres in American agriculture. Much of this land is permanently devoted to livestock, often in areas that are high in altitude or relatively arid with thin, rocky soils, or that are otherwise not appropriate for cultivated crops. However, some of those grazed acres are much more fertile and could be used for crops if the owner desired.[2]

29

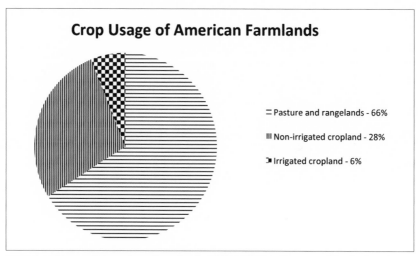

Crop Usage of American Farmlands

= Pasture and rangelands - 66%

III Non-irrigated cropland - 28%

⇒ Irrigated cropland - 6%

3.1 Crop Usage of American Farmlands (2007 USDA Census of Agriculture)

Roughly, the remaining 34 percent of our 922 million agricultural acres is in harvested cropland. A good deal of this is in crops—like wheat and soybeans—that do not necessarily require irrigation. Only about 6 percent of America's agricultural land is actually irrigated.[3]

In an average year, our farmers plant about 86 million acres of corn, 64 million acres of soybeans, and 51 million acres of wheat.[4] There are about 7 million acres in sorghum, 5 million acres in fruits, nuts, and berries,[5] about 4 million acres in vegetables, potatoes, and melons, about 900,000 acres in grapes,[6] about 700,000 acres in nursery stock, and 600,000 acres in cut Christmas trees and short rotation woody crops.[7] As of 2008, about 5 million acres (about 0.5 percent of the total) were in all types of organic production.[8]

Each of the nation's 2.2 million farms and each of the hundreds of different crops has its own marketplace and market issues. Each has its own requirements for farm infrastructure and investment. Each has its own unique soil, climate, season, and cultivation needs. Each has its own particular environmental impacts. The incredible diversity in farms, markets, crops, and the places where they are grown makes it very difficult to generalize about agriculture's relationship with the environment and even more difficult to find universal solutions to farm–environmental problems.

Competition and Uncertainty in the Business of Agriculture

Farming is a risky business. One must appreciate the economic setting within which farmers operate to understand how a farmer will respond to environmental problems. Adding to the normal uncertainties of agriculture, there are two broad, interconnected trends which have characterized much of American agriculture over the past fifty years. These are farm industrialization and the extent to which most farm products now compete on the international marketplace.

Most farm products require a good deal of transportation; many are shipped over great distances as raw produce and/or in their later processed form.[9] About half of U.S. food production is exported with roughly the same amount imported.[10] So, while perhaps three-fourths of all of America's farms are small, independent family operations,[11] those families have no lock on U.S. markets and must still compete globally. These international markets include products grown by multinational agribusinesses on the one hand and, on the other, by third-world subsistence farmers earning a few dollars a day. All of this production is in competition. The price paid is almost entirely out of the farmers' control.

The vast majority of farmers' crops are sold into anonymous wholesale markets. Quality requirements are generally standardized by huge food conglomerates. So, once those requirements have been met, business success for nearly all of our nation's farmers is very heavily about volume and production cost.

America has a mild climate, and we have historically had an extensive and fertile land base with low land costs because of our modest population pressure. But with an increasing population and comparatively strong non-farm prosperity, our internationally competitive land-cost advantage has diminished. With the elevated U.S. standard of living, our labor costs have risen as well, leaving our farmers heavily dependent on an uncertain immigrant workforce. Nonetheless, our farms have still had three major advantages: well-educated operators, easy access to technology, and low-cost credit. All three of these are made possible by our progressive and usually dependable democratic government and by our, therefore, mostly stable first-world economy.

As one might guess, these economic forces have produced an American agriculture industry that is technology-intensive and minimizes the use of manual labor, and that is capital-intensive and borrows heavily.

The result can be seen in most modern American commercial farms. A modern potato farm, for example, requires a huge initial investment. It can require a complex, water-efficient irrigation system that saves on the cost of water, reduces the cost of fertilizer and chemicals, saves on labor, and applies water evenly across the field, producing a uniform and optimal crop.

The potato farmer may plant crops using a GPS-guided tractor that injects fertilizer and chemicals into the soil exactly where each potato plant will grow and then positions each seed potato precisely where the fertilizer and chemicals were injected. The amount of fertilizers and chemicals that are injected may also be computer- and GPS-controlled to match the varying soil conditions across a single farm field, avoiding excess application with yet further cost savings. The tractors, computers, GPS systems, irrigation, and planting equipment needed to do this work can be a million dollar investment. But the production from a single potato field can also be enough to feed a small city.

These new technologies have certainly improved farm production. But they do not seem to have, in any way, reduced the business risk.[12] Our potato farmer is probably in debt,[13] and may have heavily leveraged the equity in the farm business, in the land, and in the anticipated crop. The farm is still vulnerable to droughts, floods, freezes, and a host of unexpected turns in the weather; to widely fluctuating market prices; to new challenges from pests or plant disease; and (as most farmers will add), to unexpected shifts in government policy. So it is not uncommon for a long-standing, prudently-operated, generally successful farm business to find itself suddenly balanced on the brink of bankruptcy, with a desperate need to cut costs to meet a forthcoming payroll or bank payment.

Take a look at a modern dairy farm. At one time, a profitable dairy might have had two hundred cows grazing on perhaps two hundred acres, a land-to-animal ratio that would allow, with good management, for the soils and grasses to take up animal waste before it runs off into a nearby stream or infiltrates the groundwater. Today, a typical dairy might be two thousand cows on more like fifty acres.

The cows on such a dairy will spend most of their time closely confined in large paved facilities. They will be fed using costly feeding equipment. They will be milked by automated milking machines. The milk will be stored in sterile, refrigerated tanks. Each cow may be equipped with a personal transmitter that records time spent eating, movement about the yard, milk production, and other details that allow the farmer to track the animal's productivity and health. Animal waste will be collected and stored in large waste lagoons that hold many thousands of gallons. From these, the waste will be either applied to nearby fields during the drier and more active vegetative season or will be transported elsewhere for such application. All of this infrastructure requires a huge investment, much of which will be necessarily financed by debt. The price of milk fluctuates notoriously and dairy cows are vulnerable to the occasional spread of animal disease, both of which

Modern dairy milking parlor. *Courtesy of USDA-NRCS*

add a special dimension of risk and further expense to this dairy farmer's operation. So, again, it is easy to see how this business might sometimes be highly profitable and at other times be desperately at risk.

There are exceptions, but our dairy and potato farm examples are models for typical, successful, modern, commercial U.S. agriculture—a model that is replicated, in a different form, for nearly every other major agricultural crop—tree fruits, grains, vegetables, and other livestock.

Given the economic underpinnings of this industry, it seems likely things will stay this way for a long time to come. Small-scale, local, direct-market farming is certainly flourishing, but it still represents a tiny percentage of U.S. farm value and an even tinier percentage of the farmland base. If the agriculture industry is to address environmental issues in a serious way, this must happen in mainstream commercial family farming.

Environmental Risks, Opportunities, and Costs

Farmers are often predisposed toward good land stewardship. Their profession brings them close to the land and to nature. There are long-term economic benefits to the farm from good conservation. There are personal health advantages for the farm family. And there are social pressures that can be especially significant for farmers given their tradition of multigenerational ownership and the close-knit nature of small, rural communities.

But the competition and industrialization discussed above create economic pressures that simply cannot be ignored. These pressures unavoidably constrain even the best-intentioned farmers' sensitivities toward the environment. So, knowing the business pressures they face, we need to ask ourselves: What is agriculture's potential for causing environmental damage?

If something is going to go wrong, what might that be? Let's look at a few examples:

- *Water quality:* Surface waters can be polluted by runoff from farm fields. Heavy rains or excess irrigation can wash off small particles of soil to which harmful chemicals will adhere (especially if they were applied too generously). This runoff can include pesticides, nutrients like nitrogen and phosphorous from chemical fertilizers, fecal coliform from livestock or from natural fertilizers like applied dairy waste. Chemicals or animal waste can be applied in excess, at the wrong time, or in such a manner that, in addition to washing off in the next rainstorm, they are also driven down into the soil, below the root zone and living topsoil, where they ultimately (sometimes soon, sometimes decades later) end up polluting ground water and drinking water supplies. Or surface water connectivity may return them to the surface somewhere downstream.

- *Air quality:* Farms are linked to climate change. Agriculture's climate impacts can be made much worse through the use of poor practices. Excess synthetic chemical fertilizers can produce nitrous oxide, a highly potent greenhouse gas. Livestock manure produces methane, another potent greenhouse gas. Beyond climate issues, concerns are sometimes expressed over dairy or livestock odors (usually by non-farm neighbors), over pesticide/chemical drift from aerial crop spraying, over dust from tilling in dry and windy weather, or over smoke from field burning (a practice sometimes used to cut a cycle of plant disease, to eliminate stubble or weeds, or to stimulate plant growth[14]).

- *Wildlife habitat:* Large monocultures can be unfriendly for wildlife as it removes cover, food, resting places, and safe migration routes. Livestock fencing can block or divert the natural migration of large terrestrial mammals. Chemical and pesticide pollution can poison fish, can suffocate them by changing the level of dissolved oxygen in the water, and can destroy their sense of smell and ability to navigate. Removing tree and shrub cover alongside streams and rivers can stimulate the growth of unnatural vegetation that chokes the stream and prevents its use by fish. It can also increase water temperatures, which also affects oxygen levels. It can eliminate macro-invertebrates needed by fish for food. Both the removal of vegetation and unfenced livestock can erode stream banks, infiltrating spawning areas with sediment, and damage streamside vegetation that filters out sediments and pollution in agricultural surface water runoff. There are, in fact, a host of habitat impacts that can result from farming activities along riparian areas, impacts that affect not only fish but also terrestrial species that count on the edges of streams to survive. And, like nearly every other human activity, the existence of agriculture generally displaces other, more natural environmental conditions that may be more desirable as wildlife habitat.

- *Wetlands:* Many environmentalists, and our nation's environmental laws, consider and treat wetlands as an environmental value in themselves. They are, in fact, a composite of many values, often acting in synergy to contribute powerfully to clean water, aquifer recharge, flood detention, wildlife habitat, and other critical environmental needs. Historically, we have treated excessive surface water as an enemy, draining swamps and converting them to arable croplands. In recent years, strong regulation under the Clean Water Act has greatly slowed this practice.[15] With current regulation, we have much reduced the new degradation of wetlands going on in farm country and elsewhere. Continued farming and other land uses, of course, continue to displace those former wetlands.

- *Human health*: Anyone who tracks the daily news is aware of our ongoing string of food scares and recalls—*E. coli* on fresh vegetables, chemicals on fresh fruits, tainted meat, bad peanuts.[16] Americans are probably especially nervous about (and vulnerable to) these kinds of concerns given that we are also used to an extraordinarily safe food supply and tend not to take precautions that might be customary elsewhere in the world.

  There are also less obvious but more subtle dangers such as the buildup of residual chemicals in our systems from agricultural pesticides and their impacts on our health over time. Most of us are conscious of the possible dangers of these cumulative effects, but we rely upon agencies like the Environmental Protection Agency (EPA) and Food and Drug Administration (FDA) to minimize them. In recent years, the Food Quality Protection Act (FQPA) adopted in 1996[17] has slowly been clamping down on the use of some of the more dangerous and persistent organophosphate pesticides. Consumer worries, the expense of recalls, and exposure to potential personal injury liability have made the large food distribution firms increasingly cautious about pesticide use.

Since World War II, mainstream commercial agriculture has embraced the use of chemical pesticides. But today's farmers are beginning to back slightly away from them as new, integrated pest management (IPM) techniques, some of them pioneered in the organic foods industry, are emerging to take their place.[18] Even so, America's commercial agriculture system is, at least for the moment, still deeply dependent on chemical pesticides. And there is no question that many of these can be dangerous if not properly applied or if they aren't scrupulously removed before eating—dangerous to the people who consume the food, to the farmers and farm workers who apply them, and to the food processors who prepare food for market.

Almost without exception, every single one of the potential negative impacts of agriculture listed above can be substantially reduced or eliminated with use of a suite of "best management practices" that have evolved over the years—mostly through active engagement of working farmers. They are available from a variety of sources and have been scientifically evaluated, also with the help of farmers, and thoroughly described. By far the most comprehensive and methodical assemblage and description of these practices is the USDA/Natural Resources Conservation Services (NRCS) Field Office Technical Guide.[19]

For farmers willing and able to use the USDA practices, there can sometimes be cost share assistance available to help with the expense. And sometimes (as illustrated by the "Conservation Economics" examples in this book) adopting these practices may actually help the farmer's bottom line. But quite often these practices add considerable expense to the farmer's operation. It is not surprising that a risk-averse farmer might choose not to use them. And it would also not be surprising if these kinds of costs were the first ones cut when a farm business finds itself under financial stress.

With all this risk, one can understand how there could be many specific instances around the United States where agriculture has been implicated as a significant cause of large scale environmental problems. A short list of the more notable of these would need to include the following:

- Agricultural runoff coming down the Mississippi River has been identified as a principal culprit in the massive dead zone that has developed in the Gulf of Mexico.[20]

- Farm pollution is believed to be the major contributor to pollution in the Chesapeake Bay.[21]
- Cattle are considered a major cause of greenhouse gasses.[22]
- Agricultural pesticides are linked to harming endangered salmon in the Pacific Northwest.[23]
- Agriculture impacts in wetland and riparian areas are tied to problems with fish habitat.[24]

These few specific examples need not be discussed in detail here, other than to note that, as one might expect, they and others like them do exist. For purposes of this chapter the key is that we understand the nature of farming and its potential environmental risks and that we appreciate that these risks do sometimes produce damage in the real world.[25]

Later on there will be more about the tools available to prevent that damage and the costs involved in using those tools.

CONSERVATION ECONOMICS

How Trumpeter Swans Paid for a New Barn

The Gordon Dairy near Elma, Washington, has always been blessed with frequent visits by migrating trumpeter swans. These impressive animals are the largest seabirds in North America. Females typically weigh in at twenty-two pounds and are five feet in length. Swans are susceptible to poisoning from eating spent lead shot and have lost a good deal of their habitat. While they're not listed as under threat (except in Minnesota), their populations are currently in decline.[26]

Trumpeter swans are particularly fond of dairies. Grazing cattle keep the grasses down so it is easy for large birds to land and take off. Manure-fertilized pastures and harvested cornfields are rich in the nutrients they need for their long migrations. Large, open dairy fields provide the space for them to see predators coming and to take flight. And the presence of cattle seems not to bother them at all. Nor are the cattle the least bit troubled by the swans. It turns out that some 85 percent of swans in the Northwest Coastal area have come to depend specifically on dairy farms.[27]

The Gordon family was fond of the trumpeter swans that would land on a fifty-five-acre field visible from the front window of their home.

Swan field at Jay Gordon dairy near Elma, Washington.
Courtesy of Jay Gordon

This particular field turned out to be a particularly important stopover for swans along the Pacific Flyway.

Jay Gordon not only operates the family dairy, but he is also the much-respected executive director of the Washington State Dairy Federation. Jay had met Martha Jordan, the local leader of the Trumpeter Swan Society and a passionate swan advocate.[28] Martha knew of some money available for protection of trumpeter swan habitat.[29] She proposed that the Gordon family be paid to place a conservation easement on the field and perpetually protect it both for swan habitat as well as for grazing for their dairy cattle.

Jay gave this a lot of thought. Like many farmers, he considers his ownership of the family farm temporary. He feels he represents his father and grandfather before him and is steward for his children and grandchildren to come. In the end, Jay decided to go ahead, with the family's understanding that the money they received for the easement would be used to build a new barn/work building that would help the farming operation. They'd call this the "swan building" so future generations of Gordon family dairy farmers would always remember how the farm had benefited by protecting the wet pasture below the family home.

This made the trumpeter swans "partners" in the Gordon Dairy. And it made something true for the future that had been true as long as anyone could remember: that trumpeter swans were a permanent feature of the Gordon Dairy.[30]

For Farmers Only

[ENVIRONMENTALISTS, DO NOT READ!]

Our Linked Environmental and Political Future

The United States is a complex, increasingly populous, highly industrialized society. Fifty or one hundred years ago, our collective impact on the environment was much smaller than it is today. But in the modern world, our combined environmental impacts, farmers and urban residents included, have dramatically increased. It seems almost certain that those impacts, and the perceived and actual need for protections against them, will proliferate in the years ahead.

Recognizable environmental damage from human activities surrounds us all. But urban residents typically see more of it, and seem more sensitive to and concerned about it, than do rural residents who are surrounded by natural resources that remain comparatively intact and where change seems to move more slowly. So we should not be surprised that, while farmers live closer to nature, the political pressure for environmental protection mostly comes from urbanites.

Here's what farmers can probably anticipate into the future: environmental conditions will worsen; public concern about them will deepen; and, as current trends toward urbanization continue, the urban political majorities inclined to take action will grow.[31]

Meanwhile, agriculture is a major American industry as well as a massive land use that poses actual and potential environmental risks that affect the rest of society. Our nation's vast and growing urban population has limited understanding of agriculture—less with every passing year. At the same time, the best, most cost-effective opportunities we have left to address these problems are to be found on our agricultural lands. And our farm population (and its political influence) continues to steadily decline.[32]

Given these long-term trends, clearly agriculture needs a long-term strategy to deal with them.

The Courts

One defensive strategy, common for small groups, is to rely on the courts. And there is a place for litigation. But, as a general rule, the American legal system is not much use in seeking better allocations of responsibility for social problems like environmental damage.

Being a farmer, a construction worker, an airline pilot, a restaurant owner, a landlord, a commercial fisherman, or a member of any other line of business, profession, or economic interest group, confers no special legal protections. These occupations and business endeavors are roles that any of us can change at will. This is unlike being of a particular race, religion, gender, disability, or age group, for example, where there is a history of discrimination and for which "strict scrutiny" is therefore required. Instead, for economic groups, the courts defer to legislative discretion on such matters.[33]

Suppose the Tennessee Legislature decided that their state's agriculture industry should bear a greater share of the social and economic costs of addressing, say, water quality in the Mississippi River. There might be a hundred reasons such a choice could seem unfair. Nonetheless, the courts would probably let it stand. It would be treated as a legislative political choice. Judges will not usually substitute their opinion about what is most "equitable" in addressing social needs over the decision of a duly elected legislature.[34]

There are rights in real property and Constitutional protections for the "taking" of real property, but as we shall discuss further in Chapter 7, there are real limits on that legal strategy as well.

Legislative Policy—"Just Say No"

A significant interest group strategy in Congress, state legislatures, and local councils and commissions is to simply count on blocking adoption of policies that might be harmful. This can be highly effective. It is always harder to pass legislation than it is to kill it. Few elected officials will stand up to a strongly motivated opposition, even if it only represents a small minority of voters. Small, highly motivated groups can generate substantial revenue in campaign contributions or for independent campaign advertising. And, by being active, visible, and vocal, they can have a disproportionate impact on our democratic political process.[35]

This is the legislative approach most commonly used by minority economic groups. It is sometimes referred to by lobbyists as "just say no." In using it, interest group leaders and lobbyists focus on critical lynchpin pressure points in the legislative process (local, state, or federal) to simply stop action.

To pass through a legislature, a bill needs a long succession of "yes" decisions. In the very easiest case, you need a sponsor, referral to a favorable committee, a timely hearing, positive testimony, an executive session with a positive committee vote, favorable action in a possible finance committee and rules committee, a leadership decision to send it to the floor, and a yes vote on the floor. Then it all starts over in the other house of the legislature. And you still need to avoid a veto.

None of this will happen unless each of the legislators involved is actually asked for their help. Each of them will need to be convinced. So, for the proponent of this bill to succeed, there's a lot of work ahead. They're going to need to ask for and secure literally dozens of "yes" decisions to make it pass (hundreds if you also count the many votes required).

Killing the bill, however, can often take but a single "no."

This strategy also works when motivating interested constituents to contact their legislators. People are slow to get involved if you're offering a way to make things better. But if a bill would make things worse, if something you have is at risk, people will jump to oppose it. It can be incredibly complicated, costly, and time-consuming to explain why some new law should pass to people who have never before considered the issue. But it can be cheap and easy to convince a small, highly interested group, already familiar with the issue, why things should stay the same.

While it always helps to have allies, alliances with other interest groups aren't that critical for a "just say no" strategy. When opposing new legislation, getting other groups or interests involved can actually complicate things. The moment you start seeking coalition support, you need to consider other people's needs. Instead of just voicing a clear and decisive "no," others may want to tinker with the legislation, to make it "better." The original bill may have posed a clear, horrific threat which can be easily understood and categorically hated. But "small" amendments can turn it into something that now has pros and cons and is harder to defeat.

Nationally, agriculture has used "just say no" to help maintain significant water quality and wetland exemptions under the Clean Water Act,[36] the Comprehensive Environmental Response, Compensation, and Liability Act,[37] and the Clean Air Act (livestock greenhouse gasses).[38]

The Downsides to "Just Say No"

As effective as it can be, this strategy has big disadvantages. For one thing, it makes powerful enemies. Each time a politically active minority group pulls out the big gun of "just say no," it can be sure it will step heavily on the toes of several other large, popular, well-connected interests.

Getting all those "yes" decisions to pass a bill requires working with as many and as diverse a collection of social interests as is possible. One must be inclusive, and make sure the bill will be supported by interest groups on both sides of the political aisle and from all points of view in the debate.

Every time such a bill gets killed, all the supporters in that major collective effort are made very unhappy. The more a group uses "just say no" the more people it angers. Over time, this can degrade its reputation and credibility, build up a reservoir of resentment, and accelerate a loss of influence, perhaps making the group ineffective at just that point in time when its influence is most needed.

Because "just say no" is so effective, it can be tempting to use it too often.[39] For every interest group, there are core threats to its very existence. At the same time, there are also bills that may seem philosophically disagreeable to many of the group's members, but that really have little or no direct impact on their vital business interests. These ancillary issues can, however, sometimes still generate a lot of heat among the membership. The group may be tempted to use "just say no" when they should be keeping their powder dry.

When overused, "just say no" can eventually stop working. Legislators grow tired of the negativity. They become unsure whether the opposition reflects a position that is important to a group's fundamental interests, or reflects the opinions of just a few members. Other organizations may shun a group with a reputation for antagonism. The group may lose members who disagree with its politics and who feel disenfranchised by an overbroad policy agenda. It may be ignored by the general press or by community leaders when participation is needed on legislative or other advisory committees. Should the occasion arise when such a group actually needs to get something affirmatively passed, it can find its prospects for accomplishing that greatly diminished. Nobody wants to help. Many will be delighted to oppose.

Reframing the Issue—a Longer-term Approach

Perhaps we could reframe agriculture's environmental challenge in the years ahead. If the question is *whether* Americans will protect the environment, it may be logical for the agriculture industry to simply oppose such protections as unnecessary. But where both the need for environmental protection and the public inclination to provide it are on the rise, it may be wiser to acknowledge that need and advocate for solutions that are friendly to agriculture.

In a choice of remedies, voluntary incentives are the obvious farmer-preference. But incentives are anything but a slam dunk. Securing programs and funding for incentives requires a willingness by the public to pay the costs of environmental protection. It means taxpayers must accept that they share at least some of the blame for our problems. A typical citizen's reaction may be: "nobody pays me to behave responsibly toward the environment; why should I pay the farmers?"

In short, to get incentives, farmers may need to actually pass legislation. They will certainly need to secure government appropriations. To do either, they are going to need friends. A viable agriculture industry public policy strategy might focus on winning friends—especially environmentalists. This requires a willingness to compromise, to seek common ground with non-traditional allies, to remain bipartisan, and to use aggressive tactics only for the industry's most critical issues.

Legislators love groups that behave this way. Their representatives and lobbyists are welcome in legislators' offices (whether they contributed to the last campaign or agree with their politics or not) because they provide value. They are invited into coalitions. Their advice is sought on potential new policy. Even though they may represent only a small minority interest, such groups can end up wielding great influence.

A Farm–Environmental Coalition

A farm–environmental alliance seems much more possible today than it did even a decade ago. Local, direct-market, and organic farmers have new political clout and new connections with the environmental community. Consumers are increasingly aware of food security and food safety issues and are much more knowledgeable about environmental issues associated with agriculture. And the mainstream environmental community is increasingly conscious of the need to retain working farms if we are to preserve a healthy environment.

If the agriculture community has the faith of its conviction that farms are good for the environment, then perhaps it's time for farmers to enlist environmentalist help in protecting those farms.

Preserving Hope

One of the more disturbing trends in American agriculture is an increasing fatalism among farmers, a tendency to give up on the future. They face increasing environmental problems and growing environmental activism, declining political clout, rising land prices, and simultaneous pressure to borrow, invest, and industrialize. It is easy to feel that agriculture has no future when you feel that you, personally, have no future in agriculture.[40]

Nothing, of course, could be further from the mark than the notion that agriculture is dying—not unless most of us plan, someday soon, to stop eating. Farmers should feel hopeful, not discouraged. And the organizations that represent farmers in the public arena have a responsibility to represent those long-term hopeful prospects of the majority of today's farmers and future farmers who plan to remain in agriculture for a long time to come.

Can Environmentalists Be Trusted?

Some farmers may question whether, given their differences, environmentalists can be trusted to deal fairly with agriculture. There are examples throughout this book of local communities that have created highly successful coalitions in which farmers and environmentalists worked well together. Many of the people involved are named, so if you want to know firsthand how that worked out for them, I suspect they'd be delighted to hear from you.

But let me also relate a personal experience.

Back in 1995, I worked for the commercial fishing industry and was asked to lead its campaign against a Washington statewide initiative (I-640). This measure would have put most of our fleet out of business.

I-640 was highly deceptive. It had been written by sports fishermen to look like it was designed to save salmon. But its real effect would have been to eliminate much of the commercial salmon fleet and to reallocate many of the fish they were catching to the sports fisheries. Survival of the commercial fishing industry depended on convincing voters that this was a selfish measure that did nothing for environment.

Several years earlier, the fisheries trade association I led had cooperated with environmentalists when our salmon "gillnet" fishermen had an environmental challenge of their own. Migratory seabirds tended to dive underwater and get caught in gillnet fishing gear. This violated the Migratory Bird Treaty Act.[41] The gillnet fishery was at risk of being shut down. Our fleet needed an alternative design for their nets that did not catch birds. And they needed credible research to demonstrate that the new system would work.

The gillnet fleet promised the Audubon Society and the U.S. Fish and Wildlife Service that they'd do this. But the research was expensive and they had no money. To fund it, the fishermen voted overwhelmingly for our state's first commercial fishing "commodity commission" using the same law that authorizes such commissions for farm commodities.[42] And they created a new net system that greatly reduced the loss of seabirds but could still catch fish.

Years later, when I-640 showed up on the ballot, we knew we were in trouble if real, mainstream environmentalists sided with the sports fishermen.

The only people who had the credibility to convince the public that this was not an environmental measure were the environmentalists themselves.

There was nothing in this initiative that would have hurt the environment. If anything, passing I-640 might have further reduced the now-diminished "take" of migratory seabirds by eliminating the non-tribal commercial fleet entirely. So there was no real reason for environmentalists to help us.

But they did. The state Audubon Society asked its independent local groups not to take a position against us, and none did. American Rivers and the Sierra Club joined in our television advertising and called out I-640 for what it was—a flagrantly self-interested deception that would not benefit salmon.

Without their help, we would have lost. With it, we won with 57 percent of the vote. These same environmentalists had caused us all kinds of anguish some years earlier over seabirds. But we'd taken their concerns seriously and made the changes they needed.

Later, when we badly needed their help, they came through for us.

For Environmentalists Only
[FARMERS, DO NOT READ!]

Why Farmers Can't Just Go Somewhere Else

One of the things sometimes noted by environmentalists is that our farms seem so frequently to be located in areas of environmental sensitivity. Farms are often found in river floodplains. We have farms atop former wetlands and in riparian areas along streams and rivers. There are farms protected by dikes in floodplains, former tidelands, and river estuaries. Farms are also found in semi-arid environments that may be vulnerable to soil erosion and loss of vegetation. All of these areas can be critically important for birds, fish, and other wildlife.

This may incline one to ask: "Why can't we just get those farms out of these sensitive areas and move them to where less damage will be done?"

Of course, during the early settlement of America, farmers sought out the richest, most productive soils and climates, with available water, where land was cheap (or free), and where there was access to markets. And because this is where the economic activity was, this is also where a great many of our major cities appeared. So, of course, we set ourselves up for our current farm–city conundrum.

Since then, farmers have increasingly been forced to grow crops on the land that is left over after the rest of us have occupied everything else that we find preferable for non-farm purposes. Non-farmers obviously prefer land that does not flood; that is flat, firm, and easy to build on; and that is close to roads, utilities, and urban services. Under price-pressure from development, land that fits that description is effectively removed from agriculture. That properties of this kind could be highly productive for farming is essentially irrelevant in the development market. Urban growth, sprawl, economic needs, transportation needs, and the expectations of the 99 percent of the rest of us who have our own uses for real estate, have driven farmers off most of that land and have guaranteed its conversion to other uses.

Today's farmers seldom farm in the places they would choose. As we know, it is possible, for example, to grow wheat on land that has no irrigation and that gets only fifteen inches of annual rainfall. But that doesn't mean that this is where a wheat farmer would prefer to farm if there were better land available somewhere else. In one location, a non-irrigated acre might be lucky to produce thirty or forty bushels of wheat a year. An acre somewhere else might easily produce 120 bushels. If you were a farmer, which would you choose?

We all need to recognize that if our farmers are located in areas that seem environmentally sensitive, the rest of us share some responsibility for that.

The environmental footprint of agriculture is, after all, an extension of the food and fiber footprint of urban and suburban America. If we think the areas our farmers farm today are sensitive and should be protected for natural environmental values, and if we plan to continue to eat, we need to find some kind of accommodation that allows us all to share in the cost just as we all share the benefits.

A Second Look at "Just Say No"

In the preceding section for farmers, I described how farmers have sometimes used "just say no" to block adoption of environmental laws. This deeply frustrates many environmentalists who may feel that these negative tactics thwart the will of the majority. Nonetheless, while "just say no" may be frustrating, it also reflects the structure of our legislative process and may, in a perverse way, be a desirable hedge or safeguard against transitory public passions. This was, after all, one of the reasons the framers of our Constitution created our bicameral Congress, the executive veto, and judicial review. It also is a way for democracy to respond to the strength of a position rather than just to the number of its supporters.

And it isn't just a one-sided strategy. Environmentalists, too, have used this strategy to great effect. It has, for example, been used by environmentalists to prevent weakening of some of our most fundamental environmental laws like the Endangered Species Act, the Clean Water Act, and the Clean Air Act. There is more about this later in the book.

CONSERVATION ECONOMICS

How Modern Irrigation Helped Save a River

The Yakima River in eastern Washington State flows through one of the most intensely farmed and irrigated regions in the United States. By 1996, large amounts of agricultural sediment were entering the river and the lower Yakima was placed on the Clean Water Act's section 303(d) list of polluted waters for turbidity and other contaminants. In 1998, a recovery plan was established which included a series of five-year incremental goals that, at the time, seemed highly challenging. Failing to meet those goals looked like it could result in greater regulation.

With support from concerned local farmers and landowners, two local irrigation districts (Sunnyside Valley and Roza) adopted a joint policy that called for individual farmers to submit water quality plans and that created the potential for reduced water delivery if the plans were not implemented. Farmers submitted more than 200 such plans and voluntarily converted over 20,000 acres to high-efficiency sprinkler and drip irrigation systems that reduced soil erosion and pollution. They also installed settling ponds, filter strips, and other measures to reduce erosion. All this work was funded through a broad partnership of local, state, and federal agencies and by contributions of some $6 million from the landowners themselves.

By 2003, monitoring by the Department of Ecology had demonstrated that three of the four agricultural drainages had met the "total maximum daily load" (TMDL) goal for turbidity. The fourth, while it fell short, had shown a sediment reduction of some 80 percent. Total suspended sediment in the Yakima River had been reduced by between 50 percent and

70 percent from its 1995 levels. By working together, this community was achieving miracles.

Meanwhile, a great many of the farmers were realizing increased profits through reduced water usage, labor savings, reduced chemical and fertilizer costs, and improved crop quality and yields—among the benefits of their new, more efficient irrigation systems. What started out as an environmental challenge turned out, for many, to have become a sound business investment.[43]

Gravity fed, furrow irrigation, Arizona. *Courtesy of USDA-NRCS*

CHAPTER 4

Opportunities Lost When Farms Disappear

When farms go out of business, the land does not return to native wilderness. So when one considers the environmental harm that can be done by successful farms, it is important to also consider the environmental benefits that can be lost should they fall out of agriculture.[1]

The Irreversibility of Farmland Loss

When land falls out of agriculture and ends up subdivided, its elevated price assures that this loss is a one-way street. Each resulting parcel also ends up in separate ownership and, as with other private lands, each parcel faces a different fate decided by its new owner. All those separate ownerships also eliminate any real chance that these subdivided parcels could ever be reassembled into a farm-sized property. Once they have been developed or converted to a more intensive use, that fate is irrevocably sealed.

In 2004, American Farmland Trust did a brief analysis of what it would take to restore fifty acres of suburban land to agriculture once it had been developed for housing. The difficulties are, for all practical purposes, insurmountable. First, it is probably not possible to actually reassemble the subdivided parcels back under a single ownership without the use of eminent domain. Then there is the immense cost of repurchasing these developed properties. After that, we must remove the homes, driveways, roads, sewers, power system, and other supporting infrastructure. Then the soil must actually be restored to a farmable condition (a developer typically removes and sells the top soil as the first step in preparing land for construction). Even assuming the parcels could be reassembled and omitting several significant costs including the initial purchase price, the rough expense of restoring this hypothetical fifty-acre parcel to agriculture, in 2004 dollars, came to over $1.17 million per acre, or $57 million for the entire parcel.[2]

Pavement truly is forever! With farmland loss, we can't go back. If we fail to protect our farms, either by choice or by default, the consequences are permanent.

The Environmental Benefits of Working Farmland

Between 1982 and 1997 America lost twenty-three million acres of agricultural land to development—an area the size of Indiana.[3] What are the environmental consequences of this loss?

Water quality: The vegetation on our farms filters surface and ground waters. As healthy plants grow in healthy topsoil, they take up and convert chemicals and organisms that might otherwise become pollution. Vegetative cover is a highly reliable pollution protection for both surface water and ground water, either of which can be critical for human drinking water supplies or for fish and wildlife. Working agricultural lands can remove not just the pollutants that may be applied on site, but also those that occur in rain or as runoff from neighboring lands. So, if a farm is well-managed, it need not itself pollute. And it can also help eliminate other, off-site pollution. The same cannot be said for a well-managed city. Even with strong controls on point sources and careful management of nonpoint sources, urban areas still generate considerable water pollution.[4] It is extraordinarily difficult, perhaps ultimately impossible, to prevent it.

Aquifer recharge and flood detention: As land use intensifies, buildings, streets, driveways, parking lots, hard-packed ground, and other impervious surfaces, and highly developed drainage infrastructure, can all hasten surface water runoff. By comparison, healthy, loosely packed soils supporting dense, healthy vegetation detain these waters, giving them time to soak into the ground and slowing their accumulation as floods.

Wildlife habitat and migration: Farms can provide habitat, resting places, feed, cover, and migration corridors for fish and wildlife. Protecting farmland from development can prevent the blockage of key corridors for wildlife species. A mixed landscape composed of some natural areas mixed in with areas of active, working agriculture can be highly desirable habitat for migratory fowl, more effective, in fact, than either a fully agricultural or even an entirely natural landscape.[5]

Wetlands: Historically, farming has not been kind to wetlands.[6] But urban development is now the chief cause of wetland loss. In our current heavily regulated setting, farms have actually become a primary source of wetland mitigation and restoration.[7] Studies of the effectiveness of wetland replacement strongly suggest that the usual preference for on-site wetland mitigation may be flawed. A wetland, even one with a buffer around it, is highly unlikely ever to continue to be (or to become) highly productive if, beyond the buffer, it is surrounded by a landscape committed to development and impervious surfaces.[8] If we can avoid the wholesale conversion of lands that are currently in productive agriculture, the restoration to wetlands of small, unproductive areas surrounded by well-managed, working agriculture could produce a much better result.

Sprawl prevention and climate: Given our often feeble nationwide efforts at landscape-scale growth management, the existence of working farms is often the main practical barrier that constrains urban sprawl. Protecting those farms can pay huge climate and other environmental dividends by reducing commuter transportation miles. Absent serious zoning or purchase of development rights programs, resistance by working farmers to subdivide and sell may be all that currently prevents the fragmentation and unplanned development of many of the surviving agricultural areas surrounding our nation's cities.

Local food—American food: Secure and reliable access to fresh, high quality, local, and American food is also an environmental issue: think transportation, climate, and energy.[9] And access to local food affects community quality of life. The local farms that supply this local food are the ones most immediately at risk for development. Should America become a net importer of food,[10] let's remember that there are environmental impacts from eating food that is not American just as there are from eating food that is not "local."[11]

Opportunities for Future Environmental Improvement

The loss of working farmland also costs us important opportunities for future improvements in environmental management and restoration. Once land is developed, these opportunities evaporate. Since our most price-threatened farmland is located in areas within commute or recreation distance from urban areas, these farms are also most likely to be in the same watersheds, flyways, habitats, floodways, and other environmentally contiguous areas as are their neighboring human population centers. So the opportunities they offer to mitigate for or to offset urban environmental damage are often also strategic.

For three-quarters of a century, the USDA/Natural Resources Conservation Service (NRCS) and other agencies have been assembling techniques for farmers to improve environmental performance on their land. There are today several hundred best management practices, each designed to address one or more specific environmental resource concerns, usually in a way that permits continued working agriculture. Each is based on scientifically grounded quality criteria that describe the desirable environmental conditions that the use of the practice should be able to achieve.

With technical help from NRCS or from a local conservation district,[12] farmers can adopt as many or as few of these practices as they wish and can get some limited financial help. They can use them to address issues of water quality, soil loss, air quality, wildlife habitat, and a wide array of other environmental concerns. A farmer can also implement a full conservation plan that assembles a set of these practices, designed specifically for their farm and aimed at eliminating negative environmental impacts while allowing continued, economically viable farming.

For example, if a farmer has a water quality/runoff or soil loss problem, the NRCS or conservation district expert might recommend strip cropping, grass buffers, cover crops, limited tillage, an improved irrigation system, rotational grazing, or sediment ponds. If there is a need to improve fish or wildlife habitat, the farmer might restore riparian buffers, plant field borders with native vegetation, fence pastures for rotational grazing, use habitat friendly rotational cover crops, restore in-stream habitat, or restore a wetland on a wet, non-productive area of the farm. If there are climate concerns, the farmer might use satellite-guided precision fertilizer application or change to natural fertilizers to reduce nitrous oxide emissions, install an anaerobic digester to eliminate methane emissions, or adopt "no-till" practices or "conservation rangeland management" to sequester carbon in the soil. As one might expect, each of these practices also has a suite of co-benefits so that addressing one particular environmental concern will typically improve conditions for others as well.

As mentioned earlier, the detailed explanations, science, and technical application of these techniques are fully laid out in the USDA/NRCS Field Office Technical Guide publicly available online.[13]

Making Use of Farm–Environmental Opportunities— the New York City Watershed Project

One of the more striking illustrations of a community taking comprehensive advantage of the above opportunities is the New York City Watershed Project.

The City of New York gets about 90 percent of its drinking water from the Catskill Mountain and Delaware watersheds, rural agricultural areas about two hours north of the city and covering 1,900 square miles. The city owns less than 10 percent of the land in the watersheds. The balance belongs to some 77,000 local and summer residents. There are about 350 farms in the area that cover a large part of the land and represent an important economic base.

New York City needs this area to be carefully managed and to remain mostly undeveloped. Since 1907, the city has vigorously protected its water supply by acquiring some 57,000 acres of land, razing homes, using eminent domain, even relocating entire villages. Needless to say, these actions engendered a good deal of mistrust among local residents.

Then, in about 1993, the city faced a serious problem. To meet the standards of the Safe Drinking Water Act,[14] it was looking at spending between $3 billion and $8 billion on a drinking water filtration facility, plus operating costs of several hundred million dollars annually.

Or it could restore the water quality at its source—a potentially much cheaper answer.

New York City's first reaction was to propose a series of new, rigorous regulations on the farmers in the region. It was said that these regulations would have forced farmers to retire some 35 percent of their land and would have driven many out of business. The reaction in these rural communities was predictably vigorous, with farmers proposing to blockade New York City with tractors. The potential collapse of the farm economy promised increased subdivision, new construction, and a rising population in the area.

Fortunately, the city was persuaded that a substantial community dialogue was needed. Ultimately, a Watershed Agricultural Council was created to oversee a series of mostly incentive-based actions including:

- Purchasing agricultural easements structured to keep farms in well-managed agriculture and out of development;

- Riparian buffer protection that paid the full rental value of the land, an initial signing bonus, and up to 150 percent of the cost of installing new practices required to protect the buffer;

- Farm conservation planning with fully funded incentives for implementing the practices called for in the plan; and

- Marketing assistance to help participating farmers sell their crops directly to gourmet restaurants, food stores, and in farmers markets and at other venues in New York City.

Today, farmers in the region are quite happy with this program. As of about 2004, it had enlisted an almost miraculous 92 percent participation among the area's farms. And it was credited with reversing the decline in the city's drinking water quality. The cost to New York City was a tiny fraction

CONSERVATION ECONOMICS

How a Dike Setback Preserved Four Farms

Flooding is a problem for farmers along the Nooksack River, which flows through Whatcom County, Washington, not far from the Canadian border. The traditional landowner strategy here, as in other parts of the country, had been to build a good, strong dike, ideally just a bit stronger and higher than the one built by the neighbor across the river. So long as the water overtopped first onto somebody else's property, your land might stay dry. This practice has ended and the height of dikes is now limited. But flood problems continue.

Meanwhile, the Nooksack (with its tributaries) is one of the largest, most important salmon rivers in the Puget Sound area. Its dikes are often so close to the river's edge that they mostly eliminate off-channel habitat, riparian vegetation, or other river conditions needed by the endangered salmon that must rest, hide, feed, grow, and spawn here. By channelizing the river, they also speed its flow and worsen flooding further downstream.

Four neighboring farmers along Bertrand Creek, where it meets the Nooksack, needed a long-term solution to their flooding problem. Their dike was overtopping in the spring floods nearly every other year. By the time the fields dried out, it was often too late to plant a crop. When the dikes breached, erosion damaged both the dikes and the fields, so there were ongoing costs for maintenance, repair, and lost soil.

Meanwhile, the fish needed habitat. The farmers teamed up with the Nooksack Indian Tribe, Whatcom County's flood control department, the local diking district, the Whatcom Conservation District, the local watershed improvement group, the Corps of Engineers, and others, to come up with an answer.

Their project moved the dike protecting these properties substantially back onto the farmers' land and away from the existing edge of Bertrand Creek. The farmer whose land was most affected was paid for a conservation easement. The area outside the dike and next to the creek could then be restored to natural conditions with riparian plantings, replacement of large woody debris, and opening up off-channel ponds and fish passages. The new dike was stronger, yet also slightly lower than the one it replaced. But, because the river now has room to spread, the new dike provides much greater protection for these farms. Instead of facing floods every other year, these farmers should now be able to plant crops in fifteen out of every eighteen years. And, because the new dike is built to exacting Corps standards and is nicely armored against erosion damage with native vegetation, the farmers will also save on future maintenance.

Large woody debris in stream, Montana. *Courtesy of USDA-NRCS*

of what would have been spent on a technological water filtration plant. The benefits for watershed communities: restoration of stable, prosperous, rural agriculture and the protection of many local environmental values including the pristine waters within the region itself.[15]

For Environmentalists Only

[FARMERS, DO NOT READ!]

Are Farm Businesses Really Vulnerable?

The claim that new regulation will drive one industry or another to its knees has been used to fight environmental protection before. It's probably sometimes true and sometimes hyperbole. So a battle-scarred environmentalist may be inclined to take this argument with a grain of salt.[16]

The unique business vulnerabilities discussed in Chapter 3 should, however, be enough to justify a second look at this concern when it comes to agriculture. And, while we are considering those vulnerabilities, let's remember that a farm doesn't need to fail for its owner to decide to sell. Perhaps the land has gained in non-farm value and the owner just gets tempted during one of the inevitable "down" years, or becomes discouraged after hearing of yet another new regulatory requirement. Perhaps the new rules cause the children of the family to decide that taking over the farm isn't as appealing as a promising job in the city. Maybe there was a neighbor who would have bought it for farming, but instead has second thoughts because it just seems like the business is getting too tough.

The business competition this farm faces isn't just coming from other farmers. It is also competition from totally different industries with different uses for this land.

Suppose you own a four-hundred-acre farm. With a lot of work, it has been earning you an average net annual income of $75,000 or so. Not bad for a small business. But new environmental regulations can have a way of being very intrusive. Perhaps you have to set aside forty of those four hundred acres for wetland, or wildlife habitat, or streamside salmon buffers. Now you're only farming 360 acres, but your fixed expenses remain the same. You're sure not going to pass that cost along to the multinational corporation that buys your crop. Where you feel this loss will be in your net income. When that 10 percent loss of land produces a 30 percent reduction in your net profit, how might you feel then about accepting that $3 million offer for your land? At a 5 percent return on investments, that money would bring in $150,000 a year. You could retire tomorrow. You could go get a comfortable job in town for the next few years, then move to Florida.

Having $3 million invested in stocks and bonds, even in a shaky market, can look a whole lot safer than using that land as mortgage security the next time you need an annual farm business operating loan.

Are Our Farms Dispensable?

Even if you believe the claim that regulation will drive farmers out of business, a tough-minded environmentalist might also shrug off the loss of commercial enterprises that can't meet environmental standards in the modern world. One might legitimately feel that the survival of a "dirty" or non-compliant business, or even an entire industry, just isn't worth the burdens and consequences that its environmental damage visits on the rest of us.

At the end of Chapter 2, we considered the purely environmental consequences of losing farmland. And in this chapter, we have looked at the environmental opportunities we lose when farms disappear. Those consequences and lost opportunities are diametrically different from what we'd expect to happen in the same situation in other industries. The bottom line: Losing our farms is decidedly not a good environmental option.

Moreover, the case for protecting agriculture is also different from the case we'd make for many other industries. We'd all like to see the United States continue to be self-sufficient in food. We'd like our local communities to have access to local food. We'd prefer to see our agriculture industry remain less corporate and, where possible, operated by smaller, independent family farmers. And we'd like to retain the environmental advantages of an undeveloped agricultural landscape.

If we agree that these are important values, we need to think about how we can help agriculture succeed, rather than allowing it to be replaced with something much worse.

For Farmers Only

[ENVIRONMENTALISTS, DO NOT READ!]

As a farmer, you may find this chapter reassuring. You should. It is good to know that agriculture can help the environment while remaining profitable. And it is especially satisfying to feel that environmentalists might come to appreciate this. If so, maybe they'll be a bit more careful with the future of working farms.

But keep in mind that the environmental advantage of agriculture depends on what you compare it to. If it's a choice between a farm and a forty-acre shopping mall, the farm comes out well. But if the alternative is a wetland, a native prairie, or a forest wilderness, the comparison may not look so good, at least not to an environmentalist.

The Need for Some Regulation

It would be good if the environmental community came to realize that reducing farm environmental impacts isn't just a matter of having fewer farms. And it would be very good if they also came to accept that there are limits on the practical use of regulation. That acceptance would mean that farmers might be able to live with the regulations that do get passed and that many more environmental improvements could be accomplished with voluntary incentives and environmental markets.

But you know, better than anyone, that working farms (like nearly all human land uses) have negative environmental impacts. Some of these impacts are substantial, especially when spread across the huge areas covered by American agriculture. Like everyone else, agriculture must share in the burdens of protecting and improving the environment. So we can't simply say: "Great! Farms are good for the environment. Environmentalists should just go away and worry about someone else who isn't." Instead, the conclusion we need to draw is: "Great! That should moderate the regulations we're likely to face. So let's enlist the environmental community in helping us secure the incentives we need to finish the job."

Avoiding Land Conversion Out of Agriculture

You may have noted in the above chapter that, among the most important environmental benefits of successful working farms are the opportunities they offer for future improvement. Yes, there are some environmental benefits farms provide, just because they're farms. But for others, improvements are needed. It is important that we not conclude that what farmers are already doing now is good enough. Clearly it isn't.

Fortunately, working farms can usually make improvements just by adapting better farming practices. If we end up with wholesale conversion of farmland out of agriculture, whether to other private non-farm uses or to purely environmental ones, that will only be because we have missed those opportunities.

How Can We Get Both Profitable Agriculture and a Healthy Environment?

What would it mean to adopt the goal of achieving profitable farm businesses and, at the same time, a healthy environment? For farmers, it would mean adopting new conservation practices in the years ahead. Sometimes these new practices may actually strengthen farm profitability. Sometimes they will have little or no impact on profitability. Sometimes making environmental gains may require significant capital investment or extra care and labor that will not pay off in lower costs or a better crop. And sometimes they may even require the use of land that is now in crops or livestock. If we do this properly, that last outcome should be very limited.

To the extent environmental improvements increase operating costs without any productivity benefits, farmers will clearly push for incentives rather than regulations. And to the extent there is pressure for land conversion farmers will fight to avoid it. If conversion is unavoidable, farmers will want to replace the lands that are lost, ideally in the same community, so they can also avoid the disappearance of local farm-support infrastructure businesses and the collapse of local farm economies.

But these disagreements and negotiations must occur within the context of a farm–environmental understanding in which all sides presuppose these two mutually accepted goals:

1) We will retain a healthy, profitable, economically sustainable agriculture industry along with the land it requires to operate;

2) Our farms will bear their fair share of the burdens of protecting and improving the environment.

Neither of these goals is possible unless we are all prepared to accept both of them.

CHAPTER 5

Voluntary Incentives—Pro and Con

What Are Conservation Incentives and Where Do They Come From?

American agriculture has a lot of experience using incentives for environmental conservation. Most of it has been quite positive. The most important farm conservation incentives programs have been those traditionally included in the federal farm bill, a body of legislation passed every five years addressing many issues affecting agriculture.

The farm bill's conservation programs originated with creation of the Soil Conservation Service (SCS) in the 1930s as a response to the Dust Bowl disaster. The SCS was the predecessor to the current Natural Resources Conservation Service (NRCS), which works with landowners to advise them on how to conserve natural resources—like soil, water, air, plants, and animals—on their land, while continuing to engage in economically viable working agriculture. Another federal agency, the Farm Service Agency (FSA), administers farm price support and payment programs including the Conservation Reserve Program (CRP) and Conservation Reserve Enhancement Program (CREP), which are described below.[1]

Following federal creation of the SCS (now NRCS), small local governments called conservation districts were created throughout the country. Like NRCS, conservation districts also provide conservation technical assistance for private landowners and they can sometimes bring state, local, and private money to the table as well. But one of their big advantages, and a big reason they were created, is that they are independent local governments run by boards, generally composed of farm landowners, elected or appointed from the local community. Thus they create a landowner-friendly point of contact in local, rural communities for environmental incentives programs generally.

Conservation districts partner closely (and are often co-located) with NRCS, FSA, and other state and federal agencies that deal with local landowners. Conservation districts are stronger in some parts of the country than others, but even where they are strong, the bulk of funding for conservation, especially for that portion that is spent directly on landowner incentives, is still typically federal.

Some of the principal federal programs that provide the conservation incentives discussed in this book are:

- Environmental Quality Incentives Program (EQIP) shares the cost of implementing a wide variety of environmental conservation practices. EQIP is the largest of these programs, with the broadest mission and the largest annual budget.[2]

- Conservation Stewardship Program (CSP) provides payments to farmers who adopt a selected array of conservation practices in the management of their lands that address at least two specific natural resource concerns.

- Conservation Reserve Program (CRP) leases land from farmers and restores it for wildlife or other environmental purposes.

- Conservation Reserve Enhancement Program (CREP)—a part of CRP—leases and restores locally designated highly sensitive lands (such as streamside riparian buffers).

- Agricultural Conservation Easement Program (ACEP) helps purchase agricultural easements to keep land in farming and out of development and provides easement protection for wetlands and for other conservation purposes.

Sometimes these programs lease or actually purchase interests in land. Sometimes they will pay the full cost of a project. But mostly these are referred to as "cost share" programs because they will usually only pay a part (typically up to 50 percent) of the cost outlay incurred in initially implementing conservation practices or constructing environmental improvements. There may be local funding to increase that percentage. But usually the farmer pays the other 50 percent or more. NRCS, conservation districts, and other incentives program providers try to make it as easy as possible for landowners to come up with the other 50 percent. So, sometimes the landowner can contribute "in-kind" by offering the use of farm equipment or by contributing the landowner's or employees' unpaid labor. Still, the landowner's financial contribution to a project can be quite significant.

What Are the Advantages of Voluntary Conservation Incentives?

There are some important advantages to incentives.

- *Voluntary participation*: The most desirable quality of incentives is, of course, that they are voluntary. They do not require that people be compelled to do things against their wishes.

- *Landowner contribution to cost:* Current incentive programs usually have the big advantage that a significant part of the cost of a project is covered by the landowner. Public expense is reduced by leveraging this private contribution. Because the cost of installation may only be a part of the actual landowner expense incurred in creating, maintaining, and using the practice over time, this landowner's share may actually turn out to be considerably greater than the government's typical 50 percent share of initial installation.

- *Landowner interest in success—cost and effectiveness:* Because incentives are voluntary, the landowner is fully on board and becomes a partner in the effort, both financially and otherwise. It is in the landowner's interest that these practices succeed and that they do so inexpensively. The landowner also knows, better than anyone, what is likely to work on his or her land given its specific circumstances. So the work that gets done tends to make sense for that location. If something is suggested that isn't practical or will cost too much, the landowner will usually know about it and is motivated to speak up. This built-in safeguard assures that the public money is well-spent.

- *Conservation economics:* Conservation practices will usually cost the farmer money. But they can, sometimes, also be sound business (as demonstrated in the various "Conservation Economics" sidebars throughout this book). While they improve the environment, they may also enhance farm productivity, especially over the long term. For example, a riparian buffer planted with vegetation and restored to improve fish and wildlife habitat might also stabilize a stream bank and end erosion that has been eating away the edges of a valuable farm field. Or it might create a forested barrier along the river's edge that reduces water damage to the rest of the farm and stops debris that would end up on fields after frequent flooding. The use of limited tillage, strip cropping, or planting a conservation cover crop in the off season might help wildlife habitat and keep sediment and nutrients out of the water. But it might also retain moisture and improve the topsoil, keeping it on the field growing crops and increasing productivity. Providing habitat for raptors or beneficial insects can also help control pests. Adopting good environmental stewardship may help the farmer market the crop. The existence of such economic benefits of environmental stewardship helps further reduce the cost of the incentives required and thus saves us all money.

- *Environmental lift:* One of the principal advantages of voluntary action is that it makes possible the actual affirmative restoration of lost vegetation, damaged habitat, and eroded or otherwise degraded land. With voluntary incentives, farmers can implement positive environmental improvements that may actually roll back previous losses. With the exception of some permit mitigation, regulations are typically able to only prohibit future damage. Preventing future and additional damage is important; we don't want things getting worse. But an active, willing, participating landowner can actually make things better. This is how we get trees planted, wetlands restored, renewable energy sources built, creative new solutions devised and installed, and other new physical environmental improvements.

  It also elevates our starting point for preventing future degradation.

- *Known cost:* From an economic policy perspective, incentives also offer the advantage that we actually know their immediate cost. The economic costs of regulatory action can often be hidden in higher prices for products, failed businesses, lost employment, and other depressed economic activity. This must, of course, be balanced against the fact that the longer term costs of environmental degradation are also usually hidden. But at least with incentives, we have a pretty good idea, right up front, what we're spending now, as a society, to get the environmental improvements we feel we need. It is all laid out right there in the agency budget.

  When these costs are buried in the increased business expenses of a regulated industry or in higher consumer prices, our only measure of cost may be the decibel level of political outcry from the industry's lobbyists.

- *Outcome monitoring and financial oversight:* Because they are usually paid for with public funds, and because some of that money potentially benefits private individuals, incentives also require fiscal rigor to survive in the political arena. Those expenditures must be justified to voters and lawmakers. Of course, regulatory agencies do make an effort to identify and quantify their accomplishments.[3] And it is always hard to find unbiased money to pay for monitoring environmental performance. But measuring performance can seem pointless when that performance is simply required by law. So it is an advantage for incentives that their clear need for accountability motivates incentive program managers to carefully track their cost and to look for strong measures of program effectiveness.

- *Site and need-specific adaptation lowers total social cost:* Using incentives for environmental improvements on private lands can also be cheaper overall. Of necessity, regulations need to be "one size fits all." They must apply broadly enough to adequately include the behavior that is of concern. But in order to get that breadth, and because the world is a complicated place, they also often encroach onto and affect activities that do not need regulating. That can add unneeded expense and inconvenience to the burdens borne by those who are regulated, by their customers, and by society as a whole.

  When regulations are truly needed, we can probably swallow some of that added expense and inconvenience as a part of the cost of living in a safe and clean society. But they can be particularly impractical when applied to cover the many site-specific conditions, limitations, and opportunities that exist on thousands of unique individual parcels of land that are used in a wide variety of activities across a highly diverse agricultural landscape.

  Voluntary incentives avoid these unnecessary overlap losses. Because the landowner is an active participant, incentivized actions tend to be well-adapted to the special conditions and circumstances on each particular property and are less likely to unnecessarily interfere with important economic needs for the land. Incentives are typically administered by technical experts on an individual property-by-property basis. This adds program staff expense. But it also helps assure that the money is spent on work that is well adapted to the specific site. Unwarranted public and social costs can be avoided and unanticipated social benefits can be maximized simply by approving only the best and most productive projects. Regulations cannot typically consider such matters.

- *Community engagement:* Incentives can also stimulate and leverage collective community engagement. If people feel they are being dictated to by outsiders, change can be difficult. An unwilling citizen does only the minimum, may drive up enforcement expense, can be a source of ill will throughout the community, and can organize locally and become a long-term political (and cost) liability. Encouraging and incentivizing good citizenship, however, can produce positive social pressure and enlist willing, even enthusiastic community participation and leadership with amazing results at minimal public cost.

- *Fairness*: Finally, incentives can sometimes be fairer than regulations. There are times when the regulated industry may not really have caused the problem. Because they are in a position to fix it, however, they may, nonetheless, end up being the particular minority targeted by the political system to do so. Fairness is complicated. Some of these complexities are addressed in Chapter 7. For now, let's just note that having incentives available as an alternative to regulation makes it possible to shift the cost of environmental improvement from a particular group to the rest of society when that is what seems most rational and fair.

The Struggle to Target Incentive Cost-share

As we've seen, sometimes a conservation practice will provide significant benefits for the farm business while also helping the environment. In other cases, the benefits may be mostly environmental, largely serving the general community. Where there is little benefit to the farm, the net costs of using the practice may make it difficult for the farmer to justify adopting it. An in-stream restoration project, for example, might be of critical importance for saving endangered fish and thus of great value to the general community. But it may be of no value at all to the farmer. The installation work and long-term upkeep may be a considerable cost and nuisance. If the project succeeds, the increased presence of endangered fish passing through the property may actually end up heightening public scrutiny and increasing public pressure for unwanted (and perhaps costly) regulation.

Conversely, a modern irrigation system that saves water needed in-stream for fish, or that greatly reduces pollution in irrigation return flows, might cost many tens or even hundreds of thousands of dollars to install. But it might also be a sound investment for the farmer who can save on costs of water, labor, energy, chemicals, and fertilizer, and can improve the quality and market value of the irrigated crop.

The optimal approach would be to view this as a kind of marketplace and to match the level of cost share incentive offered with the likely independent motivations of the landowner. For a cost-share program manager, however, it is difficult to sort out these considerations in advance for each individual practice and for each specific instance of its use. And there usually isn't sufficient money to make the incentives appealing enough to enlist enough applicants for the program to make sense.

To avoid having to make those kinds of choices, NRCS and local conservation districts often apply a flat 50 percent cost share limitation on the total amount that will be spent on a single project or on any given farm. This, in practice, can tend to become "the amount" they will pay, generally. Accordingly, the NRCS projects that are most popular with farmers become the ones that provide the most on-farm benefit. And projects that do not provide such benefits will often require contribution from other sources of funding to accomplish; funding that, quite often, is simply not available.

Chapter 7 discusses how this might be improved. As it stands, the current approach creates both advantages and disadvantages for the system. Sometimes it doubtless maximizes the share of the cost that is paid by the landowner. But in other cases it probably limits landowner interest in participating in projects that may have been of considerable public value.

Weaknesses and Limits of Voluntary Incentives

Incentives for environmental stewardship in agriculture also have their issues and limits.

- *Limited funding:* The first and foremost of these weaknesses is their cost—or at least their direct public fiscal cost. It is a constant political challenge to secure adequate incentives funding since they compete with funding for other important public priorities. Because funding can be difficult to get, conservation cost share programs are able to cover only a very small percentage of the potential annual demand for conservation assistance in the United States.[4]

- *Missed opportunities:* Because the cost of installing a conservation practice will often be only a small part of the total overall expense of creating and maintaining it, a cost-share limit of 50 percent of installation cost can be a big constraint. There may, for example, be lost use of grazing or crop land, increased labor in ongoing management, reduced crop performance, or increased energy costs. So a 50 percent NRCS contribution may end up covering only a very small percentage of the actual long-term expense of the practice. As a result, landowner interest is often limited; many needed or preferred projects are missed.

- *Unclear landowner motivations:* Among our cooperating landowners, we can never be sure who actually changed their behavior and decided to participate by reason of the incentives they received. A "cost share" incentive will reach out best to those landowners who are already somewhat inclined to take action. But we cannot know for sure exactly why any particular participant decided to act or how many of those that did so might have taken action anyway even without the incentive. So, from a public finance perspective, it can be hard to confidently measure an incentive program's cost-effectiveness.

- *The contract fulfillment conundrum:* The fate of publicly-funded incentives programs depends heavily on both the willingness of farmers and ranchers to participate and on political support for the programs. Managers of incentives programs often find themselves needing to prove the worth of their programs using anecdotal evidence. For this they must rely on whatever political "goodwill" they can muster among their satisfied farmer participants.

  With program managers so dependent on the goodwill of their landowner clients, it can be challenging to enforce incentives contracts where, for example, a landowner fails to maintain, over time, a practice that was first installed with public money.[6] Overall, NRCS seems to do fairly well at securing contract fulfillment from its clients.[7] But when such a situation arises, program managers are forced to balance the benefits of rigorously enforcing the contract against the potential disadvantage of driving away other potential landowner clients in that community who might see such enforcement as overreaching. At the same time, weak contract enforcement can undermine the credibility of their program.

- *Strategic impact:* Cost-share programs can also be hard to make strategic. Their success depends upon well-intentioned citizen-landowners who are willing to share in their expense. Unfortunately, those public-spirited citizens who are interested in voluntarily participating may be sprinkled widely and thinly across the landscape. Their land may not always be located in the key, critical location where the most environmental leverage can be achieved. Or the willing landowner may not be the one whose land would be the best able to address the specific critical problem which represents the most important community concern. With more money to spend, the programs would receive more applicants. They could then be more selective in funding only those projects that offer the most strategic outcomes. Since they are chronically underfunded, however, their limited credibility for strategic cost-effectiveness becomes a self-fulfilling prophesy. (More about this in Chapter 9.)

  Incentives can also come to be an empty promise. The natural and usual local community reaction to an environmental problem is for threatened citizens to urge that it be addressed with incentives. But in the face of difficulties in actually getting the funding, the hoped-for incentives can end up not forthcoming.

There have, for example, been many efforts to address nonpoint pollution under the Clean Water Act using incentives. The needed funding, however, very often never shows up in the amounts hoped. This isn't much of a testimonial for incentives. So it should come as no surprise that some environmentalists have concluded, in another self-fulfilling prophesy, that incentives just don't work.[8] Many environmentalists have come to object to the use of voluntary incentives unless their funding is essentially a sure thing. Of course, it seldom is.

CONSERVATION ECONOMICS

How a Fish-friendly Tide Gate Revived Farming for a Whole Community

Snohomish County Drainage District No. 13 (DD 13), just east of Everett, Washington, is a small, local government run by volunteers for the purpose of keeping the six hundred acres within its boundaries dry enough for homes and farming. DD 13 lies along the lower Snohomish River. Much of its land is below high tide. All of its nineteen farms are vulnerable when the river floods.

DD 13 drains into Swan Tail Slough, a waterway at the foot of a bluff along its eastern edge. The slough empties through a tide gate. When the tide is low, pressure inside pushes the gate open so water can drain out into the river. When the tide rises, outside water pushes the gate closed keeping the district dry. A large pump helps complete the process.

Farming has been a way of life here since European settlers built these dikes in the late 1800s. Before that time, rearing salmon used Swan Tail Slough for refuge from the rapid flows, predators, and other hazards of the main channel. There is a desperate need for such off-channel habitat for salmon, some of which are now listed under the Endangered Species Act. So current rules require operators of facilities like the DD 13 tide gate and pump to obtain renewed approval from the U.S. Corps of Engineers for any major changes or replacements. This includes a full environmental impact analysis.

DD 13's heavy, rusty, fifty-eight-year-old tide gate was wearing out and in serious need of replacement. It barely opened and largely blocked salmon out of the slough. The old pump was obsolete. Replacing the gate and pump was going to be expensive. Residents would find it very difficult to afford on their own. And they were concerned that, even if they could find the money, they'd never secure approval to replace the gate. They feared their farms could soon end up inundated and unusable for agriculture, which was said to have happened in another nearby area along the river. Many of them had come to believe that their tiny farming community was essentially doomed.

With help from Snohomish County, NOAA Fisheries, the Snohomish Conservation District, and other partners and funders, DD 13 won official approval and secured grant funding assistance for a new, efficient, salmon-friendly tide gate and pump. The new, lighter gate opens wide to let more water out even on a moderate tide, helping flush the stagnant slough and improve its quality. It also allows salmon to pass freely in and out.

Not long after the new gate went in, there was a near-record flood. At its peak, only a narrow ribbon of dike and houses stood above the water. As the flood receded, residents walked the dike and watched the new gate open wide and drain the district at a rate they had never seen before. Soon after, salmon fry were entering Swan Tail Slough in great numbers.

Before this project, many of DD 13's farmers had given up hope. Some hesitated to invest in or even maintain their farm businesses. Most had concluded that the county government wanted them to fail at farming and to give in to restoration. Many had become vocal adversaries of environmental protection.

Today, however, this community is acquiring a new sense of pride and self-identity. The farmers are marketing their products locally and promoting them as grown with respect for salmon and the environment. They are reaching out to their residential neighbors on the surrounding hills to help reduce the chemicals and pollution that harm the salmon in Swan Trail Slough. And landowners who, before this project, bitterly opposed doing anything that would "let salmon into our district," are now making their private land available and serving as volunteers in riparian habitat restoration along the banks of their slough.

2:00 a.m. low-tide installation of new tide gate at DD-13, Snohomish County, Washington. *Photo by Ryan Christian, courtesy of Snohomish Conservation District*

For Environmentalists Only

[FARMERS, DO NOT READ!]

At this point, you may be thinking: "OK, so perhaps incentives are fine. But isn't there also a place for regulations?" There is! Please read on; the next chapter deals with that.

But incentives also have a role to play.

The Foundations for Skepticism About Incentives

There are many reasons environmentalists have come to mistrust incentive programs, some valid, some not so much. Let's look at some of those reasons:

- *Regulatory successes:* One reason many environmentalists prefer regulation may be a desire to repeat the successes of some of our major national regulatory environmental laws like the Clean Water Act, the Clean Air Act, the Marine Mammal Protection Act, and the Endangered Species Act. There have definitely been big gains.

  But, as successful as they have been, these major legislative landmarks have also, in some regards, been less effective than we might have hoped. One could point to the rapidly expanding list of endangered species or mention the limitations of the Clean Air Act for creating new sources of carbon sequestration. But perhaps among the strongest illustrations of the weakness in our current laws is in the failure of the Clean Water Act (CWA) to reign in nonpoint pollution. The CWA was, of course, designed mostly to target point sources. And it has done a great job. But nonpoint is today's most significant water quality problem.[9] It is erasing many of the CWA's gains and is the most significant issue for agriculture. Yes, perhaps we could achieve more with stronger rules and enforcement. But it is still difficult to see the CWA as the best model for how to control nonpoint pollution.

- *Mistrust of voluntary action:* Partly, the environmental community's focus on regulation arises from frustration with slow overall progress. The blocking tactics of many large industry groups (including agriculture) that seem to oppose efforts to protect the environment are, no doubt, particularly frustrating. Having experienced these tactics, it is hard to then embrace measures that depend on voluntary action by the same people who have resisted change and denied the problem.

- *Cultural differences:* Environmental confidence in regulations is partly cultural. People who mostly live in heavily populated areas and who work for and deal with large institutions daily can become accustomed to living by regulations and less likely to see them as particularly intrusive. An urban resident's daily experience with city traffic may be more than enough to make them a believer in the importance of rules.

- *Underfunding:* But the most important reason environmentalists lack confidence in the effectiveness of voluntary incentives may be the very concern that they actually share with farmers—incentives are so badly underfunded.

Incentive Funding and Strategic Effectiveness

The starting point for conservation incentives does not typically focus on large, landscape-scale problems. Rather, the traditional approach is to identify and work with each individual landowner. We view their operation, discuss the issues, and assess the improvements that could be made on that one property. We provide individual attention, adapt to the specific circumstances, support and encourage the landowner's personal sense of social responsibility, help to identify some of the potential business benefits, and add in a small financial sweetener in the form of a partial monetary incentive. The hope is that, if we do this diligently and with enough landowners, over time we can change the world.

This has proven to be a terrifically effective technique. It is the one believed to be responsible for transforming the U.S. agricultural landscape following the 1930s Dust Bowl. This is the working model for most conservation incentive program professionals. It is the foundation for most existing NRCS and conservation district work around the country.

As we've seen, however, this approach tends to sprinkle these small successes thinly across the landscape and is limited in its capacity to address large problems that are bigger than a single landowner or whose solution requires a more targeted and more comprehensive approach.

But this process can actually be more strategic than may at first appear.

NRCS and conservation district personnel have developed strategies to help. NRCS's national, state, and local offices throughout the country adopt strategic plans that identify the key "resource concerns" that they see as of primary importance. Conservation districts go through a similar process. The creation of specific national programs like the Wetlands Reserve Program (WRP), or the Wildlife Habitat Incentives Program (WHIP), or the Conservation Stewardship Program (CSP), (along with many others) each represents an effort to call out specific environmental issues for special, more targeted treatment. And at the local level, NRCS and conservation district staff typically work with local leaders to agree on key issues or geographies where they should focus their limited financial resources.

Strategic focus can also be gained through the targeted use of personnel. For example, when a key priority watershed or community has been identified as critically important, local conservation professionals will sometimes make personal contact with every single landowner whose help might be needed. They may do this by attending or organizing small, local, community meetings. They may call landowners on the phone or seek introductions from others in the community. Many times they simply go door to door.

In this way they enlist a few of the more willing landowners and build on their positive experiences, testimonials, and credibility to create examples for others in the community who may be initially hesitant. Slowly but surely, they often leverage their initial successes and secure the cooperation of a solid critical mass of the key landowners in a targeted community or watershed. Every conservation district in the country can relate a list of amazing success stories that have followed a model much like this.

This staff-intensive approach, however, also requires adequate funding. It requires that someone generate the community network needed to make this succeed. These staffers are not highly paid, but they do need to be trained professionals. And they need to have worked in the community long enough that they have come to know the landowners and to understand the programs that are relevant and available. To make this approach succeed, these local district offices need funding that is adequate to provide those personnel and also that is stable enough to keep them in place over time. Most simply lack that kind of funding.

In addition to staff, these programs also need the incentives themselves. A small increase in the dollar or percentage share amount of a financial incentive can work wonders in increasing the critical mass of landowners interested in participating. Unfortunately, conservation incentives programs rarely, if ever, have the wherewithal to offer greater incentives to landowners whose properties may be particularly critical or whose participation is particularly necessary to address a strategic environmental need. This will be discussed in greater detail later in this book. For now, however, it is important to be aware that if current incentives programs were better funded their ability to be strategic and to address environmental problems at the scale needed to be decisive could be dramatically improved.

Given this background, one would hope that, as an environmentalist, you might reserve judgment on the effectiveness of environmental incentives until you've seen how they work when they are adequately funded and until you've seen how a farm–environmental coalition might help secure that funding. One good example is the New York City Watershed discussed in Chapter 4.

For Farmers Only

[ENVIRONMENTALISTS, DO NOT READ!]

The Place for Incentives

If you are a farmer who is working on environmental issues, you probably already support incentives. Certainly the conservation district and nonprofit professionals who advise farmers on conservation stewardship usually believe in this approach.

But, to the extent one truly cares about protecting and improving the environment at a landscape scale, it has to be asked: "How are we doing with that?" Spelled out in this book are numerous instances in which this approach has worked wonders. So we know the system can work. But if we were hoping for dramatic environmental gains on the broader scale— solutions to the kinds of widespread environmental problems identified in Chapter 3, for example, the answer has to be: "Not very darn well!" Farmers have contributed to some amazing gains, but we seem to be climbing a sand hill. Many of our society's biggest environmental problems just seem to be getting worse. Why? You'd probably agree, it's because there usually just isn't nearly enough money. So let's consider the reasons for that.

One of the reasons we find it hard to get substantial funding for incentive programs certainly seems to be the circular one mentioned above: that these programs aren't seen as highly strategic because they are dramatically underfunded. And they're underfunded because they aren't seen as strategic.

So legislators aren't as impressed as they might be. And the environmental community doesn't fight for funding as hard as it could.

But there is also another significant reason for that underfunding as well: the agriculture industry doesn't really fight for incentive funding either.

Clearly the mainstream agriculture industry cares deeply about avoiding new regulations. In the fight against them, farm industry leaders commonly argue for incentives as a better alternative. But as soon as elected officials back away from new rules, the agriculture industry's interest in funding those incentives often seems to weaken. It isn't at all clear that the key mainstream leaders in our farm community care enough about actually solving our underlying environmental problems to fight for the funding needed to make the incentives programs work. Once the immediate threat of regulation goes away, other priorities move to the front burner.

If incentives are to be a credible alternative to regulations, the farm industry needs to get serious about supporting them.

The Place for Regulation

Let us also not buy into some fiction that, to the extent we have to do something about the environment, we ought to be able to do it all using voluntary incentives. There is a legitimate place for regulation. As we've seen, there is a strong case to be made for voluntary action and for limits on the use of regulation. But for some things there must be rules. And efforts by farmers to weigh in against excessive regulation will fall on deaf ears if we don't acknowledge that regulation also has an important role to play.

Dealing with the Cost of Incentives

Those of us who believe in incentives also need to face up to the "small" matter of their cost.

As the good conservatives they often are, most farmers don't like taxes. Nor do the legislators who usually represent them. With some notable exceptions—such as the farm bill commodity price support programs—the agriculture industry typically opposes costly public programs, sometimes even when those programs are in their own self-interest. This is probably at the heart of the reticence of the American mainstream commercial agriculture industry to vigorously and consistently fight for adequate incentive funding.

So it isn't just the misgivings of the environmental community that undermines our incentives programs. This belongs on the doorstep of farmers as well.

CHAPTER 6

Regulations—Pro and Con

A friend of mine who works for a regulatory agency is fond of saying: "Just give me a clear rule and a few million dollars for enforcement and I'll fix agriculture's environmental problems in a hurry." The logic of this seems unassailable. Make it clear what you expect people to do and that they'll get punished if they don't.

Just as we have a good deal of national experience with incentives, we also would seem to know how to regulate on environmental issues. The Clean Water Act,[1] Clean Air Act,[2] Endangered Species Act,[3] and Marine Mammal Protection Act[4] are four excellent examples of federal environmental laws that seem to have had remarkable success. Each has survived generally intact since its introduction in the early 1970s, and each has brought about dramatic improvements in the quality of our environment.

But, like incentives, regulations, too, have their strengths and weaknesses.

When Regulations Work and When They Don't

The Clean Water Act (CWA) is a good working example. As mentioned in the previous chapter, our national success at cleaning up point-source pollution with CWA regulation has been excellent. But it has had a lot less success with nonpoint pollution. It's worth asking why.

In the initial stages of implementation, the CWA required U.S. polluters to adopt at least the "best practicable technology" (BPT) to clean up their act. BPT still needed to be "practicable"—if a technology was unproven or was terribly expensive, it didn't have to be adopted. Nonetheless, the BPT requirement drove the wastewater treatment industry to develop cost-effective systems for treating pollution. Industrial and public utility point-source pollution has been greatly reduced. Today the nation's water quality is dramatically better than it would have been had the CWA not been passed in 1972.[5]

But, for point sources, getting to clean water can also require a second stage of CWA implementation. Suppose all the point-source polluters have adopted BPT but the waterway is still polluted. In that case, the regulatory agency must determine the maximum acceptable daily "load" of each pollutant which that waterway is deemed capable of bearing while still meeting water quality standards. As mentioned in Chapter 3, this is called a "total maximum daily load" (TMDL). Each polluter discharging that pollutant is assigned a maximum allocation or amount of pollution that they will be individually allowed to contribute to that combined community load. In reaching their individual load allocation these polluters are required to adopt a yet-higher standard of technology called the "best available technology" (BAT). This means they must use whatever water purification/treatment technologies it may be reasonably possible to use, essentially regardless of their cost. If that doesn't work, they must reduce their operations.

Even using BAT, there is no guarantee they will receive their National Pollution Discharge Elimination System (NPDES) permit to operate. Because no matter what technology they use, these polluters must still demonstrate that their operations will not exceed their assigned daily load allocation. If they adopt BAT and still can't get there, they must do something more (like water quality trading, for example, discussed in Chapter 9). If there are no other options and they still can't reach their allocation, they must reduce operations or they get no permit. And, whoever they are, they are sometimes out of business—at least at their current location.

The consequences of failing to get a permit can be so unacceptable that it is worth almost any expense to comply. For a public wastewater utility to close down, for example, could cause tremendous damage to the community it serves. Ceasing operations or refusing to accept waste from some of their customers is, for many, simply not an option. So they're likely to spend almost whatever it takes.

So why does this system work so well?

1. *Motivation to comply*: There is plenty of motivation to meet the standard. Failure may simply not be an option.

2. *Access to resources*: The major point-source permittees are large institutions (like public wastewater treatment utilities, major manufacturers, food processors, energy producers, or other large industrial facilities) with access to the funding required to comply. They can often pass along higher operating costs to their ratepayers or customers.

3. *Competitors face the same standards*: For businesses, their competitors across the country often face similar restrictions.

4. *Ease of enforcement*: Violations are usually easy to identify and to prove—just test the water coming out of the "point source" (e.g. at the end of a discharge pipe).

5. *Limited number of permittees:* Since there are only a limited number of relatively large point source polluters, locating them all, requiring permits to operate, and getting them each to compliance is a finite and manageable task.

A Watershed-based Approach

The heavy reliance of this preferred CWA approach on technology is somewhat ironic. The typical treatment plant can be a complex mix of pipes, concrete settling and treatment tanks, refrigeration systems, pumps, aerators, filters, computers, and other chemical, electronic, and biological processes. These depend on electric power, ongoing maintenance, highly expert personnel, and continued attention and monitoring. Yet both the environmentalists who champion this approach, and their environmental agency counterparts who are responsible for its implementation, are deeply schooled in the advantages of natural systems.

One has to wonder where they got their remarkable faith in technology.

There are other ways to handle some of this. Watershed carrying capacity could be increased through improvements in the natural conditions along the waterway. We could improve channel complexity, restore riparian buffers and vegetation, increase flow, and restore and improve off-channel estuaries, for example. In many cases, nonpoint source polluters along the river might be called upon to manage their land in a more environmentally friendly way that reduces their and their neighbors' contributions of pollution.

A more watershed-based and "natural" approach would have some great advantages. In addition to helping remove the targeted pollutants, it could also create new wildlife habitat, sequester carbon from the atmosphere, reduce flooding, address other, non-targeted water quality issues, and secure a host of environmental benefits that might be of great value, even if they are "ancillary" to the immediate purpose of improving water quality. And, in many cases, this might all get accomplished at a much lower community cost.

The watershed restoration approach, however, also has disadvantages. How do you measure the outcomes if you can't do so at the end of a pipe? It would require involving a lot of other people and interested groups in the process—for example all those landowners who own properties along the upstream banks of the waterway. It might mean enforcing the CWA against a large number of unidentifiable nonpoint source polluters. The whole thing could easily end up bogged down in community process, controversy, and litigation. (More about these alternatives in Chapter 9.)

For both the regulatory agency and the permittee, it seems much easier to just solve the problem on site, right there at the NPDES permittee's own facility. The permittee can hire established contractors who understand and are quite capable of building the kind of facilities needed. They can set a budget and plan how they'll raise the money. The whole project and completed facility will be under the permittee's control; if something goes wrong, they can get it fixed rather than having to rely on a lot of other people to get the job done for them. These apparent certainties make it easy for regulators to set compliance deadlines and to have confidence in their "reasonableness." The completed facility can be readily inspected to assure it is continuing to perform. If anything fails, it should be easy to find the responsible party and to get the problem fixed in a hurry before much damage is done.

With the manageability of the outcome, the clarity of the regulatory requirements, and the ease of enforcement, this regulatory system works quite nicely—even if it is very far, indeed, from the best and least costly system we might imagine.

Regulatory Fairness

At first look, a regulatory system like this also seems quite fair. When the vast majority of the water pollution comes from known and identifiable point sources, it is easy to see who to blame, and hard for any individual polluter to claim that they are being harshly dealt with. Regulations make it clear: here's how much you're contributing to the problem; here's your proportionate share of the fix. In practice, of course, there is much argument about how these load allocations get set. But at least the CWA approach makes an effort to be rational and fair.

This certainty of responsibility creates another type of fairness as well: fairness for the conscientious citizen. Clear, predictable, and consistently enforced regulations create unmistakable standards of conduct and call out irresponsible behavior. People who behave properly know that others will also be required to do so.

The power of this kind of fairness was illustrated a few years back in the dairy industry in my home state of Washington.

Around 1996, Washington dairies began to face serious CWA enforcement against poor management of their livestock manure. The U.S. Environmental Protection Agency (EPA) and the State Department of Ecology (DOE) ramped up their enforcement and began issuing violation notices and major fines. Most of the modern dairies were being forced to deal with high land prices and intensifying competition by reducing the acreage of their farms while increasing their number of cows. This concentration of cows also concentrated animal waste above what the smaller land areas could handle and created a need for more systematic waste management.

While many of these dairies could be considered nonpoint sources, the steadily increasing concentration of their operations also made it easier for determined regulators to identify a specific source of manure pollution. Some of the fines on dairy farms caught polluting local streams and rivers were in the range of $25,000 to $35,000—big money for a family farm.

Fuel was added to the fire by a widely-publicized lawsuit brought by a local citizens group against the Yakima area's Bosma Dairy. Ten local dairies received notice of intent to sue. Eight settled out of court and one left the business. But the Bosma Dairy fought the case all the way to the Ninth Circuit Court of Appeals.[6] Bad practices in the industry and the resulting enforcement actions became big news. Stories ran in the mainstream media. Political pressure began to build.

Facing lawsuits, ongoing fines, the possibility of unworkable legislation, and continuing negative press, the Washington State Dairy Federation enlisted the help of legislators in proposing a bill that would, for the first time, require every dairy farmer to be licensed and to adopt and fully implement a "dairy nutrient management plan" (for "nutrient," read "manure"). The plan had to be professionally prepared and certified to be in accordance with NRCS specifications. If a dairy didn't get licensed, its owners would be fined. If they didn't have an approved plan, they would be fined. If they didn't build the physical improvements needed to make the plan work, they'd be fined. If inspectors found that the plan wasn't actually being implemented in practice, there'd be a fine.

As an inducement, legislators committed to several million dollars in state incentive cost-share funding over a six-year period to help farmers build some of those needed improvements. But the essence of the bill—supported by the dairy industry—was still regulatory.

When the dairy bill was first introduced in 1997 it failed to pass. It had solid official support from the Dairy Federation. But several influential individual dairymen came to the statehouse, on their own, to oppose it. Some of these opponents were dues-paying members of the Dairy Federation who simply disagreed with their leadership. Their opposition was enough to stall the bill.

Following the 1997 legislative session, a smart and gutsy Dairy Federation executive director undertook to cut to the heart of the issue. She tracked down and assembled a bunch of color photos taken in the field by EPA and DOE enforcement personnel; recent pictures taken at actual dairies throughout the state. They showed farm fields deeply layered with solid animal waste. They showed liquid manure being applied to fields in the middle of a pouring rain. They showed irrigation guns spraying manure directly across open streams. They showed overflowing manure storage lagoons. There were even manure lagoons being drained directly into local streams.

In the State of Washington, where salmon are an icon and clean water is prized, these pictures were potentially highly inflammatory.

Acting without instruction from her board, the Dairy Federation executive copied this stack of pictures in color onto 8½" x 11" pages and sent the entire collection out by post to every dairy farmer in the state. She made no comment on them. But at just a glance, for a knowledgeable dairy farmer, those pictures said it all. This was why the dairy industry had a big problem, why there had been so much bad publicity and community anger, and why they were facing all the recent intense regulatory attention and enforcement.

The Dairy Federation executive thought she might end up fired for what she'd done. But not one farmer called to complain. The locations of the pictures were not stated, but these were real and recent photos of local farm fields, so it was a safe bet that the owners of those farms (and their neighbors) knew exactly where those pictures had been taken. Every farmer whose land had been in one of those photos had to have been deeply embarrassed. No doubt some farmers were very relieved not to find a picture of their property in that packet. And every other farmer who was trying to do the right thing was angered at the irresponsibility of some of his or her colleagues.

The pictures had not been sent to the press. But it had to be disturbing to think that this kind of information could be so easily made public. None of these farmers wanted their neighbors or their communities to think (or to know) that they were doing stuff like this. And after the whole industry saw those pictures, nobody was going to show up at the Legislature and be publicly seen as, in effect, endorsing such practices, least of all the farmers who were actually doing them.

And nobody did!

The following year, 1998, the legislature brought the bill back to life and, with renewed Dairy Federation support, easily passed the Washington Dairy Nutrient Management Act.[7] There was little or no opposition.

Yes, you noted correctly that this essentially regulatory bill was proposed and supported by the state Dairy Federation, the dairy industry's own trade association. And, yes, Republican legislators (with help from Democrats) prime-sponsored the legislation and herded it through to passage. Moreover, all this happened during one of those rare periods when Washington State's House of Representatives was evenly split between Republicans and Democrats, creating great opportunities for deadlock. It was a time when action on anything might easily have been prevented with determined opposition from the dairy industry.

So one might justifiably ask: why did they do it?

Of course the dairy farmers were chagrinned and intimidated by the painful fines and lawsuits and wanted them to stop. They wanted to take control of whatever legislation did emerge so they could make sure it would be workable. And they were keenly embarrassed by the terrible publicity.

But most of all, they were angry with those colleagues in their midst whose irresponsibility had brought all this down upon them. They were fed up with allowing a few poor citizens in their group to reflect poorly on the whole dairy industry. And they decided that the only way everyone in the industry would be treated fairly and equally is if all of them were clearly and decisively held to the same high standard. This worked especially well in the dairy industry because markets for fresh milk tend to be local. They all knew their most immediate competitors would be subjected to the same legislation.

Regulatory Constraints

Perhaps the most significant constraint on the usefulness of regulation is that there is only so much of it that we seem willing to accept. Regulations can be intrusive and unwelcome, however righteous their purpose. All of us understand the need for rules and are willing to live with some. But there are limits:

- *Clarity*: If we may get chastised, embarrassed, fined, or otherwise punished for doing something wrong, we want the rule to be unmistakably clear. We want to know the exact limits of what it is we're not supposed to do so we can avoid doing it while also being confident about our conduct when we are acting lawfully.

- *Enforceability*: We don't want to live with rules that are seldom enforced or unenforceable. We don't want a world where the majority of us are breaking the law every day, where police power is, in effect, unlimited because everyone violates some law, and where law-abiding citizens become "chumps" constantly put to disadvantage by those who ignore the rules.

- *Enforcement cost and bureaucracy:* There are limits to what we want to spend on enforcement. But more importantly, there are limits on the extent of the government enforcement "presence" with which we're willing to live in our daily lives.

- *Coverage:* We don't want there to be so many rules covering so many areas of life that complying with them becomes overly burdensome or difficult to track or that they constrain too many of the activities of our daily life and too greatly limit our freedom to make our own choices.

- *Complexity:* We don't want the rules we face, either individually or taken together, to be so complex that they get too difficult to understand or that it gets too burdensome to make sure of exactly what we need to do or not do to be sure we're complying.

Inspection and Licensing

To mirror common usage, I've used the term "regulation" in this book to refer broadly to any legal rules constraining human conduct. Technically, however, only the rules adopted by a regulatory agency like the Federal Trade Commission, the Consumer Product Safety Administration, the Federal Aviation Administration, or the Environmental Protection Agency, for example, through their delegated authority, are regulations. And one of the implicit concerns is that, because such regulations are usually adopted by administrative officials who are only indirectly answerable to voters, they can seem dictatorial.[8]

Such regulations are quite often limited in their application to those who engage in a certain profession or activity (like physicians, realtors, druggists, pilots, accountants, electricians, drivers, etc.) Typically, though not always, they are also associated with some system of licensing that may require all those who wish to engage in this activity to register their personal information and demonstrate their qualifications. There may also be a system of inspections to assure that the licensee is complying with the rules.

This is how it works for point-source permittees under the CWA. Similarly, the Washington Dairy Nutrient Management Act, discussed above, required all dairy farmers to register with the state, to keep a current nutrient management plan, and to operate in accordance with that plan. And it included a system of inspections to make sure that they were doing so.

Strict Liability

One of the reasons regulations can seem especially burdensome is that you can still be guilty of a violation even if you don't know about the rule or know that what you're doing is wrong.[9] This is unlike violations of most ordinary criminal laws. In order to be guilty of assault, for example, you must know what you're doing is wrong and proceed to do it anyway. You must have guilty intent. Violating a regulation, however, does not generally require that the offender act with wrongful intent. You can be punished for running a red light regardless of whether you even saw the light at all.

This is called "strict criminal liability" and it is usually applied only in a regulatory context. We do this partly because the penalties and the stigma associated with a regulatory violation are considered less significant. And, even though the rules may be detailed and rigorous, strict liability seems acceptable because the narrow or clearly defined group of people to whom they apply must have some specific training, license, or certification or can, for one reason or another, be expected to know about them. Perhaps people in this position should, therefore, be held to a higher standard of conduct with respect to this specific, limited area of activity.[10]

Regulation can, however, quickly become onerous when applied broadly across society. When regulations have very broad application, as is the case with traffic rules, for example, most of us begin to balk unless we're convinced that there is an unmistakable need for these rules and that, without them, the risks would also be obvious, immediate, and potentially personal as well. (For traffic violations, this definitely seems the case.)

Strict liability creates a big challenge for environmental regulation when it moves beyond controlling large institutions like steel mills, energy facilities, public utilities, and the like. Fairly enforcing regulations on environmental performance by individual citizens can be much more challenging and is likely to face a good deal more public resistance. For one thing, meaningfully enforcing broad rules of that kind can quickly intrude into areas of our lives we consider to be private.

We're probably not prepared, as a society, to accept having as many police officers out looking for pollution in our yards or for chemicals in the backs of our garages and under our bathroom sinks as we now have on our highways spotting violations of the rules of the road.

Regulatory Limits in Controlling Nonpoint Pollution

The Clean Water Act, again, provides an excellent example. As we've seen, it has not been particularly effective in dealing with nonpoint pollution.

In an urban setting, it is sometimes possible to collect a good deal of the nonpoint surface water pollution that runs off of city streets, rooftops, and other impervious surfaces. Much of this can be channeled into a surface water drainage system. Those drainage waters can then be treated, managed, and addressed by regulators as point-source pollution. Even there, however, that effort is often only partially successful. Some of these systems can be overwhelmed in heavy rainfall events and they may miss a good deal of the water. Efficient collecting may not be possible where the population is more widely spread out.

Nonpoint pollution is extraordinarily hard to identify or prosecute in court. (Imagine the waste oil, exhaust, tire wear, and other leavings from your car as you drive down the freeway, and you get the idea.) Those signs one often sees stenciled on the pavement next to urban drainage grates that say "Dump no waste—drains to stream" illustrate how controlling nonpoint pollution can end up depending heavily on public education and voluntary compliance.[11]

When environmental regulatory agencies like EPA—or its state sister agencies—set the allocation for local point sources under a TMDL, that allocation will often reflect this weakness. It can end up much lower, and the resulting cost and difficulty of meeting it much greater, than would have been necessary were nonpoint polluters also sharing the pain. This can create immense pressure on point-source polluters who operate under these permits. Since (like Eric Nelson in our Introduction) it is they who are most firmly in the regulators' grip, and it is they, and their customers or ratepayers, who end up sacrificing to meet that onerous load allocation.

Many times a local public wastewater utility or local industrial plant discovers that it must spend tens or even hundreds of millions of dollars on a new, high tech, wastewater treatment facility that might not otherwise have been required. So regulators, and communities, increasingly struggle to find other ways to reduce that sacrifice by getting nonpoint polluters to bear their share of the burden.

In mapping out plans for TMDL compliance, regulators often set a load allocation for nonpoint polluters as well. They often do this, however, knowing full well that meeting that nonpoint allocation using the hoped-for voluntary incentives is problematic. It seems likely that many of these plans will fail to meet their built-in deadlines.

Farmers ought to be very worried about the consequences of such failures. Where a farm community faces a nonpoint load allocation under the CWA, they should fight very hard indeed to get the proposed incentives funding in place. If they don't meet that nonpoint allocation with the promised incentives by the specified deadline, they may easily face legal action in the courts that may result in painful regulation of their farming practices.

The Potential for Regulation of Agriculture—"Ag Practices Act"

Regulatory control of agricultural nonpoint pollution is difficult. But it is not impossible.

Yes, it may be challenging to identify and measure the pollution that comes from a specific farm. But it is not hard at all to require that all farmers implement certain conservation practices in managing their lands, practices that are known to measurably improve water quality if applied across the farm landscape.

These practices can include:

Buffers: Require that farmers maintain a minimum width of undisturbed buffer between farming activities and any waterway and that livestock be fenced out of this area.

Tillage: Require the use of no-till farming in growing certain logical crops.

Soil cover: Require the planting of cover crops during critical off-seasons or the use of strip cropping on vulnerable hillsides or over a given slope.

Farm plans: Require adoption and use of an approved farm conservation management plan written in accordance with NRCS specifications and meeting specified quality criteria.

All of these farm practices have been thoroughly studied, so we can be fairly certain what the effects will be if their adoption is required. All could be easily inspected for compliance. This was essentially the approach taken in Washington under the Dairy Nutrient Management Act described earlier.

This approach is sometimes referred to as an "ag practices act." For obvious reasons, the farm industry generally opposes it. It is seen as government interference in the details of farming. And one can understand why. It intrudes rather directly on the farmer's discretion in deciding how best to grow a successful crop. It could easily overreach, requiring the same practices of everybody where action by only some of them is really necessary. It would very likely reduce both the opportunity and the motivation for individual farmers to find and use more effective, less disruptive methods to prevent pollution and help the environment—methods that might work much better on their particular farms in their specific geographic area with the actual problems they face, problems that might not be typical in other locations and, hence, not considered in describing the required practices. And it would take its toll on the economic survival of some farms—perhaps with undesirable consequences.

Nonetheless, it is important to keep in mind that if the public decides to regulate agricultural nonpoint pollution, it is quite possible for it to do so.

Regulation as a Motivation for Incentives— Washington's Ruckelshaus Process[12]

The potential for worrisome regulation can, of course, also create powerful motivation for communities to intensify their struggle to fund voluntary incentives.

In the State of Washington, local "critical areas ordinances" (CAOs) are the regulatory land use management tool through which counties enforce many local, state, and federal environmental requirements. The inclusion of several species of Northwest salmon on the Endangered Species List has created a challenging legal and political battle over riparian buffers. The agriculture industry was faced with new CAO regulation that might have required substantial buffers along local streams and rivers. Meanwhile, the environmental community was struggling to get serious progress on salmon recovery in the face of considerable resistance to regulation, especially at the local government level where these CAOs are implemented. State legislators were in the unenviable position of having to compel local counties to protect salmon.

To end this decades-long deadlock, the 2007 Washington State Legislature established a two-year (later extended to three years) moratorium on new amendments to local critical areas ordinances affecting agriculture.[13] It directed the William D. Ruckelshaus Center, a Washington State University–University of Washington partnership, to lead a negotiation process between farmers and environmentalists seeking some kind of deal on salmon habitat in general and buffers in particular.[14]

With the eyes of the public and the Legislature upon them, and the clock ticking, in late 2010 the negotiation group came up with a basic conceptual agreement that was formalized into legislation in the 2011 session.[15] It included the following elements:

- Local communities are offered the option to avoid new CAO amendment and enforcement and to receive significant state funding for a voluntary, incentive-based local conservation program to deal with key environmental problems. If the community opts out, it must proceed with creation and enforcement of needed CAO requirements.

- If the community opts in, it proposes priority watersheds and issues and suggests work plans which set benchmarks for environmental protection and improvement.
- A state oversight and technical review committee reviews and approves these work plans and the proposed benchmarks and tracks progress in meeting them.
- The moratorium on CAOs continues until the state funding is provided.
- If, after funding is received and after implementing their plan, a watershed fails to meet the agreed benchmarks, the local community must return to the usual CAO process or proceed with some other new state-approved approach.

This program, rather elegantly, uses the threat of future regulation as a motivation for local communities to address their environmental problems. But it also secured the support of both farmers and the environmental community for state funding for incentives. If, with the incentive funding, a community fails to meet its approved benchmarks, it will fall back into the hands of the existing CAO regulatory process.

For Environmentalists Only

[FARMERS, DO NOT READ!]

The regulatory option is where farmers and environmentalists seem to face their greatest dissonance. So there are some major frustrations when farmers and environmentalists discuss these issues.

Pollution as a "Moral" Issue

High among these frustrations is the farmers' sense that they are being judged. Of course, if you're doing damage to your community, you should be judged. But many environmental activists feel deeply that any kind or amount of pollution, environmental damage, or harm to wildlife is just plain wrong and simply shouldn't be allowed. If it isn't already illegal, it ought to be. This viewpoint suggests that people whose activities have any negative impact on the environment are bad people, and that it doesn't really matter what excuses may be offered. They should just be stopped.

Certainly, most would agree that irresponsible and socially damaging behaviors deserve to be treated as morally wrong. But not all activities that have environmental impact are immoral. Certainly not all are illegal, nor should they be. When one applies indiscriminate moral judgment to activities that affect the environment, it is easy to forget that all of us, no matter who we are, affect the environment. Preventing all those impacts is not a desirable, let alone a practical, thing to do.

For example, it can come as a surprise that the Clean Water Act (CWA) and Clean Air Act (CAA) do not actually prohibit the release of pollutants. To put it plainly: if they did, we would all be obliged to die. At least three of the biological prerequisites for life would have to end—eating, breathing, and elimination. Most other generally accepted daily activities like transporting ourselves from place to place or heating our homes and offices would also have to stop. Fortunately, the purpose of the CWA and CAA is not to stop the release of pollutants.[16] Rather, their objective is that we collectively meet responsible air and water quality standards, a goal that is a good deal more reasonable.

In fact, the EPA and its sister state environmental agencies routinely issue permits to discharge pollutants: Title V Operating Permits under the Clean Air Act, and National Pollution Discharge Elimination System (NPDES) permits under the Clean Water Act. It is not the purpose of these permits to stop the discharge of pollutants, but rather to appropriately reduce it, to allocate those discharges across society, and to control who is allowed to discharge, how much they discharge, and where and under what circumstances they do so. The Endangered Species Act works in a similar way—it doesn't require the cessation of all negative impacts on endangered species. Rather, it issues permits for "takings" and limits those permitted takings to a level that will allow the species to recover.

Human life and economic activity necessarily involve environmental impacts. What we need to do is control those impacts and to do so in a way that is fair and that doesn't cause unnecessary social and economic dislocation.

In other words, this isn't a moral equation. It is a practical, scientific, social, and political one.

Political Vulnerability and Defensiveness

This sense by farmers that they are objects of unreasoning moral outrage also strengthens their determination that they not be made the scapegoat for problems that aren't their fault.

Remember, farmers quite often live on and farm land that has been in their family for generations. The landscapes and rural communities in which they reside change slowly—there are no huge new buildings periodically piercing their skyline; no new residential communities are springing up wherever they look. At least outwardly, their farms may not look a great deal different than they did in their grandparent's time. The startling landscape changes that are happening across our country are much more apparent in urban areas, where the impacts of growth, sprawl, technology, and rising populations are clearly visible. When farmers hear about worsening environmental problems, they focus on the farm practice improvements they've made, which are many. It is difficult for them to associate those problems with their conduct on their farms and in their communities.

At the same time, farmers are very aware that the weakening of their numerical and political influence creates the potential for them be become a political target and end up the fall guys for problems that ought to be addressed by others. So, if we want their help, we need to be very clear that they are only expected to bear their fair portion of the burdens.

If we do that, they will stand up and do their share.

The Principled Nature of Environmental Advocacy

Another frustration for farmers is that environmentalists seem to have no practical "skin in the game." The consequences for farmers of an environmental policy decision can be quite real. The outcome may affect their actual income, perhaps a lot. In the worst-case scenario, they could end up bankrupt and be the last of several generations to farm the family land. It is important to remember that, for farmers, this isn't a matter of theory or of principle. The outcome affects their livelihood, their family, their self-worth, and their very way of life.

Farmers don't see environmentalists as being exposed to the same risks. From a farmer's perspective, the environmentalist can afford to focus on theory and principle; the outcome seems unlikely to call for any personal sacrifice. When farmers think about who they are up against, the usual stereotype that comes to mind is of an urban resident who may know very little about rural life or farming, who has probably never been in business, and who may have little idea of what it takes to succeed in business. The environmentalist seems like someone whose contact with the environment is mostly recreational, who is probably supported by a well-paying urban job, and whose life and lifestyle will continue unaffected by the outcome of their disagreement.

This is the person with whom the farmer is, directly or indirectly, negotiating.

This helps explain one of the farm community's most common complaints about dealing with environmental representatives. To farmers it seems like every time they reach a tentative agreement, at that point when everyone goes back to their boards or to their memberships to cement the final deal, environmentalists always come back wanting more.

This is because the environmentalists in a negotiation can easily understand the farmers' needs; they are essentially the same for all the farmers affected. If the result seems fair and doesn't too badly damage their economic survival, the farmers can probably live with it. But the farmers' picture of the needs of their environmental adversaries is not nearly so clear. With their environmentalist counterparts motivated mostly by principle, it's hard to know what they really want. What *is* the principle? It may be different for each of the group's members. How much environmental protection is enough? When things are a matter of principle, more is always better; no amount less than everything will ever be enough.

So when environmental negotiators go back to explain things to the people they represent, they inevitably face up to that wide diversity of principled viewpoints. They end up coming back to the farmers for "just one thing more."

Farmers come to feel that they will never satisfy the environmental community until their entire farm has been totally converted to pre-Columbian wilderness and they, too, are on a salary in the city.

Cost IS an Issue

Farmers also sense that economic impacts just don't seem to matter to environmentalists. And, in the face of ongoing environmental degradation, it is easy to view economic impact arguments against regulation as self-interested and cynical.

But economics do matter! The cost of environmental protection dictates how much of it society can afford. If we make it too expensive, the plain fact is, we're going to get a lot less.

Of course we need to make investments, now, in our environmental future, just like we need to invest in education, public health, transportation infrastructure, or drawing down the national debt. There will always be limits on how much we can invest today, no matter what we're investing in. There may be disagreement about what those limits are or on what we prioritize. But there are limits.

Consider, for example, our nation's recent experience with climate legislation. The United States did not join in the Kyoto Protocol mainly due to worries about its potentially harmful economic impacts. More recently, the risks of climate change (widely understood on both sides of the political aisle) were squarely placed before the U.S. Congress in the Waxman-Markey Bill—the American Clean Energy and Security Act of 2009 (HR 2454), also known as the climate bill. The bill's death in the Senate could be easily explained by economic concerns, especially in view of the then current global recession.

Conversely, many of our greatest political successes in securing new laws protective of the environment have followed sustained periods of economic prosperity.[17]

So, if we are to secure meaningful environmental protections, we simply have to pay attention to their costs—both fiscal and economic. Where we can't make a strong "cost impact" case, success will continue to elude us.

Finally, economics matter if we care about fairness. And fairness matters if we really want to get something done.

It isn't just the total cost that's important. It is also important to know who should pay it. Farmers, like most everyone, are willing to share the burdens of a social problem. The public, and the public's elected representatives, are going to expect them to do so. But, also like most everyone, farmers will balk if they feel they're being taken advantage of. So if we are to successfully enlist public and farm community support for more rigorous environmental policy, it isn't enough just to show that there is a problem and that fixing it is economically sensible. We also must be confident that we know where responsibility lies and that we can fairly assign the burdens of the fix.

If that seems a high standard to meet, it is also a political reality we face.

For Farmers Only

[ENVIRONMENTALISTS, DO NOT READ!]

There isn't much doubt that there are national environmental problems for which agriculture is significantly responsible. Just one highly visible example in the water quality arena is the dead zone in the Gulf of Mexico.[18] Agricultural runoff of nitrates and phosphorous throughout the Mississippi watershed is heavily implicated. The recent USDA Conservation Effects Assessment Project (CEAP) shows substantial improvements have been made through incentive-based conservation, but grave problems still exist.[19]

It simply isn't possible for farmers to stand aloof from this problem. Too many people's lives and livelihoods (Gulf fishermen, communities, and tourism businesses, for example) are suffering damage.

This is but a single example. Agricultural runoff is a problem facing communities throughout the country.

The Nonpoint Argument

The agriculture industry's response to water quality complaints of this kind is often to point out that most agricultural pollution is nonpoint and that nonpoint pollution from farms is no different from anybody else's nonpoint pollution (city people included). Since we can't (and don't) control nonpoint for other people, why should we pick on our farmers?

This argument seems plausible to farmers partly because they don't feel like they are that much different from anybody else. There are 2.2 million farms in the United States. Most of them are owned by the people who farm them. Their farms are also their homes. They raise their families there, send their kids to local schools, participate in their communities, all much like their urban counterparts. No urban resident wants to see an EPA enforcement officer at their door, looking to inspect their toolshed for lawn chemicals or to see if the family cat has killed a migratory bird.

Neither do farmers.

But farms *are* different from urban and suburban households. To begin with, farming is a business. Business enterprises of every kind, even small ones, face some kind of regulatory attention to those issues specific to their particular activities. Farms, by their nature, significantly alter and disturb relatively large areas of land. They produce products (usually food) that enter the stream of commerce and are consumed by large numbers of people. They hire employees. They store and use large quantities of fuel, fertilizers, pesticides, and chemicals. They till, drain, dike, fertilize, plant, irrigate, and graze the land. All these activities suggest potential impacts on consumers, on employees, on the environment of the farm and of the lands that surround it, and on the public.

It is true that the public has, so far, been unwilling to bankroll (and face) the considerable enforcement that might be required to adequately control nonpoint pollution. But nonpoint pollution is still pollution, and it is causing a lot of harm. To claim that it is "just nonpoint" isn't really an argument so much as it is a sort of camouflage. And it is a vulnerable claim. It assumes that farm pollution is just the same as other people's pollution. But if it isn't just the same, then maybe it should be treated differently.

Imagine, for a moment, that you are an environmentalist or that you work for a state environmental regulatory agency. Perhaps your field of expertise is water quality. You care deeply about the environment and about clean water in particular. You have worked for most of your professional life to enforce the Clean Water Act as well as local state laws against pollution. Every day you deal with regulated industries, like industrial plants, wastewater utilities, hydropower producers, and city surface water managers.

For these people, you lay down the law: they either control their pollution or they lose their permits. No exceptions!

Your work sometimes causes a lot of pain. You've seen major industrial facilities forced to move or be run out of business. Some of their local employees have lost their jobs. You've seen cities forced to raise taxes to cover required improvements in their surface water management. You've seen public utilities forced to dramatically increase their rates and to face angry protests from ratepayers in their local service district. Some of those ratepayers could ill afford that hike. And every year that passes, it becomes more and more obvious to you that the principal cause of the pollution in these rivers is no longer the people you are regulating. Every year the largely unregulated nonpoint polluters become a bigger and bigger part of the problem. Much of that pollution, often most of it, now comes from agriculture.

You've also watched the agriculture industry succeed, again and again, in fighting back regulation. And to the extent farmers can be regulated, you're told by your government agency superiors that there just isn't enough money in the budget to enforce the law against them. Farmers are just too costly to catch and to prosecute. If you're an environmental activist, you and your organization have fought and lost frequent battles over stronger rules and over budget appropriations for enforcement. If you're an employee with the state's environmental agency, you live with those losses and watch the problems grow worse while your hands are tied.

Now along comes a farm lobbyist who argues that farmer pollution is "just nonpoint" the same as everybody else's. How do you feel about that?

Or imagine, instead, that you live in a medium-sized inland city. Maybe you're retired and live in a modest suburban home. Maybe you're struggling to raise a family. Maybe you like to keep a nice green back yard. Or maybe you own a small business, perhaps one that uses a fair amount of water, like a restaurant, for example.

And you vote.

One day, you receive your utility bill in the mail and are staggered by the amount. Your water/wastewater charges have more than doubled! There must be some mistake! But, no, when you call customer service, you're told that your utility has been required to build a costly new sewage treatment plant in order to meet the water quality standards for the river that flows through town. This is going to cost over $100 million, a lot of money in your community. And the increase you're seeing in this utility bill is just the start; your bills are likely to go up again, and substantially, in the months and years ahead.

Suppose you then read an article in the local paper and discover that most of the pollution in your river is actually caused by upstream farmers. But because they are nonpoint polluters, and thus are difficult to catch and to prosecute, the government has been forced to reduce the TMDL discharge allocations for point sources—local businesses and public utilities like the one that provides your sewer service. That is why that new wastewater treatment facility has to be built. If the farmers were doing their part, that plant might not be needed.

As one of those local urban residents, how do you feel about that? If you call the legislator who represents your town and explain all this, how do you think that legislator is likely to respond?

The Need for a Stronger Agriculture Political Strategy

As the TMDL requirements of the Clean Water Act are steadily implemented all across the United States, situations just like this are arising again and again. There is a point in time, not so far down the road, when a "just say no" political strategy isn't going to work anymore. When that happens, the first priority will be for farmers to convince their legislators (and the public) that the best way to improve agriculture's environmental performance is to raise taxes and provide the agriculture industry with voluntary environmental incentives.

The question is: will anyone still be listening?

Your local Farm Bureau representative makes an appointment with one of these legislators in the hope of making a case that farmers like you shouldn't be regulated, that instead, the legislator should vote to raise taxes so the government can afford to pay you and other farmers to reduce your pollution. These new taxes will be paid by those same citizens who have been calling to complain about their higher utility rates. The legislator will, of course, know full well that for a fraction of the fiscal cost to government (perhaps without needing any tax increases at all) you and your fellow farmers could just be regulated and directed to reduce pollution, perhaps with an ag practices act.

How do you think your Farm Bureau lobbyist's incentives proposal will be received?

As a farmer, you probably knew, even before you read the previous chapter on incentives, that there are many ways in which incentives can be much more effective than regulations. You already knew that while they cost a good deal more in government revenue, incentives may be much cheaper in overall economic impact on the community. And you knew that there are definitely times when incentives are much fairer, times when the general public really ought to cover more of the cost of environmental protection. So when the issue comes up before a legislative hearing, you will make those arguments.

But what will the expert from the state's water quality agency offer in testimony as the best approach? What will the local environmentalists argue? What about the local NPDES permittees, the businesses and utilities whose pollution allocations have been so dramatically and expensively reduced— what are they going to say? What are the mayor and city council members going to say (none of whom have any farmers in their districts)? And most important of all, how will our retiree, our young parent, and our local restaurant owner testify in response to your proposal that they pay more taxes so your costs of doing business don't need to go up?

As you answer these questions, keep in mind that the water quality example we've been using is but one among many similar accumulating environmental wake-up calls for today's farmers.

How Restoring a Wetland Grew Healthier Livestock

Sweet Grass Farm is a small specialty cattle operation located on San Juan Island in the northwest corner of Washington State.[20] About fifteen acres or so of this farm are in a large seasonal wetland that dries out for about half the year. This area (like many historical wetlands in the United States) has been used for generations to graze cattle during the dry part of the year. Wetland areas are not widely seen as advantageous for farming and were historically drained or filled rather than being managed as wetlands, so it is fortunate for the environment that this one had never been drained.

Scott Meyers, the owner of the farm, has been experimenting for years with ways to reduce his livestock impacts on the wetland while actually improving its productivity for grazing. He carefully manages his grazing during the summer months and excludes his cattle entirely in the winter while nurturing and reintroducing the natural wetland vegetation. He does this knowing that almost anything he does that might affect a wetland is highly suspect to many environmentalists, making him a potential target for regulation.

A local environmental nonprofit[21] partnered up with Scott to do a study of the impacts of his approach on natural wetland function and on nearby saltwater fish habitat. Scott wanted to know how his management practices might be improved. The results showed that his careful management of this area had produced remarkable success for most natural wetland functions, including substantial beneficial contributions to prey for salmon that rear and feed along the saltwater shores below the farm.

At the same time, Scott has noted that the rich grasses that appear in the spring, as the wetland dries out, become extraordinarily nutritious grazing for his cattle during the dry season. He harvests these grasses and uses them to feed his cattle in the wintertime. The cattle grow stronger and healthier, well worth the wait and the extra effort.

Scott has become an advocate for what he calls "wetland ranching." He encourages fellow ranchers to duplicate his experience and thereby help return seasonal wetlands on their land (sometimes referred to by farmers as summer pasture) to more natural wetland function.

CHAPTER 7

Choosing Between Incentives and Regulations

Given the strengths and weaknesses of each, sometimes the regulatory approach will work better for addressing agriculture's environmental issues, sometimes it will be incentives. Neither seems either adequate or appropriate to do the entire job alone. If farmers and environmentalists are to break their deadlock, they need a common understanding about the circumstances in which incentives will be best, and those in which we should look to regulations.

At the moment, we don't even have the language to discuss this choice.

As a first step we must end the current debate over which is better: incentives or regulations. The question is meaningless. Each is better for different things. We need a new debate over when each is most appropriate and how to make each more effective and less burdensome.

The Political Struggle over Incentives Funding

During the years I was executive director for the Washington Association of Conservation Districts, it was an important part of my job to lobby our state legislature and to convince them to fund our conservation district programs. At the start, our political strategy seemed obvious. Since conservation districts are the agencies that offer voluntary incentives, we could enlist the help of the agriculture community. And since the incentives we were seeking would be good for the environment, we could enlist environmental groups as well. With both on board, we would be unbeatable.

Sadly, it wasn't that easy.

Incentives cost money. And securing appropriations is never easy. The rural, Republican legislators closest to the farm community were less than enthused about any new spending. Their constituents in agriculture made it easy for them because mostly what the farmers wanted was just to avoid regulation, and arguing for incentives seemed to suggest that there actually may be a problem that needed attention. While the urban Democrats might conceivably have spent the money, their environmental constituents were unimpressed with incentives' mixed record for strategic effectiveness. What they really wanted were meaningful, enforceable rules and arguing for incentives funding seemed to undermine the purity of the case for regulation.

In the end, legislators from both parties could be counted on to continue current limited funding. But none of them were prepared to make these programs grow as needed. Our conservation districts would walk away at the end of each session feeling like we had received a collective congratulatory pat on the head for our good work, but never with the breakthrough that would empower us to change the world.

Thus was the "baby" of incentives thrown out with the "bathwater" of regulation.

Identifying Criteria for Making the Choice

What we need is a strategy to decide between these two approaches—in the various circumstances where they may be used—that we can count on to be as fair, effective, and inexpensive as possible.

Without such a strategy, the choices we make between incentives and regulations will continue to be largely irrational. Elected officials will base their decisions on a good deal of political bias and scant real information. The power to influence those decisions will remain in the hands of the constituent groups who can most effectively manipulate the political process. Decisions will waver from one direction to the other depending on current political winds. Some of our most consequential public policy choices on agriculture and the environment will continue to be made quietly, behind the scenes, and mostly by default.

And both farmers and environmentalists will each continue to see the other's preference as a threat.

As long as we lack the confidence that we can solve our environmental problems using the fairest, most effective, least socially costly means, it will continue to be difficult to get those problems solved. And we will continue to lose sight of the critical need to do *something*. A sound strategy for making the choice between incentives and regulations will get environmentalists a lot more environmental protection. It will get farmers the insulation they need from excess regulation. And it will get both farmers and environmentalists some measure of protection for the future of what needs to be our mutually treasured agriculture industry.

A starting point would be to agree upon criteria by which to judge the desirability of incentives and regulations. Participants and the public can then apply those criteria in making their case for one or the other.

What might such criteria include?

If we're interested in securing the broadest possible political support, our first criterion needs to be fairness. The incentives versus regulation choice requires us to ask, for each of the issues we face: Is this a problem that should be paid for by the general, taxpaying public? Is it one that should be paid for by a specific responsible group? Or is it a mix—and why?

To get at the fairness issue, we need to ask questions like:

- Who caused the problem in the first place? How is causation shared?

- Who is responsible for its continuation now? How is current responsibility shared?

- Are there people who are profiting from the use of public domain natural resources and who should stop doing so or who should be paying for that use?

- Are those who might be asked to step up able to pass their higher costs through the marketplace along to others who might be currently benefiting, even if indirectly, from unduly low prices for goods and services?

- Will a new regulation affect all of the members of the regulated group in a way that is mostly proportionate to their share of responsibility, or will it unduly penalize some in order to get at those who really ought to be shouldering most of the burden?

- Will there be unacceptable regulatory overlap affecting legitimate, responsible behavior?

- Will a preference for incentives be paid for by the people who, generally, ought to be paying? Can this be addressed by selecting an appropriate funding source?

Perhaps there are other questions, as well, that can help us advance a constructive conversation about fairness.

The concept of fairness is, of course, always going to be a muddy one. But keep in mind that the case that is made for a healthy environment is often grounded in social equity. We justify undertaking these burdens today because we feel future generations should not be forced to pay for our extravagant use of environmental resources, that society's poor and middle classes should not be disproportionately affected by a degraded environment, that environmental damage by first-world countries should not destroy the future economic opportunities for second- and third-world countries. We're never, realistically, going to get a society that is always and completely fair. But if we do not at least try for fairness in solving these problems we also erode the very foundations for our strongest arguments for a healthy environment.

Our second critical criterion must be *cost*. It is almost always the short-term cost of environmental protection and restoration that stymies progress, regardless of the long-term gains. Like everyone else who operates in the political setting, we all need to heed the Clinton-era political dictum: "It's the economy, stupid!" To understand the cost, we must ask questions like:

- What is the fiscal impact—either for incentives or for regulatory enforcement? What other needs do we have that will go unmet?

- What is the economic impact? How disruptive will this be?

- Will there be overlap affecting behaviors that need not be regulated? What is the expense of that?

- What are the short and long term costs of failing to protect our natural capital now and how can they best be measured?

Tied to cost is *effectiveness*. To judge effectiveness we need good science and metrics.[1] Because these decisions are usually made by non-specialists in the political arena, we currently tend to fall back on simple measures like how many trees were planted, how many acres were converted to conservation stewardship, or how many lineal feet of stream bank were restored. We should be measuring results: how many more members of a species are surviving, how much closer we've come to meeting clean water standards, or how much we have reduced flooding.

In weighing effectiveness, we must consider the issues discussed in the previous two chapters, looking at what works best in each circumstance. For example, if one wants to control something like point source pollution, new development, or destruction of existing habitat, the best bet may be regulation. If one wants to get a degraded wetland restored or new vegetation planted along a stream, one might chose incentives. If the objective is to motivate adoption of new farm management practices that are more wildlife friendly or that will help filter surface water, the choice may be more complicated. But in each case, we'll want to use what seems most fair, is least costly, and works best.

Weighing effectiveness also means we need to consider the best mix of regulations and incentives.[2] Some regulation will be needed to deal with the bad actors we will always find in any group. But we mustn't allow "strategic" and "cost effective" to translate into spending our limited incentives funding on bringing the bad actors up to speed. This has the effect of penalizing responsible citizens who take action at their own expense without help or reward. Without adequate incentives, of course, no one gets any reward and the entire burden of getting the problems fixed falls on the shoulders of those who end up subjected to regulatory enforcement.

These three questions of fairness, cost, and effectiveness will not always be answered in the same way. There will be competing considerations. We might choose an approach that is costlier if we think it is fairer. We might choose one that is less fair but more effective. Let's just do our best to make these decisions consciously and publicly. Once we begin making considered decisions, some of these questions may begin to answer themselves.

Improving the Process for Decision-making

Of course every policy decision is, ultimately, political. But we frequently make these choices without much consideration. Elected (and even appointed) policymakers are usually lay people focused on many issues and hurrying through their own complicated lives—not experts in environmental science or in agriculture. In a democracy, the public also influences these decisions and will never be sufficiently engaged to really pay attention to the details. Issues like fairness, cost, and effectiveness will never be easy to explain.

But since we do need to consider these issues, perhaps the most important improvement we could make would be to create a clearer process for doing so.

One of our obstacles is that current incentive and regulatory programs are typically housed in completely separate agencies as well as at different levels of government. For example, most of our major federal cost-share incentive programs for agriculture are handled by USDA-NRCS, an agency that exercises no (or very little) regulatory authority over land management. Regulatory authority is exercised by agencies like the U.S. Environmental Protection Agency (USEPA), the U.S. Fish & Wildlife Service (USFWS), or the U.S. Army Corps of Engineers (Corps). While some of these regulatory agencies may have some environmental restoration grant money to offer, their primary focus is on rules and enforcement.

This silo structure is typically mirrored at the state level, with state departments of agriculture or conservation commissions taking responsibility for incentives programs, and state departments of ecology, environmental quality, or fish and wildlife primarily responsible for regulation.

Of course we want our regulatory agencies to be vigorous and determined in their enforcement of the law. So it helps if they have a clear enforcement mission. And we want incentives agencies to work well with landowners. If you want landowners to invite you out to look over their private operations, it's best they not be worried that you may see something illegal and call in the environmental "police."

But the disadvantage is that each agency inevitably fights to protect its own turf and its own funding. Each serves, takes on the perspectives of, and becomes loyal to its own public constituency—that particular collection of politically active citizens and groups that supports and/or is affected by its programs and its budget requests. Each hires people who are true believers in the solution their agency has to offer. Every problem comes to be seen as a nail best dealt which by their agency's particular hammer.

One would think that, when an environmental problem is identified and public sentiment builds to see it addressed, all the relevant agencies of government (and their respective constituencies) would sit down around a table, share their expertise, and talk through how best to solve it. But that almost never happens. More typically, the constituents of one of these agencies (e.g. fishermen, hunters, bird enthusiasts, recreationalists, farmers, environmentalists, etc.) raise the issue with their most familiar agency or with a friendly legislator. If the matter merits attention, a proposal shows up for the first time in public as a bill offered in the legislature or as a new rule in the agency regulatory process. It immediately becomes intensely political. Everyone gets defensive, and any opportunities to thoughtfully compare the proposed bill with other possible approaches have evaporated.

People can get frustrated with too much "process." But perhaps our farm–environmental problems need earlier and more complete involvement of all the parties affected and a more careful and open consideration of the kinds of criteria discussed above. We could encourage greater public engagement. We could insist that the fairness, effectiveness, and cost (fiscal or economic) of the chosen approach be explicitly considered and then explained in public and in writing. We could make a habit of encouraging the public to read, understand, and critique those explanations in public discourse. Future choices could be guided by the best among the rationales used in earlier decisions.

Some communities have tried to improve these processes.[3] Where nothing currently exists, some inter-agency process could be established through executive order if not by legislation. Participants could consider and recommend the best approaches to farm–environmental problems and influence the direction of regulatory and legislative decisions. And when an approach to a problem is adopted, they could insist that, whatever it is (incentives or regulations), its implementation be adequately funded.

All this would help create the public confidence we need in the fairness of our choices between incentives and regulations.

Combining Motivations—Michigan's MAEAP

When farmers adopt conservation practices their motivations are typically mixed, a mix that will vary from person to person and circumstance to circumstance. One person may simply wish to improve the environment. For another, there may be community pressure. The practices involved may lower a farmer's costs or improve productivity. For some, there may be consumer preferences or environmental standards required by the marketplace. Some may be influenced by the cost-share money available. And for many, there will be the hope that by taking action they can reduce the risk of regulatory enforcement.

The State of Michigan consciously combined several of these motivations in a single program called the Michigan Agriculture Environmental Assurance Program (MAEAP).[4] By becoming "MAEAP-verified," a Michigan farmer can receive assurance that he or she will not be subject to environmental fines, will be broadly protected from civil penalties under Michigan's environmental laws, will be exempt from inclusion in a water-quality TMDL (see Chapter 6), will be prioritized for available cost share funding, and will receive a "verification" that can be of potential marketing value and a public indicator of community responsibility.

MAEAP verification is voluntary. A farm conservation plan is adopted and there is third-party verification that the plan is being implemented. As of this writing, Michigan has nearly 10,000 farms starting the verification process with 1,000 of them having completed it with substantial environmental gains.[5] Why has it been successful? There seem to be a variety of reasons, but a survey of participating farmers indicated that for 58 percent of them, securing the promised regulatory insulation was one of their principal motivations.[6]

Uncertainty about real or potential exposure to environmental prosecution is a significant issue for farmers. What MAEAP illustrates is how marshaling this among multiple motivations in one program can be highly effective.

MAEAP participating farmer, Scott Lonier. *Courtesy of MAEAP*

For Farmers Only

[ENVIRONMENTALISTS, DO NOT READ!]

Well-managed working farms do not pollute! We have some three-quarters of a century's experience with best management practices that can guarantee they don't. We know perfectly well how to avoid environmental damage from agriculture.

But for whatever reasons, many farms aren't using these practices—whether they be NRCS practices or otherwise.

As a result, a great many of our farms do pollute and cause other environmental problems. Yes, a farm may be a lot better for the environment than a manufacturing plant, a strip mall, or a housing development. But farms occupy many times more territory than all those other land uses taken together. In a world where we have diverse human land uses, we all, farmers included, have to do a lot better.

As the means for doing better, farmers obviously prefer voluntary incentives. But since not nearly enough farmers are actually using them, the agriculture industry needs a plan to make sure we get more incentives and, hopefully, less regulation.

Unconstitutional Takings

Faced with this dilemma, one might ask whether there is something in the U.S. Constitution that might protect farmers from excessive regulation or redirect government attention toward incentives.

One possibility is the Constitution's Fourteenth Amendment stricture that all citizens are entitled to "equal protection of the laws." As we saw in Chapter 3, however, equal protection mostly prevents discrimination against traditional political minorities. It provides very little protection for economic groups.

But what about the Fifth Amendment limit on the taking of private property for public use without just compensation? Perhaps a regulatory set-aside of private land for, say, a riparian buffer would constitute a taking under the Fifth Amendment.[7]

There are cases where such takings claims can succeed.[8] But courts explicitly defer to the discretion of government legislative authorities to make reasonable decisions that are for the health and welfare of the public. They are slow to reverse such decisions. The usual standard in regulation of land use activities, for example, is that such regulation is permissible, and no compensation is required, if the owner can still make some "economically viable use of the land" and if the requirements "substantially advance legitimate state interests."[9] It isn't enough that an individual's real property has lost value because of a government action.

Clean water, sustainable wildlife, air quality, human health, and other environmental values are decidedly legitimate state interests. So for a plaintiff to show a complete elimination of any "economically viable land use" or that there was no "legitimate state interest" is extraordinarily difficult.

Constitutional takings law is, therefore, a very thin reed upon which to lean in protecting the future of the nation's agriculture.

Political Barriers to Stronger Incentives

Without a strong constitutional legal argument, future opportunities to secure stronger incentives (and to avoid undue regulation) seem likely to depend on farm industry political efforts in Congress and in local legislative bodies. There are, however, some very real human barriers to securing stronger incentive programs through legislation.

The first of these barriers is the fact that most farmers and ranchers tend to be fiscally conservative and not fond of taxes and government spending.

Farmers often oppose taxes even when the money would mostly come from non-farmers and the spending mostly benefit farmers—as is the case with incentives. We'll come back to this in Chapter 8. But, for now, let's note what many farm supporters of incentives may well know, that it can require some courageous political leadership for conservative farmers to stand up in rural communities and in their local Farm Bureau organizations and argue for substantial government spending (and taxes) for incentives.

A second barrier is that the agriculture industry has been too long on the defensive.

As we've seen earlier, the "take no prisoners" political stance minority economic groups often take in defending themselves can be inconsistent with the pursuit of an affirmative legislative agenda. For farmers, this stance is no coincidence. Many of them have come to feel isolated from and at odds with their urban fellow-citizens. Farmers also understand their vulnerability to citizen suits by determined groups. And short funding for environmental enforcement has led some regulators to occasionally pick a farmer out for intensive enforcement in an effort to make an example. (I've had regulatory personnel tell me directly that they do this.) In the face of these unpredictable, sporadic "attacks," individual farmers can come to think of themselves as "shadow" violators, never certain when they might come to the attention of the authorities or if their conduct breaks some mysterious law or other.

These experiences can make farmers defensive and secretive about their personal farming operations. It can also influence the actions (and the rhetoric) of the trade associations that represent them, encouraging frequent use of "just say no," and causing the whole negative cycle to repeat itself.

No apparent benefit for agriculture, nor any improvement in the environment, results from all this pain.

A third barrier is that agriculture has been driven into a corner so many times, farmers sometimes seem to have lost faith in their industry's future.

An average American farmer is now fifty-seven years of age—not far from retirement. Many have come to believe that there is no real future in agriculture. When talking with farmers I have many times heard the sentiment: "If I can just be left alone to farm for the next few years, perhaps then I'll be able to sell out and retire." With this perspective, farm leaders may lack the confidence that broad-based, community supported, ag-friendly legislative measures are even possible. If the industry tried for the alliances needed for a positive legislative effort, would there be anyone still willing to join them? Delaying the inevitable by continuing to use "just say no" as long as possible may seem like the only real alternative.

Fortunately for all of us, however, American agriculture is far from dead. And farming is (or could easily become), hands down, our nation's "greenest" industry. In fact, farmers' strongest allies should be environmentalists. Despite the bitterness of past battles, there is still widespread public support for the agriculture industry—support that could quickly become much stronger if farming came to be broadly perceived as good for the environment.

I hope that, as a farmer, you will note that each of the barriers described above is a limitation that agriculture has placed upon itself. Perhaps it isn't the rest of the world that has to change for agriculture to forestall the need for damaging regulation.

Maybe it is the agriculture industry itself.

For Environmentalists Only

[FARMERS, DO NOT READ!]

Many times I've heard environmentalists ask "why should we offer incentives that pay people to do the right thing?"

The answer, of course, is that we shouldn't.

Unfortunately, the right thing isn't at all clear. The responsibilities we might ask people to live up to are relative. Choosing who should bear society's environmental burdens (or even figuring out who is doing so already) is very difficult.

But we, nonetheless, have to try.

We've seen how determination to avoid being forced to solve environmental problems can lead to denial that the problems exist. For environmentalists, the situation may be simply reversed. They are rightly passionate about getting environmental problems solved. But in their determination to solve them they can come to feel it is unimportant who ends up forced to pay for that solution and at what cost.

Obviously these problems do exist. But, just as obviously, it does matter who solves them, and how much it costs.

Breached Dikes on the Mississippi River

Decisions of this kind are matters of social justice. The U.S. Army Corps of Engineers was faced with a difficult choice during the 2011 flooding on the Mississippi River. Whether they made the right decision may be debated for years to come.

Dikes, river channelization, thousands of square miles of expanding impervious surface, and drainage systems throughout the central United States are, predictably, making the Mississippi ever tougher to manage. In the midst of a record flood in early May 2011, the Corps of Engineers chose to blow out the dikes at Bird's Point that protect hundreds of Missouri farms and 200,000 acres of farmland rather than allow the destruction of the town of Cairo, Illinois.

This decision may have saved on total property damage and perhaps also saved lives. But tell that to the farmers whose lands were flooded and made un-farmable, whose homes and businesses were destroyed, and who suffered some $85 million in crop losses and $156 million in economic damage.[10] And tell it to the politicians whose constituents live in Missouri, as opposed to Illinois.[11]

Presumably the farmers were not chosen to bear this sacrifice because they were more responsible for the flooding problem than the residents of Cairo. One might argue that the open, vegetated farm fields up and down the Mississippi Basin contribute a lot less to flooding than do the impervious roofs, streets, driveways, and parking lots in places like Cairo

Instead it seems likely that the dike-blowing decision went this way because there were fewer farmers than there were residents of Cairo, and because the total property value of what they stood to lose seemed lower than what was at risk had the town been flooded. With time to consider it in advance, maybe the citizens of Cairo (and their insurers) would have happily offered to compensate the farmers for their losses.

No one is claiming that allowing their farms to be flooded was the farmers' social responsibility or that, because blowing the dikes was the "right thing" to do, the farmers should just suffer the consequences and receive no payment for their losses. (At this time, compensation is still very much in question. So is the height of the replacement dike and whether it will afford the same protection as did the one that was destroyed.)

When addressing environmental problems, we, as a society, make decisions like this every day. But taking time to think these choices through and explain them to the public can be important if we care about protecting individual rights and treating our citizens with respect.

Salmon Buffers in the Pacific Northwest

The fight over salmon buffers in the Pacific Northwest provides another illustration.[12]

Salmon spend most of their lives in the ocean, but they spawn and rear in freshwater lakes and streams, streams that require cold, unpolluted water and natural complexity for the fish to survive. Farmland in the Northwest is often located in low, flat areas in floodplains, along rivers, or near streams. Tens of thousands of miles of salmon streams lace Northwest landscapes and run right through the region's farms.

That makes the Northwest's twenty-year battle over riparian buffers extraordinarily painful. Buffers seem logical if the salmon are to be saved. But these aren't the comparatively narrow grass buffers typically used to filter pollution in some other parts of the country. To protect salmon habitat, these buffers must create shade to cool the stream and provide streamside microclimates where fish-friendly riparian conditions can emerge and where the smaller creatures that fish eat can thrive. They must include large, woody debris that can help create resting places and make stream beds more complex and fish-friendly. These are buffers that, depending on who you talk to, may need to be at least 150 feet wide (three hundred feet if you include both sides of the stream).[13] They might require the planting and protection of tall stands of native trees, like two-hundred-foot Douglas fir. Livestock may need to be fenced out.

If you lose a three-hundred-foot-wide swath of land bordering a stream that runs through your forty acres, you've just lost perhaps a quarter of your farmland, depending on the shape of the property and the course and location of the stream. That may easily be the fourth of your land that generates your actual profit margin.[14] Farmers whose families have, for generations, been working the soil right up to the water's edge have an opinion on this. And, for at least two decades, the debate has swung back and forth between simply requiring "no-touch" buffers through regulation (which many farmers consider a flagrant unconstitutional "taking") to voluntarily buying protective easements, leasing buffers under the federal farm bill's CREP program, or simply condemning the land outright.[15]

One doesn't have to go far afield to see why this entire debate gets under a farmer's skin. Just drive across one of the busy Lake Washington floating bridges that lead east out of Seattle and look around. What you'll see is miles and miles of lakeshore, almost all of which is lined with multimillion dollar waterfront homes. None of these has such a buffer or anything close. Instead, there are manicured lawns that run right down to the water's edge, docks, boathouses, fortified bulkheads, homes that are themselves often much closer to the water than 150 feet, and waterside activity that is surely inconsistent with the welfare of the sockeye and other salmon that swim through this lake every year to the various streams and rivers that feed it from the surrounding countryside.

Or drive along Lake Union or the Lake Washington Ship Canal that passes through Seattle and out to Puget Sound. These shores are lined with industrial properties, marinas, shipbuilders, floating homes, restaurants, offices, and a host of other business properties built right down to the water's edge and often out floating in the water itself or resting on docks above it.

As it happens, one of those thousands of waterfront homes on Lake Washington belongs to Microsoft's famous founder, Bill Gates. So the farmers whose lands lie upstream and who have spent the past twenty years fighting over buffers have begun to ask: "What are you asking Bill Gates and his neighbors to do?" To be fair, the Gates property is heavily vegetated and by no means a serious offender along this Lake Washington shoreline, and there are increasingly stringent requirements on new construction along the lake and canal. But the answer for most existing properties is: "not much."

The take-home message for a farmer is that it isn't about the need for sacrifice, it is about who is going to make it. If you're a farmer, and you weren't an opponent of riparian buffers beforehand, that one-mile drive across Lake Washington could quickly turn you into one.

There is little doubt that the political and economic clout of these landowners and businesses is at least one of the reasons we allow those waterfront uses to continue. But as it happens, all of Lake Washington, the Ship Canal, their shorelines, and the uplands behind them are within the urban boundaries of Seattle, Bellevue, and several other suburban cities. One of the reasons those houses and businesses are there is also because we have made a conscious social policy decision to put them there. In the State of Washington, that choice was made through the public processes of a statewide growth management law. They are permitted under our State Environmental Policy Act (SEPA)[16] and our Shorelines Management Act.[17] Elsewhere in the country, we might have made that decision less consciously and more by default.

Most of us would probably agree that it is better for the environment if urban growth is concentrated instead of allowing it to sprawl uncontrolled across the landscape. In fact, the environmental benefit of concentrating growth is one of the two principal arguments offered for growth management (public service efficiencies being the other). But when one looks at the

Residential development along the Lake Washington shoreline, Mercer Island, Washington. *Photo by Don Stuart*

urban landscapes in and around Seattle, Detroit, Chicago, Atlanta, Dallas, Los Angeles, New York, Washington, DC, or any other major metropolitan area in the United States, it is hard to conclude that those places are particularly friendly to the environment. Those of us who live in cities still have environmental impacts.[18] It may be that by living closely together in one place we reduce the harm somewhat. But we still share responsibility for the wider damage being done. It seems likely that most of us would far prefer the higher taxes that might be required to provide incentives to farmers over the alternative of being forced to stop driving cars, using computers, heating buildings, drinking lattes or, even, giving up our beautiful waterfront homes on the shores of Lake Washington.

The Need to Make a Wise and Conscious Choice

Just because you want to save the environment doesn't mean your choices about how to get that done will necessarily be more righteous than those offered by someone else. It really is too facile to merely claim that everybody should be required to live up to their environmental responsibilities, and that we shouldn't have to pay people to do the right thing. What the right thing is and who is responsible is very often up for grabs. Figuring that out may, at times, be the whole point—the lynchpin for getting anything done.

Finally, as an environmental activist, you might appreciate that even if incentives weren't your first choice of a way to secure environmental improvements, they may turn out to be practical for another reason as well. This book is being written in the midst of one of the nation's big national debt debates. So there is a lot of focus on the deficit and on government spending. But in the end, if spending is necessary, and if it is much preferred over regulation, even a lot of conservatives might go along with it. There are also Republicans who care about and want to protect the environment but who just find it hard to do so without running up against their own anti-regulation views and constituencies. So incentives for conservation on agricultural lands offer one of those rare opportunities environmentalists will have to enlist conservative Republicans in helping address environmental problems.

By supporting incentives and enlisting farmers in the cause, environmentalists can put those legislators in the political position where they are able to make that choice.

CHAPTER 8

Taxes and Government Spending

Nobody likes taxes. But most of us are willing to pay them when we feel they are needed. We have to pay taxes to defend ourselves against our enemies and to control crime. We need public highways, universal education, and a court system. And we do need some protections for the environment.

So the biggest questions are: how much and who pays?

Cost of Community Services (COCS) Studies

At the local level, it is very clear that agriculture is a positive net contributor to the public purse. In local communities, the cost of government services that are provided to various land uses can be readily compared with the revenue that is received from each. In the past twenty years, over 150 separate county-level cost of community services (COCS) studies of this kind have been done across the United States.[1] These studies were originally developed by American Farmland Trust (AFT), which has completed many of them itself. But they have also since been done by many agencies, nonprofit organizations, local governments, university researchers, and private consultants. Their results leave no real doubt that farmers contribute significantly more in taxes than they receive in community services.

COCS studies are very straightforward. They compare tax revenues with public expenditures for each common land use in a community.[2] A typical study might compare government receipts and expenditures for commercial and industrial properties, residential properties, and natural resource lands like farms and forests. The study identifies what the government received in revenues from each of these land uses with the amount spent in providing public services for their benefit (such as police, fire, schools, transportation, etc.). According to AFT's nationwide tracking of these studies, for each dollar contributed in local taxes, working natural resource lands typically receive back about thirty-five cents in community services. In other words, out of each dollar contributed by agriculture in taxes, about sixty-five cents represents a subsidy farmers contribute to other taxpayers in their communities.

Farmers and ranchers are not the only ones providing such a local tax subsidy. Commercial and industrial properties also pay more than they receive—on average they receive about twenty-nine cents in services for each dollar contributed in taxes.[3]

So where does all this extra money go? Mostly it helps pay for the usually higher cost of services required by residential landowners. The residential properties included in all these studies received, on average, $1.16 in community services for every dollar they paid in taxes. Since residential properties are typically quite valuable, at least as compared with farmland, and there are a great many of them, total revenue from residential taxes is quite substantial. So this extra sixteen-cent cost per tax dollar paid represents a great deal of money and it probably isn't surprising that it takes a substantial subsidy from working lands (sixty-five cents per dollar) and from commercial and industrial properties (seventy-one cents per dollar) to make up that sixteen-cents-per-dollar loss on residential properties. This, then, is how our local county and township governments are able to balance their budgets.

This general pattern (with commercial, industrial, and resource lands paying more in taxes than they receive in community services and residential properties paying less) plays out in every single one of the COCS studies done across the country.

Keep in mind that for most commercial or industrial enterprises (including ag support businesses), the local taxes they pay on their sales, revenues, equipment, and real property will often mirror the employment they provide. Those employees need housing, so there is a relationship between the number of homes in a community and its commercial and industrial enterprise. If a new business moves in, it is likely that new employees will follow, along with new residential development.

With farms, however, that relationship is less clear. These studies have sometimes been explained by noting that "cows don't go to school." Usually the number of agricultural employees per acre of taxed land is very small. So while farmers—like their commercial and industrial counterparts—help subsidize residential taxpayers, those residences usually do not house employees who work on a farm.[4]

It also should be noted that these results are based on actual taxes paid during the year covered by the study. So they already take into account the reduced "current use" property tax rates that farmers are sometimes allowed on agricultural land.

The Significance of a Farmer Tax Surplus

One reasonable conclusion to draw is that retaining a healthy local agriculture industry and protecting farmlands from sprawling development would, just as a purely fiscal matter and ignoring the other economic issues, be good fiscal planning that would save all taxpayers money over time. To the extent that those farms might be replaced by houses, the cost of new government services to those new residences would far outstrip any new tax revenue that the new housing would generate. At the same time, the farm-generated subsidy would be diminished.

This differential between the cost of public services and the revenue for different land uses frequently drives local community leaders to argue for a kind of "balanced growth." The idea is, at least in part, that the community will seek new economic development in the form of new commercial and industrial enterprises and will allow new residential construction at a level that balances the higher fiscal impact of housing against the new net tax income it will see from new businesses.

Even assuming such a strategy can actually be managed, one still wonders about the place for agriculture, which requires low cost, open, undeveloped land to survive. Balanced growth of this kind, after all, still contemplates that there will be development of more industrial, commercial, and residential land. This usually results in less private working natural resource land and a steady loss of the public tax revenue subsidy those open, undeveloped lands currently provide.[5] In other words, such balanced growth may not turn out to be so balanced after all. As each farm develops, such communities are pushed, inevitably, further and further into the red.[6]

There are particular consequences for so-called "bedroom communities." These suburban communities are generally within commuting distance of large commercial and industrial centers to which their residents travel for jobs or shopping. But, to get there, they may need to cross a county or other taxing district line. For those suburban communities, it is the neighboring county (the one with the commercial and industrial activity) that receives the lucrative business tax revenue. The county containing the residential community is forced to pay the higher cost of services for all those homes without the aid of the commercial and industrial tax subsidies that would make up for it. For such a bedroom community, adding yet more residential capacity by allowing the subdivision and development of its remaining farms can be a very bad bargain.

It is also important to recognize that the public service expenditures reported in these COCS studies do not separately identify the added costs to be expected for new residential development. The amounts received in community services for each dollar paid in taxes in these studies represent a collective average for all existing residential properties. So these figures average in community service costs for existing small older homes, apartments, and townhomes located on small lots in and near urban areas (and near existing urban public services). Those services are probably provided at very low cost. These lower costs are averaged in with the much higher costs for services provided to newer, sprawling residential developments typically located on much larger lots that are a greater distance from police, fire, and other government services. These developments are also far from schools, and require a greater travel distance for transportation, sewer, power, and other public infrastructure.

The cost of new public investments in the infrastructure required to support each new single family residence being built in the State of Washington was estimated in 2000 to be $83,000 per new home. Meanwhile, the per-home average public "impact fee" being charged developers at the time was about $2,500, leaving a net fiscal impact to be picked up by the rest of us, a net subsidy for each buyer of one of these new homes of over $80,000.[7] This sum is a part of that extra sixteen cents in community service costs received by residential properties. But it is obviously much greater for developments out on the urban edge, the ones most likely to have an impact on agriculture.

So our farmers are not only providing the low cost land upon which many of those new homes are being built, they are also providing at least a part of the $80,000-plus per-new-home subsidy that keeps them affordable for their new owners. It is easy to see why homes in a sprawling suburb may be comparatively cheaper than ones closer in to town.

It all leads one to wonder: if we don't want sprawl, why do we subsidize it? And why do we cause our non-sprawling farmers to pay for it?

The COCS studies discussed above were done at the local government level (usually for counties or townships). So they do not measure the comparative position of agriculture for taxes versus subsidies at either the state or federal levels.[8]

How this same calculus might play out at the federal level is probably anybody's guess considering the many kinds of complex subsidies, tax breaks, and special services provided (think home mortgage subsidies, oil exploration investment credits, special treatment for capital gains, and, of course, price supports and other subsidies under the farm bill).[9] Given the broad nature of most federal spending, and federal reliance on income taxes, it would be very difficult to allocate those costs and revenue among particular land uses or business types.

It also may be difficult to make such comparisons when looking at state-level data, although it does seem likely that most state spending would somewhat mirror the spending by their counties, except with a somewhat larger proportion of their expenditures being for services that would be difficult to allocate to particular land uses.[10]

Note, also, that these studies look only at the direct fiscal impacts of the specific land uses involved. They do not consider the broader indirect fiscal impact of losing other support business activities that may disappear as farms disappear. We know, for example, that the indirect economic impacts of agriculture tend to be higher than for many other industries.[11] For one thing, farmers' economic impacts tend to remain local. Presumably they generate local tax revenues from other sources as well. One would anticipate that the loss of farms would also result in the loss of the other local businesses (processors, service businesses, suppliers, equipment dealers, etc.) that support those farms. Because the beneficial indirect economic impacts of agriculture are higher, the loss of those benefits would also be disproportionately greater than whatever gains are made in alternative economic activities that may replace the farms.

With agriculture making these substantial and disproportionate contributions to the public purse locally, and with this happening throughout the country, even if we assume that farmers get a significant fiscal boost from the federal government through farm bill programs, it still doesn't seem likely that agriculture begins, overall, to approach oil,[12] insurance,[13] aerospace,[14] or several other major American industries in the aid they receive from American taxpayers.

Thus, in dealing with government, farmers need not be embarrassed to ask for help with conservation stewardship incentives, with purchase of development rights programs to protect agricultural lands, or with other programs that might strengthen the farm industry.

Transforming Public Attitudes Toward Agriculture

A strong economically and environmentally healthy agriculture industry would be of great value to the future of our country. So investments in that future ought to be ones all of us, farmers, environmentalists, and the public, could happily make. In our efforts to be fiscally responsible and work within our means, let's not overlook the possibility that a farmer–environmental-ists alliance could shift the world in a way that would dramatically increase the American public's collective political desire to make such investments.

How Migratory Bird Habitat Grew Healthier Crops

The Skagit Valley, in northern Puget Sound, is an important agricultural area with rich soils, a long history in farming, a supportive community, and perhaps 100,000 acres in a diverse variety of crops. Much of this land and crops are in lowland areas on the Skagit Delta below the high-tide line, areas that were first protected with dikes by early settlers.

This delta is also a critical area for migratory shorebirds, whose his-torical habitat was largely consumed when these dike-protected farms were originally drained and converted to cropland. Even with those losses, the Skagit Delta today provides support for some 70 percent of those birds on their annual migrations. Much of this habitat is on active, working farms.

Swans in farm field. Skagit County, Washington. *Photo courtesy of Martha Jordan*

Farmers in this area already rotate their cropland. By planting a non-commercial cover crop or leaving the land fallow in off-years, they can cut the cycle of pests and disease, renew soil fertility, and improve production. These rotations sometimes take place over a three-year period with so-called money crops only grown in one of those years.

The Nature Conservancy partnered up with three respected local farmers and several other community groups to demonstrate how both farmers and shorebirds might be able to benefit from their use of the same land.[15] The participating farmers agreed, for one of their three rotation years, to flood one of their fields with two to three inches of water. This would grow wetland vegetation and create habitat for migratory birds. In effect, bird habitat became one of their rotation crops with the land in agriculture one year, lying fallow another, flooded for birds in a third year, and then returned to agriculture.

It turns out that these periodically flooded fields create highly productive habitat for the birds. And when those fields are rotated back to cropland, their fertility and productivity for agriculture is remarkably improved.

For Farmers Only

[ENVIRONMENTALISTS, DO NOT READ!]

The Need for Government: A Free Market

To accept that there is a place for taxpayer-supported incentives, we all need to acknowledge that an unregulated private economy is never going to adequately protect the environment. It follows that environmental protection will require something additional that goes beyond the market, like incentives or regulation.

Of course we all know we can't have markets without at least some regulation. How many of us would be willing to buy stuff if consumers were routinely cheated, if the things we bought were frequently dangerous, or if there was no recourse when what we bought was defective or turned out to be worthless? How many of us would sell something if we couldn't count on getting paid? Where would we be if we couldn't get our contracts enforced?

There sure wouldn't be much in the way of a market.[16]

In a similar way, how long will our free-market economy last if we allow ourselves to run out of the resources to produce the things we want to buy and sell? A free market is pointless on a sterile planet.

Unfortunately our free-market economy was not designed to protect the long term. Corporate shareholders expect a profit and they expect it quickly, even those who voluntarily invest in arguably "green" enterprises. Not many people are going to wait around for twenty or thirty years for their dividends in order to make the world a better place.

Of course farmers' businesses are far more personal and more multi-generational than comparable enterprises in other segments of the economy. Still, every farmer well knows how difficult it is to invest in the long-range future of the farm while also meeting the year-to-year economic reality of paying the bills. Many farmers try very hard to leave healthy land as well as a successful farm to their children. But even so, an investment that may be good for the rest of society, but that will do little or nothing to help the farm today, can be very hard to justify.

Allocating Tax Responsibility for Incentives

As we saw in this chapter, farmers probably pay a tax surplus to local governments. So it may seem logical that these counties be involved in supporting agriculture. Realistically, however, most local governments, especially those in the rural communities where most agriculture is located, lack the tax base (if not the political will) to contribute substantially to agricultural conservation incentives. Furthermore, the environmental concerns we need our farmers to address are often global or regional, not just local in nature.

Our rationale for incentives also assumes that the particular problem we're addressing may be one we feel is mostly society's responsibility, not just the responsibility of individual farmers. So we need a revenue source that actually puts the burden where it belongs. State and federal incentive programs are paid for with taxes contributed by the larger general public—taxes on income, business revenue, sales, and real and personal property. These revenue sources come, in massively higher proportion, from urban populations than from rural residents or our nation's relatively few farmers. So the vast majority of the money farmers receive through conservation incentives flows into the agriculture industry from the outside. Yes, farmers pay sales, property, and income taxes like everybody else. But the proportion of their contributions to the funding they earn through incentives is quite minimal—as it should be if it is paying for something that is the public's responsibility.

This also, as a matter of pure self-interest, makes taxes for incentives a very good deal for the agriculture industry. This is one of the limited ways rural communities have of tapping into the massive wealth that is generated in our nation's urban areas, and of shifting the burdens (where that is appropriate) of environmental protection and restoration to the full public.

Finally, as long as we're being self-interested, let's not forget the flagrantly political dimension. To many farmers, it seems like it's all those urban liberals who vote for higher taxes. Conservative rural farmers are usually against them. Maybe it makes sense to look at it from another perspective: If urban liberals want to pay more in taxes so farmers can get compensated for generating environmental services, why not let them?

For Environmentalists Only
[FARMERS, DO NOT READ!]

The Growth Management Responsibility

As Europeans moved west across America, the settlement of every new town carried with it the conviction that this tiny village would someday become the next Chicago. Boosters everywhere believed fervently in the inevitable growth of their local communities.[17] This idea became a part of how we saw ourselves. It is written into our literature, and it survives today in small rural towns all across America, especially in the West.

Unfortunately, the reality of urban growth is a lot like corporate growth. The big towns get bigger. The smaller ones hold their own or wither away. A rural conservative worldview has emerged that urban areas are stealing away their prospects for growth and development. New businesses tend to locate near the city where there is a large, well-educated workforce to draw upon; where there is transportation for workers, products, and supplies; where there is access to support business services, etc. Without those attractions, rural employment slowly evaporates. Bright young people grow up, go off to school, and end up living in the city where they can earn more and feel more a part of the modern world. Rural communities are slowly drained of their wealth and economic vitality.

Growth management laws can reinforce these trends, so their passage often confirms this perspective.[18] Growth management has come to be seen by many rural residents as a tool by which urban areas legally seize for themselves the lion's share of opportunities for growth and its associated wealth and power, as just one more way urban liberals tyrannize and impose their biases on rural communities.

Anyone who has walked a downtown street in the older part of any of our larger cities certainly knows that urban residents aren't necessarily rich and powerful. But the evidence is clear that education, jobs, wealth, and political power have steadily migrated into our nation's cities.[19] And for people whose families, friends, schools, churches, careers, economic futures, and primary loyalties are rooted in small rural communities, it is deeply frustrating to watch the cities grow while their small town fades.

As COCS and other similar studies demonstrate, rural communities probably pay lower local taxes. And it seems likely their taxes would go up if they grew. But it is still difficult to find a local politician—a small town mayor or city or county council member—who is not convinced their community would be a lot better off if they could just attract some new business and new employment. Maybe higher local taxes are a small price to pay for rural growth, employment, and economic prosperity.

This assumes, of course, that we are not concerned about preserving either the environment or economically viable agriculture.

So when an environmentalist shows up in the office of the state legislator from one of these rural, agricultural districts, we know how the case for environmental protection on agricultural lands is likely to go down. That legislator, probably a Republican, will be thinking something along these lines: "First your cities suck the economic lifeblood out of my community. Now, when they also screw up the environment, here you are trying get us to fix your problem by imposing further rules that will probably destroy the only remaining (and struggling) industry we do have: our local farmers. There's no way you're going to get any help from me!"

Conservation Incentives as an Opportunity to Balance the Scales

Conservation incentives are one of the ways the rest of us can move some urban wealth to rural areas and redress some of that economic imbalance. Maybe some of the farmers (about one-third, more or less, depending on the locale) do get subsidies directly through the farm bill. It is also true that rural areas get some extra help with certain public services—like rural highway construction—that cost more per-capita to build over a wider, less populous area. But given the farmer imbalance in the payment of local taxes, it is still far from clear that, in public services received, they truly receive a fair shake when all is said and done.

If we're going to protect the environment at a manageable cost, our rural communities need to be economically as well as environmentally sustainable. The industry that needs to flourish is agriculture. And agriculture needs to flourish in the real world, not as some tame Disneyesque figment of the imagination. It must be made up of real businesses selling real products into highly competitive international wholesale markets for food and fiber.

There is yet another reason environmentalists need to fight for incentives funding: This may be environmental protection and environmental money that is actually possible to get! Conservation incentives provide a rare shot at bipartisan support for spending. Of course any item in a state or federal budget can affect any other. And there will always be the budget "hawks" who never agree to anything. But where there is the chance to secure support for environmental spending from rural, conservative lawmakers, environmentalists should go for it. Those opportunities are few and far between.

CHAPTER 9

Environmental Markets[1]

The U.S. population is projected to grow by 130 million people over the next fifty years. That's as many new people as the total number who lived here in 1940.[2] Environmental problems and the pressure to address them seem certain to increase. Some of the damage resulting from this growth can be avoided or prevented. But much cannot. And those regions of the country which face most of it will need to find the least costly, most effective methods to mitigate for its ever-increasing environmental impacts.

One of those methods may be environmental markets.

As we've seen earlier in this book, there is reason to anticipate that much of the pressure to make up for environmental degradation in the years to come will fall on agricultural lands. The cost of such improvements in our urban areas will always be terribly high. Public lands are already largely managed for environmental values. So what remains are the private farms and forests, which occupy perhaps two-thirds to three-quarters of all our nation's private lands.[3] If our society expects to somehow make up for the environmental degradation we know is coming, it seems likely this is where we will have to look.

Is this a threat or opportunity?

Opportunities for Farmers in Environmental Markets

If mitigating for the environmental impacts of growth simply requires that we restore to a natural state as much currently undeveloped land as possible—farming is in trouble.

A closer look, however, reveals that the detrimental consequences of population growth and development can often be effectively offset through improvements on working agricultural lands without dramatic losses of farm production.

Moreover, this may well be the least costly approach.

Of course the cost for farmers to produce these kinds of offsets on their own, and at the scale needed to make up for growth, is much too high for struggling farm businesses to carry. But because farmers are already earning agricultural income from the natural resource productivity of their land, and because they are typically already producing some of these values just by keeping their land out of development and keeping it healthy enough to farm, farmers can usually continue to farm while enhancing these values for much less than it would cost to mitigate or offset them elsewhere. Presumably this is also much less than the social/economic cost to either prevent the loss of the environmental value in the first place or to just let it happen and ignore the consequences.

There are a many arenas where markets for farm-produced environmental services can emerge:

- *Carbon offsets:* An industrial plant that needs to reduce its carbon emissions might accomplish part of their goal by paying farmers to adopt reduced tillage, lower nitrous oxide emissions from artificial fertilizer, or install an anaerobic digester that eliminates methane from cattle waste.

- *Water quality trading:* A public utility might need to expand its sewage treatment plant to meet the needs of a growing community, but finds the cost prohibitive. Rather than spending $100 million on a new, high-tech treatment plant, the utility might instead elect to spend $10 million contracting with upstream farmers who will adapt their land or their practices to achieve those same reductions and more.

- *Wetland mitigation:* A new highway right-of-way might unavoidably pass through a wetland that must be replaced. A nearby farmer might have a wet, unproductive parcel on part of her farm. She might improve the wetland function on that area of her land and sell wetland credits to the highway department to help them mitigate their impacts.

- *Habitat mitigation:* A new shopping mall might threaten to damage migratory bird habitat. By adopting appropriate rangeland management practices, and by establishing a conservation easement on his property, a rancher whose land lies along the same migratory route could sell those services to the developer, cash out excess investment in the land, secure supplemental continuing income for his operation, and continue in active ranching in the years ahead with little impact on his production.

- *Renewable energy:* A non-irrigated wheat farmer might lease small patches of his windy ridge-top land for installation of wind turbines that will produce green energy that replaces more damaging sources of energy. Given their careful installation, farming could continue with little inconvenience around and beneath the new turbines.

- *Water quantity trading:* A farmer might install a new, water efficient irrigation system or change to a different crop that uses less water. The water savings can be leased to a water trust program to increase in-stream flows for fish and/or to make up for new urban demand for water in a nearby growing community. Meanwhile, the farmer earns extra income to supplement his continuing crop revenue.

- *Flood mitigation:* A growing city might wish to expand its suburbs into a flood plain area, worsening downstream flooding. By protecting continued agriculture or by arranging for flood storage in the agricultural off season on working farm properties, the city could eliminate and even diminish the aggregate downstream flood impacts of its expansion in the years ahead while supporting profitable farming.

Transactions like these are becoming increasingly common.[4] They represent a growing marketplace for environmental services that can be produced by working agricultural lands. USDA has created a new Office of Environmental Markets responsible for helping these markets emerge.[5]

How Environmental Markets Work

Environmental markets of this kind are usually (though not always[6]) driven by regulations that limit or "cap" allowable damage to the environment. Examples of such caps might include:

- Placing a limit on carbon emissions by industrial and other air polluters under the Clean Air Act or through new state or federal legislation, perhaps pursuant to the Kyoto accord;

- Imposing a "total maximum daily load" on allowable water pollutants that can be discharged into a given water body under the Clean Water Act;

- Establishing a no-net-loss of wetlands policy under the Clean Water Act;

- Limiting wildlife habitat loss under the Endangered Species Act;

- Establishing a minimum in-stream flow for a waterway in order to protect fish habitat;

- Creating minimum percentages of renewable energy that must be included in the "portfolio" of an energy utility; or

- Requiring a local community to have no new impacts on flood risk as a condition of approval for flood insurance guarantees by the Federal Emergency Management Agency (FEMA).

Once a cap of this kind is in place, the regulatory agency is in a position to allow environmental offsets or mitigation as an alternative approach to compliance. The agency will need to be convinced that the cap will still be met using this alternative system. If they are, the offset or mitigation alternative may quite often be much cheaper. So a developer or permittee can well afford to pay third parties (like farmers and ranchers) to supply the environmental "credits" they need to stay within their limit.

One of the first environmental markets of this kind was the highly successful air quality market created in 1990 to combat acid rain in the U.S. Northeast.[7] As of this writing, there are also some fifty active water quality markets in the United States, 119 habitat conservation markets, a lively carbon market that brought in $144 billion worldwide in 2009, renewable energy credit markets driven by laws in twenty-nine states, and at least 415 wetland markets (as of 2005).[8]

Many of the on-farm conservation practices discussed in Chapter 4 can be made eligible for credit production. For example:

Precision agricultural chemical application, Nebraska. *Courtesy of USDA-NRCS*

- *Conservation tillage:* Reducing tillage of the land and planting/seeding new crops directly into untilled (or minimally tilled) ground can generate creditable benefits like preserving water, sequestering atmospheric carbon, improving water quality, providing wildlife habitat, and preventing soil erosion.

- *Precision fertilizer application:* Global Positioning System (GPS)-guided, computer-operated field equipment can reduce fertilizer use by applying only what is needed for differing soil conditions across a large farm field. This can produce carbon or water quality credits by reducing nitrous oxide emissions or preventing potential polluted surface water runoff into adjacent waterways.

- *Conservation rangeland management:* With rotated livestock grazing, widely distributed supplies of water, and a close response to seasonal impacts and changing conditions, healthy rangelands can be made to sequester carbon in plants and soil, prevent erosion and pollution, and enhance habit for native wildlife, all of which might generate environmental credits.

- *Cover crops, crop rotations, strip cropping, and contour farming:* By planting appropriate wildlife- and soil-friendly crops in rotation with the targeted profit-generating crop, by tilling and planting across hillside contours and planting rotational crops in strips that alternate with a cover crop, and with similar techniques, farmers can provide feed/forage for various types of wildlife, secure the soil, prevent erosion, and eliminate surface- and ground-water pollution. Any of these might be eligible for credits.

- *Irrigation efficiencies:* Modern irrigation systems can reduce the application of fertilizers and chemicals; reduce surface water runoff, erosion, and soil loss; and, reduce the use of short supplies of fresh water—each also creditable services.

- *Wetland development:* Farmers can improve small, wet, nonproductive patches of farmed ground and convert them to creditable wetlands without a negative impact on farm productivity.

- *Conservation easements:* By selling their development rights, farmers can guarantee that their land will remain out of development and will continue to provide multiple identified environmental benefits in the years to come. This might become eligible for carbon, wildlife, water quality, or other credits.

Contour farming, Kansas. *Courtesy of USDA-NRCS*

The Strategic Advantage of Environmental Markets

In Chapter 5, we discussed pros and cons of voluntary incentive programs. One of the big disadvantages mentioned there was that the typical cost-share approach to environmental stewardship incentives limits the number of farmers interested in participating. A reduced number of applicants limits the ability of incentive program administrators to be strategic by selecting from the best among them.

Suppose there are one hundred farmers who own land along a twenty-mile reach of salmon stream. Of that hundred, there might be only eight or ten who would be willing to apply for a cost-share fish habitat restoration project on their property. But over that entire twenty miles, there also may be only a couple of miles that are especially critical for the fish. It is probable that none of the eight or ten applicants for this program would actually own land in the critical area. Or maybe the program managers are lucky and they get one. Still, those ten farmers are located somewhere along that twenty miles of stream. The restoration projects will do some good, just not as much as might be preferable.

So long as the managers of that program are willing or able to offer only a share of the initial cost, this may be the best they're going to do.

But suppose, instead, the program managers could cover the full cost of the stream restoration project, including the business expense of its maintenance plus a small profit. Suppose that instead of being limited to just sharing the cost of installing such projects, the program could afford to pay enough that it could, where it needed to, interest a majority of the targeted farmers to participate. With the much larger willingness of landowners to get involved, this program manager could be choosy. Instead of only eight or ten interested farmers out of the possible one hundred, the projects might become attractive to eighty or ninety of them.

In that case, the program might choose to offer the incentives only to those farmers whose land was located along that critical two miles of stream. Out of the ten or so farmers located there, they could count on being able to enlist at least eight or nine, and perhaps even all ten of them.

Yes, on a per-mile of stream or on a per-farmer basis, the projects might cost twice or even three times as much. But their strategic impact in addressing the problem might be eight or ten times greater. Suddenly this voluntary incentive program has become highly strategic and very cost-efficient, even without any cost share provided by the landowners involved.

The offering to farmers wouldn't be some arbitrary share of the implementation cost. Rather it would be based on willingness to participate. What the program would pay would be driven by the market value or actual cost plus profit of the services provided. So for those practices that had the additional benefit of helping make the farm more profitable (like stream bank stabilization or flood detaining buffers, for example) the expense to the program could actually be lower because those farmers would be willing to sell their services for less. For practices that had no such benefits (like in-stream fish habitat restoration, wetland development, and habitat friendly cover crops, for example) the expense might be somewhat higher. As perhaps it ought to be.

Certainly there will always be a place for current cost-share programs which leverage participant willingness to contribute personally to the public good. But an additional market-driven system, for use when a more targeted and strategic approach was needed, would sometimes be a preferable option. Such a program could be funded with money generated to offset or mitigate for the damage done by other, non-farm human activities like industrial and municipal pollution, land development, highway construction, energy generation, and urban growth. As mentioned earlier, markets of this kind are already emerging.[9]

Baselines

It is important to note that before a seller can be paid for producing environmental credits in one of these markets, that seller needs to demonstrate to the satisfaction of regulators that a baseline of environmental performance has first been met. This baseline will be the minimum level of environmental performance that is considered to be the seller's underlying social responsibility—that level of performance that we would expect anyone, in the seller's position, to provide as their normal duty as a citizen, without being paid. Only those environmental benefits that are provided in excess of that baseline can be considered eligible for payment. Establishing what the baseline should be is an essential step in allowing the use of any environmental market. And for markets that involve farmers, it is one that will require active, thoughtful involvement by both the farm and the environmental communities.

One of the big upsides to environmental markets is that they cause us to engage in this baseline discussion. As things stand now, without such markets, there is no baseline. Or, at least, we have not consciously created one. The only generally agreed-upon standard of environmentally responsible performance that exists today is the one that is imposed by current enforceable law. Beyond that, we're all on our own—or at least so it seems. To have an environmental market, one must first establish what actions will be approved for payment and what will not. Without such markets, we apparently have insufficient reason to establish such baselines. So we're all free to disagree about what is and is not the minimum level of socially responsible behavior.

And, of course, we do disagree. This is the essence of the disagreement over incentives versus regulations that is at the core of this book.

A world in which all environmental problems were dealt with exclusively through regulation would clearly be quite a costly, painful, unfair, and undesirable one. And a world in which we tried to address everything with voluntary actions leavened by incentives would be equally unacceptable, costly, and, probably, ineffective. So each side believes they have something serious to worry about. This creates a perfect storm of enemies and disputes.

Once we've established baselines, however, the cause of much of this disagreement seems likely to evaporate. And the huge gap in our current ability to deal with the uncharted territory between incentives and regulations could disappear.

CONSERVATION ECONOMICS

How a Fish Buffer Helped Save a Cattle Ranch

Dale Reiner's cattle operation occupies an ox-bow along the Skykomish River near Monroe, Washington. Like many rivers in developing areas, the Skykomish floods more and more often these days. These frequent floods used to deposit huge quantities of debris on Dale's fields, which he had to periodically remove at great expense. They washed away his soil, and threatened to carve a new course for the river itself, which would have obliterated much of his ranch.

Among many other distinctions, Dale is a former president of the Snohomish County Farm Bureau, a former board member with the Snohomish Conservation District, and is widely liked and respected in Washington agriculture. But none of that meant much to the county when, over a decade ago, Dale began seeking approval for some measures to manage the flooding across his land.

Dale's proposals were modest. He wanted to install some fixed, widely spaced flood-detention structures along the up-river edge of his property. The structures would allow water to flow through, and at the same time capture some of the larger debris and slow the water's momentum. He also wanted to protect and improve a buffer of cottonwood trees along the river through a lease to the Conservation Reserve Enhancement Program (CREP). And he proposed to improve some off-channel salmon ponds on his land to create new fish habitat there.

Approval to do almost anything affecting a river is hard to get. Fortunately for Dale, the threatened change in the river's course would also have bypassed and required replacement of an existing multimillion dollar bridge on a major state highway. It would have destroyed several residences as well. A local salmon restoration group known as Northwest Chinook Recovery was on board to restore the fish habitat. With these allies, and after a decade of struggle, Dale finally got his project approved, including the buffers.

As we've discussed, riparian salmon buffers are hugely controversial in the Pacific Northwest. Dale's buffer is a matter of some discussion among local farmers in Snohomish County. Dale tells his colleagues that creating his buffer was one of the best business decisions he ever made. To start with, he gets paid a fair lease value for the land through

CREP. The mature and maturing cottonwoods slow the river down and collect and divert flood debris. Periodic, managed floods across his land now deposit a layer of rich river silt that grows great pasture. Dale's buffer and other improvements have saved his farm and provide riparian shade for the river and habitat for the fish. The river still floods across his property, but it no longer threatens to destroy it nor the downstream homes and state highway.

For Environmentalists Only
[FARMERS, DO NOT READ!]

Environmental markets of the kind described in this chapter face skepticism from both conservatives and liberals. Environmentalists and regulators worry that they might provide a way for environmental scofflaws to buy their way out of proper conduct. They fear that credits might be purchased (and displace other corrective measures) but might represent actions that the sellers either would have done without payment or that they should have done as their plain moral duty as environmentally responsible citizens.

With appropriate baselines, we can eliminate these concerns. We will have a system in place that assures that the credits sold are for real environmental gains and that they actually exceed that baseline. This may seem like a daunting regulatory challenge. But writing and applying an appropriate baseline need not be all that difficult. Of course the environmental community needs to be involved. But there is nothing unique or unusual about creating baseline requirements that sets it apart from any of the other multitude of regulatory challenges we face every day.

How Does the Environment Benefit?[10]

Environmentalists also worry that environmental markets just "rearrange deck chairs on the Titanic." The concern is that buying and selling offset and mitigation credits accomplishes nothing more than substituting one form of compliance for another; that even if such markets work well, they will not result in any environmental gain.

There are, however, many ways in which the environment realizes gains with an environmental marketplace:

- *Lowest cost:* By allowing the least-cost provider to sell environmental services to those who need them, the expense of environmental compliance can be greatly reduced, thus preserving scarce resources and minimizing the economic impacts of environmental rules. When something costs less, we can afford more of it.

- *Political expediency:* When the cost of addressing an environmental problem becomes too high, the political will to deal with it tends to evaporate. Environmental markets reduce that political pressure and should be seen as essential infrastructure for efforts to address many environmental problems.

- *Reduced reliance on public funding to solve environmental problems*: Environmental markets can generate funding to address environmental needs without depending on public appropriations. Once they are in place, environmental markets also can continue, even in a challenging political or fiscal setting.

- *Matching the scale of the problem:* The level of environmental market funding will reflect the scale of the need for the services—the greater the amount of activity causing environmental damage, the more funding there will be to correct that damage.

- *Matching the locale of the problem:* Because environmental markets secure their funding where the negative impacts are located—typically in the same watershed, habitat, or area of concern—the funding will also generally be spent in the same locale where the problems being created are the most severe.

- *Associated benefits:* When a farm produces (and sells) one environmental service, it nearly always ends up producing others as well. A riparian buffer created to lower stream temperature, for example, will also reduce water pollution, protect aquifer recharge, and provide riparian habitat for fish and wildlife. Conservation rangeland management designed to sequester carbon will also preserve vegetation for birds and other wildlife. Multiple markets that paid for all of these benefits would dramatically reduce the social cost of each. But even where only one environmental service can be sold, others are likely to result for free.

- *Conservative offset ratios:* <u>Purchasers of offsets in an environmental market need to be absolutely sure that they will meet the requirements of their permits. And regulators also need that certainty. So trades are generally made at conservative ratios designed to eliminate uncertainty.</u> For example, a farmer might be paid to adopt conservation practices that remove, say, three pounds of nitrogen from a waterway in order for his or her trading partner to receive credit to offset perhaps one pound. The net effect of such ratios is that trades almost always result in a substantial net gain for the environment.

- *Improved performance of current mitigation system:* Recent studies of wetland mitigation indicate that we are falling well short of the "no net loss" outcome expected under the Clean Water Act—averaging less than 50 percent functional equivalency for replacement wetlands created under existing programs requiring mitigation.[11] The current system typically leaves performance in the hands of the developer (whose interest is to get past the mitigation requirement, and past regulatory oversight, as quickly and cheaply as possible). When wetlands mitigation is provided by wetland bankers (whose interest is focused more on providing good services so they can sell more high quality "credits" in the future) performance tends to be a lot better.

- *Engaging farmers in environmental hot-spots:* Current public incentive programs tend to be non-strategic (for the reasons discussed above and in Chapter 5 on incentives) and the funding is spread thinly across the landscape. In a market, suppliers are paid more nearly what their environmental services are worth so program managers can target acquisition of the most needed services. This makes these markets a powerful tool to make strategic environmental improvements at key locations and on critical problems.

- *Establishing a dollar value for a healthy environment:* <u>Currently, the value of environmental services is vague and uncertain, measured only by academic "cost replacement" studies and "willingness to pay" surveys. So it is easy for society to shrug them off, for elected officials and regulators to ignore them, and for commercial product markets to treat them as free or worthless.</u> When, however, these services are actively traded and thereby acquire a concrete measurable market price that people regularly and willingly pay, it becomes much more difficult to pretend these services have no worth. Strong environmental markets thus seem likely to strengthen the social and political case for protecting the scarce and important values provided by the environment.

- *Protecting farmland:* Finally, environmental markets represent a way for farmers to earn supplemental revenue by making themselves indispensable as generators of environmental services. Their extra revenue can help improve their farm's profitability, diminish the likelihood that it might be sold for development, and reduce the public cost and political challenge of protecting it from development.

All these are net benefits for the environment and for our future opportunities for environmental protection.

Wetlands and "No-Net-Loss"

Environmentalists are understandably sensitive about anything that might undermine the "no-net-loss" of wetlands policy,[12] currently applied under section 404 of the Clean Water Act.[13] Wetlands are unique in synergistically providing a great variety of critically important environmental services. Their slow disappearance is an environmental tragedy.

In practice, however, accomplishing no net loss has proven challenging.[14] Replacing a mature, nicely-functioning, existing wetland with a new one, perhaps in a different location, is fraught with difficulties. Losses in functionality, especially in the short term, seem almost inevitable. So environmentalists have urged and secured strong requirements that impacts on existing wetlands first be avoided and minimized wherever possible.

But as developing U.S. cities try to constrain sprawl, development pressure on the sensitive lands inside their boundaries keeps alive the necessity that we find wetland replacement/mitigation on lands elsewhere. As we increasingly favor off-site mitigation for development impacts,[15] we are also indirectly transferring the footprint of urban development from inside the city out onto our treasured agricultural lands.

A Watershed Approach to Wetlands Mitigation

The same changes in EPA and U.S. Corps of Engineers compensatory wetland mitigation policy that have liberalized the use of off-site mitigation also encourage the use of a watershed approach.[16] A watershed approach endeavors to secure the kind of mitigation that best addresses the needs of that particular watershed.

One place where our performance could be improved is in "like kind" wetland mitigation. As a precaution against losses, environmentalists typically insist that lost wetlands be replaced by others that are of "like kind." This is usually a wise requirement. But sometimes there might be a better approach. Wetlands generate a variety of environmental services like water quality improvement, flood detention, aquifer recharge, and wildlife habitat. Some of those services may be critically deficient in that watershed and desperately needed. Others may be abundant there. Consistent with a watershed approach, suppose that, when a wetland was damaged by a construction project, regulators were to identify the most locally critical environmental services that were affected. Project mitigation could be required to produce more of those specific, badly-needed services than were lost while perhaps producing less of others that aren't needed and are still present in the watershed in abundance.

Under such an approach, the funding available from developers for wetland mitigation could go a great deal further and improve on our currently imperfect success.

In the process, we could also help our farmers and cut the losses of quality farmland because many of those functions can be produced on farms that also continue in working agriculture. Environmental community flexibility on this issue would go a long way with farmers who, in some communities, are seeing more losses of farmland to wetland restoration than they're seeing from direct development.

For Farmers Only

[ENVIRONMENTALISTS, DO NOT READ!]

Are There Benefits for Agriculture?

There are also many ways agriculture can benefit from environmental markets:

- *Alternative/supplemental income:* Many farmers could enhance environmental values as an ancillary part of their existing farming operations. So environmental markets are a chance for farmers to diversify and increase profitability.

- *More farmers benefit from conservation incentives:* Current funding for conservation incentives in agriculture only serves a small fraction of the farmers who would like to participate. With environmental markets paying more of the cost, more farmers could afford to implement conservation practices to improve their environmental performance.

- *Reduced regulation:* If more farmers are meeting baselines and generating environmental services, the agriculture industry's environmental performance would improve, reducing the need and public pressure to regulate.

- *Slowing the loss of agricultural lands:* Stable environmental markets will provide supplemental income that will help keep the farm in business and the farmer on the land and in agriculture. They will also provide a premium for those producers willing to make long-term investments and who commit to remaining on the land and in active agriculture. This will reduce loss of farmland to development and the resulting loss of critical agriculture industry business infrastructure like processors, wholesalers, suppliers, and farm service providers.

- *Funding for purchase of development rights:* Dependence on scarce public funding greatly limits the potential of most purchase of development rights (PDR) programs. Environmental market transactions often include funding for the acquisition of long-term contracts or of agricultural easements that pay the farmer to keep the land in farming so it can continue to provide the agreed-upon environmental services.

This helps keep farmers on the land while reducing dependence on government appropriations for PDR.

- *Increased community support for, and connection to, agriculture:* International sources for most farm products have led to a growing perception that Americans may no longer need American farms. Despite the current local food movement, the vast majority of consumers buy most of their food in major supermarkets. So they still tend to believe that food can come from anywhere. Suppose, however, that continuation of urban growth and the nation's economic prosperity depended upon the help of local farms not just for food but also to mitigate for the environmental impacts of that growth? An economically viable U.S. farm industry that keeps land out of development and also supplies these critical environmental services, while also providing food, would make farmers a good deal more indispensable than they are already.

- *Fairness in allocating the burdens of environmental protection:* Without accepted and credible measures for the economic value of environmental services, it can become politically easy to push off the burdens of protecting these services onto a small, underrepresented industry (like agriculture) through regulation. But suppose those services acquire a known value reinforced daily in an open, public marketplace? With an established value for environmental services, the potential economic unfairness of regulation can be easier to demonstrate. Environmental markets can thus encourage a more fairly shared and incentive-based approach to addressing our nation's environmental problems.

The Threat of Land Conversion Out of Agriculture

Unfortunately, the first experience many farmers have with environmental markets is wetland banking. Flat, undeveloped, low-cost farmland, often located in areas that were once wetlands, will inevitably become prime targets for wetland banks.

Of course, unless they were faced with condemnation, the individual farmers who sell their land to wetland bankers mostly do so happily and voluntarily. But resulting upward pressure on market prices makes it harder for remaining farmers in that community to compete for land. And the resulting removal of quality land from agriculture erodes the critical mass of local farm production supporting important farm business infrastructure.

With this experience, farmers can be forgiven if they initially view this and other environmental markets with suspicion.

The threat of conversion of farmland to environmental restoration is not likely to go away, with environmental markets or without. But without these markets farmers become nothing but an obstacle. Given the amount of money involved, they are an obstacle that is easily pushed aside. With environmental markets in place, however, working farmers become a part of the solution. As urban growth, sprawl, and development increase, pressure for environmental conversion of farmland to make up for the resulting damage will inevitably increase. With farmland so desirable for environmental conversion, it seems unlikely that "just say no" will provide much long-term hope.

And wetlands aren't our only worry. There could, in the years ahead, be a great deal more money flowing into conversion of farmland for a wide array of environmental uses. Money is power.

Agriculture definitely needs a political strategy for this, but what strategy? There are perhaps six broad principles that could be part of a long-term agriculture strategy to prevent the increased loss of agricultural land to environmental conversion:

- *Participate in environmental market development:* Most of these markets are still emerging and will be for some time to come. Farmers need to participate as they emerge to assure their rules are realistic for farmers.

- *Use environmental markets to earn money:* Farmers need to participate in these markets, use them to earn as much money as possible, and use that money to help make their farm businesses profitable so they can remain on the land and in active working agriculture.

- *Out-compete the converters:* Farmers have a big competitive advantage over those who would convert farmland to full environmental restoration. Farmers are already earning income on this same land by selling their crops. They only need to earn some additional profit from generating and selling environmental credits to supplement that existing crop income. So farmers can provide better services at a lower cost and fill that demand by out-competing the farmland converters.

- *Develop tools for working lands to produce credits:* Farmers can help conservation districts, NRCS, university researchers, regulators, non-profits, and environmentalists identify and refine the conservation practices that best allow farmers to produce credits without losing quality farmland from working agriculture.

- *Position agriculture as an environmental savior:* Farmers can position the working agriculture industry as *the* source of solutions for society's environmental problems. Make it clear that the best way for society to afford to grow and prosper is to protect and work with agriculture businesses to address the inevitable resulting environmental woes at the lowest possible cost.

- *Oppose conversion:* Farmers can consistently and vigorously oppose conversion of high quality farmland out of agriculture no matter what the cause, and fight for the tools (regulatory or incentive) that can help prevent it. At the same time, they should remain open to opportunities to convert non-productive land for environmental uses where there is no significant loss of farm production.

Yes, today's environmental markets are still a bit "thin on the ground." There are, however, already some meaningful opportunities for farmers.[17] And there is a good deal of interest and much future promise.[18] In the long term, environmental markets could be transformational for farmers. An agriculture industry broadly engaged in selling environmental services seems likely to become as effective at producing clean water, clean air, and wildlife habitat as it is today at growing wheat and carrots.

CHAPTER 10

Local Food, Consumer Influence, and Farmer Privacy

If there is an economic bright spot in American agriculture today, it has to be the local food movement. The public is reawakening to the pleasures and health benefits of fresh local food and to the greater sense of community gained through a direct connection with the people who grow it. Farmers who have access to urban consumers are increasingly selling direct to the public through farmers markets, roadside stands, and street-corner vending. Consumer-supported agriculture (CSA) farms provide weekly shares of their seasonal production to subscribers. Agro-tourism combines on-farm direct sales with activities like harvest festivals, corn mazes, hay rides, and catering for weddings and other events. Farmers can add value to their crops and sell farm-processed product direct as well. Some local farms are also making inroads with some of the large supermarket chain stores.

This is happening all across the country. And it leads one to wonder: As consumers become more directly and personally connected with the farmers who produce their food and more aware of the issues associated with its production, might they become a positive influence on the environmental practices used to grow it?

The Size and Significance of the Local Food Movement

Of course the total value of direct-market sales still represents only a tiny percentage of total U.S. production.[1] But the growth in this sector of the agriculture economy has been remarkable. For example, the total number of farmers markets in the United States grew steadily from 1,755 in 1994 to 8,144 in 2013.[2]

Sales of direct-market agricultural products across the country have been rising much more quickly than overall sales in the agriculture industry generally.[3] The total number of farmers engaged in direct-market farming rose by 17 percent in the five years between 2002 and 2007.[4] About 6 percent of U.S. farms are now selling at least some of their crop direct to the public.

145

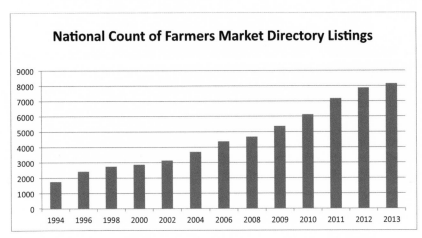

10.1 National Count of Farmers Market Directory Listings (USDA-AMS, Marketing Services Division)

Because they extract more value out of the same crop, depending on the urban community involved and on the size of the surrounding agricultural landscape considered local, a very small percentage increase in urban consumption of locally grown food can often have a significant impact on the near-local farm economy.[5]

While total local direct-market food production may be limited, local food consumers have increasing impact on public policy affecting agriculture. The many activist groups that are proliferating within the food movement around the country represent a significant new political constituency that increasingly influences federal and local farm politics.[6] Of course three-quarters of the farm bill is devoted to nutrition, so it would be expected that food advocates would be interested in the nutrition title. But there is also increasing food community recognition that other farm policies (commodity subsidy programs, the conservation title, research and extension, and marketing, for example) can have a big influence on nutrition as well. And today's local food movement is diversifying. It concerns itself with issues of food quality, food security, and access to food that involve the entire array of food issues, including the environmental ones.

This movement seems almost certain to have disproportionate impact on future farm policy and on how all farmers grow food. Since it is still a small part of the market, we need to look for how we might use this consumer influence to gain leverage.

Traditional Farm Insulation from Consumer Influence

In the usual wholesale marketplace, agricultural producers are quite isolated from their ultimate consumers. A commercial wheat farmer, for example, might sell to a large food processing firm. Once approved and accepted, the farmer's wheat will be quickly mixed in with the wheat produced by other growers. Details about its origins will be lost. It may be shipped anywhere in the country or the world where it will be included in processed foods that return to consumers under a brand name and in packaging that seldom provides a clue about the farmers that grew it or the practices used in doing so. If the final product is undesirable, the farmer faces no disgrace. If it is harmful, there is no farmer liability. And if it was grown in a way that is socially or environmentally responsible (or irresponsible), the consumer will never know. There are, increasingly, exceptions for unprocessed fruits and vegetables. But, even there, the farmer often remains anonymous.

Sometimes consumer demands are reflected in the purchasing standards of large processing or distribution firms. If there are potential health concerns (and potential liability), the farm-gate buyer will be paying attention. Or a processor or distributor may occasionally be conscious of some environmental sensitivity of their customers, particularly if there is some kind of "green" marketing campaign. But ordinarily, the chance that the environmental preferences of a purchaser of corn flakes will end up reflected in an Iowa corn grower's farming practices is essentially nil.

Local Food and the Environment

The fact that a product was produced locally does not guarantee that it was grown responsibly. But it is significant for the environment that the crops sold by these farmers may be grown on the urban-edge landscape. Keep in mind that many of our worst environmental problems are also associated with concentrated human populations.[7] So the environmental practices (helpful or unhelpful) of farmers located in the same estuary, watershed, or habitat as an urban center may be particularly significant for the environment. Consumer influences on the environmental responsibility of local farmers or on preserving local farmland can, therefore, have a disproportionately positive impact on the environment.

There are also other environmental advantages to eating local.[8] Eating local can also mean eating fresh, which may reduce environmental impacts of packaging and processing. Local (and fresh) food can reduce the current estimated 1,500 miles of average transportation for food products with possible energy savings and reduced climate impact. Local, direct-market farms are often smaller and each may grow a wider variety of crops on their land, increasing genetic diversity and improving the chance that there will be natural, uncultivated areas between cropped fields that create habitat for wildlife.

Buying local may also help protect local farmland. Keeping local urban-edge farms profitable can help keep their land in agriculture and out of sprawling, environmentally damaging development. A local farmer, especially a direct-market local farmer, is probably receiving a much larger share of the final sales value of their crop. While they must invest time and money in marketing their crop, they can also make a living selling fewer heads of lettuce or ears of corn. This allows them to earn more income per acre of land in farm production and thus increases their ability to compete in a land market that is heavily pressured by development demand.

Many of our small, direct-market farmers are also certified organic. Organic certification is not necessarily full proof of environmental responsibility, but it is certainly a good start. There are other certifications that can be useful for consumers as well. Some farmers have received one or another of the many third-party environmental certifications like Salmon-Safe,[9] Fish Friendly Farming,[10] or Food Alliance.[11] These kinds of certifications are available all across the country and help provide assurance that the products sold have been grown in accordance with responsible standards of environmental performance. The online service Local Harvest provides a directory of locally grown foods, farms, farmers markets, and CSAs.[12]

Influencing Institutional Producers

Opportunities for consumers to influence how farmers grow their food are not limited to local or direct markets. Some of the larger commercial food processors and suppliers are also using certification systems to provide consumer assurance that their products are grown responsibly. NORPAC, discussed below, for example, has a Food Alliance certification for many of its products. Consumers can find these firms and farms at the Food Alliance website.[13] One can increasingly also find commercial grocers who identify where their fresh produce was grown. This is not easy for them to do, so when they do it they deserve congratulations and loyalty.

You're unlikely, yet, to see this at all among the packaged foods which are usually highly anonymous and represent about 57 percent of total U.S. food consumption.[14] But the more origin identification we can get, at least for fresh fruits, vegetables, meats, and other similar products, the better it will be for the environment. Consumer environmental preferences can have a surprising impact even on large institutional suppliers.

How Restoring Fish Habitat Helped Sell Eggs and Milk

Wilcox Family Farms is one of the largest producers of fresh eggs and milk in the Pacific Northwest. The Wilcox family grows a number of crops on 1,800 acres along the environmentally sensitive Nisqually River which passes under Interstate 5 (I-5) about halfway between the cities of Tacoma and Olympia, Washington. While they are a mostly wholesale operation, they vigorously market their products online and maximize the marketing value of good environmental stewardship.[15] They have earned Food Alliance, Certified Humane,[16] Salmon-Safe, and organic certifications.

Wilcox Farm stream habitat, Washington. *Courtesy of Stewardship Partners*

In order to get their Salmon Safe certification, the Wilcox family completed several improvements on their farm. They restored native trees and vegetation to create shade and habitat along the Nisqually River. They reduced their use of commercial fertilizers and pesticides, fenced off livestock to create natural buffers from fish streams, and they created a system to capture and remove most of the animal waste produced by the hens and chicks in their egg operation.

Along with Wilcox Family Farms, Stewardship Partners of Seattle has recruited over fifty local farms into the Salmon-Safe certification program.[17] Certainly these farmers are public-spirited people trying to do the right thing. But just as certainly, most of them are also motivated by the knowledge that many informed consumers will pay a premium for the knowledge that their food was responsibly grown.

CONSERVATION ECONOMICS

How a Major Processor Made a Business Decision to Reduce Pesticides

Snap bean farmers in the Willamette Valley, south of Portland, Oregon, have had increasing difficulty with a fungus known as "white mold." This can severely affect their crop and, at times, result in complete rejection by the processor. Motivated to deal aggressively with this disease, growers had been increasing application of chemical fungicides with multiple sprayings.

In 2005, a large, local food processing firm, NORPAC Foods of Stayton, Oregon,[18] applied through American Farmland Trust for an EPA-funded grant that would help their snap-bean farmers reduce their use of fungicide chemicals to combat white mold. The grant was to help them better use integrated pest management (IPM) practices designed to minimize the application of pesticides that can be dangerous to health and the environment.

NORPAC is a cooperative, wholly owned by its 240 farmer-members. Its farmer-directors are, no doubt, just as profit-motivated and just as financially conservative as farmers anywhere in the country. Their IPM project called for the use of careful crop, weather, and disease monitoring to help them decide when they could forgo a second spray of chemical fungicides. Given the dire consequences of making a mistake, this ran counter to the usual farmer inclination to spray again just to be sure.

The following year, I had the chance to do a site visit to assess the firm's progress on this grant-funded project. I was curious about why these farmers would have a sufficient interest in reducing their use of pesticides that they would apply for such a grant.

At the time, one of NORPAC's major customers was SYSCO, a large national food distribution firm.[19] Among SYSCO's many customers were several Northwest colleges and universities that provided food services for their dormitories, student unions, and other on-campus facilities. Those university food service managers, and their student patrons, were increasingly vocal in asking that their food be both healthful and environmentally responsible. They represented only a very small portion of SYSCO's customers, but they were a significant voice. So SYSCO asked its suppliers, like NORPAC, to take steps to limit their farmers' use of environmentally dangerous pesticides.

There were, of course, also other factors in NORPAC's decision. Allowable chemical fungicides had recently been restricted by EPA to ones that were becoming more costly. The farmers were concerned about the health of their own families and field workers, and NORPAC was concerned about the health of its factory workers. But these co-op farmers' wish to protect the market for their products, and SYSCO's close connection to the needs and desires of its customers, was a big part of the farmers' motivation to adopt a new management practice that increased their financial risk but that was also much better for health and the environment.

Willamette Valley snap beans in early bloom, Oregon.
Courtesy of NORPAC

CONSERVATION ECONOMICS

How a Dairy Cooperative Ended Use of Synthetic Growth Hormones

Tillamook Creamery,[20] headquartered along the central Oregon coast, is a farmer-owned cooperative and a major Northwest regional competitor for Kraft cheese. In 2005, it decided it would no longer accept milk from its member dairies that used a synthetic growth hormone known as rBGH.[21]

Tillamook's decision followed a vigorous public debate fueled by PCC Natural Markets, a Seattle-based organic co-op grocery. PCC Natural Markets was also only a modest part of the Tillamook customer base. But PCC is active in the local food movement, and has an involved customer-member base. When it became clear that this small but determined band of Tillamook customers truly didn't want to eat cheese that came from cows given synthetic growth hormones, Tillamook voted to prohibit their use.

Like NORPAC, Tillamook is a cooperative composed of and run by their 147 member dairies. Their decision was made by a decisive vote of that membership, and it was clearly a decision that was heavily driven by business considerations—environmental ones.

NORPAC and Tillamook are on the commercial mass-market side of the agriculture industry. Yet their structure as cooperatives brings their farmer-members much closer to their ultimate consumers and makes them more sensitive to consumer wishes. Presumably the farmer-members of both firms were focused significantly on their own financial self-interest. But they were ready and willing to respond to the wishes of even a small minority of those consumers. SYSCO, too, deserves credit. They empowered those university students and food service managers—presumably also, at least in part, as a matter of good business.

This potential for leverage in the food processing sector has led to new efforts to stimulate major change in worldwide agriculture. The World Wildlife Fund (WWF) has a project that is enlisting the major global food suppliers and processors in adopting world-wide certification standards for environmental responsibility. They aim to avoid the challenge of directly changing the behavior of millions of farmers and the virtual impossibility of educating billions of consumers on the complexities of environmental practices. Instead they are focusing on getting one hundred or so of the world's largest food processing and distribution companies together to create agreed environmental standards for farm production. This could result in a simple, well-recognized "green" certification for consumers that can be used throughout the international food processing, food supply industry.

This effort holds a lot of promise. It could provide a realistic yet powerful way for citizens and consumers, even if they haven't the time to shop at the local farmers market, to still make a leveraged difference through their personal purchasing choices.[22]

Farmer Privacy and Independence

Despite the advantages of direct markets, many farmers like the way the wholesale agriculture marketplace insulates them from consumers. Almost every other business engaged in creating, modifying, manufacturing, or even just supplying products faces today's elevated standards of strict product liability. If a defect in a product causes someone harm, the producer can be liable regardless of how careful they may have been.[23] The producer of that product must cover the risk with insurance and is expected to pass the cost along to their customer base.

Sometimes, of course, producers do prefer to label their products. For an increasing number of products, there may be a public or private record, a tracking system, or even some other technology that can trace the product's source. It helps that, aside from potential contamination by pesticides or fertilizers, there are limited ways most farm products can be dangerously defective when they leave the farm. Still, to the extent that possibility exists, most farmers like the fact that they are anonymous.

Many farmers like their wholesale position for other reasons as well. They may be in farming partly because they prefer directing their energies to growing a crop, not to processing, packaging, customer relations, sales, and marketing. They value and nurture their skills and identities as growers. Direct consumer connections can invite scrutiny. Even if a farmer's practices are environmentally friendly, they may not be something he or she wishes to discuss with outsiders. A big part of the appeal of being a farmer is the freedom to manage your private land and grow your own crops in the manner you see fit. One of the substantial appeals of wholesale agriculture is that the only time the farmer needs to answer to anyone off the farm may be once a year when the crop goes to the processor for approval and sale. The rest of the year, they are on their own.

So it is understandable why much of the agriculture industry might prefer to retain that insulation.

For Farmers Only

[ENVIRONMENTALISTS, DO NOT READ!]

Local Food and Public Education about Agriculture

It is practically an article of faith among farmers that one of their core problems is the lack of public understanding of agriculture. The generational gap between most Americans and our agricultural roots grows as the percentage of the U.S. work force employed in agriculture steadily diminishes.[24]

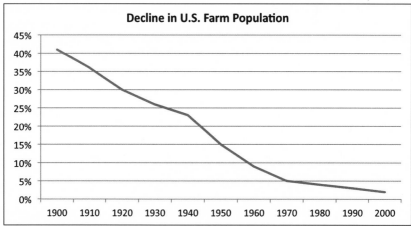

10.2 Percentage decline in U.S. Farm Population (USDA Economic Research Service)

Ever fewer of us have parents or grandparents who were farmers, or have personal experiences with life on the farm. It is conventional farmer humor to say that most people today think their food comes from the supermarket. So farmers naturally feel they get saddled with public policy driven by popular opinions and written by elected officials ignorant of the realities of the food supply or of farmers' needs.

At the same time, we have a growing local food movement that reflects a veritable explosion of consumer interest in farmers and food sources. Consumers are increasingly interested in learning how food is grown, which foods are healthiest and tastiest, and what issues might be faced by the farmers they deal with that could potentially disrupt their future access to that food. What these consumers learn from the local, direct-market farmers with whom they interact will have a profound impact on future consumer perspectives on the entire agriculture industry.

These direct-market farmers also have the potential to influence local urban-edge politics. They and their customers may be constituents of elected legislators or members of Congress who need help understanding agriculture. And, as geographically close as many of them are to urban areas, they may also be at the forefront in facing some of the agriculture industry's most difficult environmental challenges. Certainly they will have ideas about how to more effectively deal with the environmental community. Many of them are environmentalists themselves.

These urban-edge farmers are becoming the face of agriculture for much of the non-farming public.

Of course the direct local food market still represents only a tiny percentage of total U.S. farm production.[25] So one might understand why commercial farmers would not be focused on their issues. But it is worrisome that, in reviewing the 257 pages of the 2013 American Farm Bureau Federation (AFBF) Policy Book, one finds essentially no discussion about local food, direct local marketing, farmers markets, local food access and security, or any of the concerns that are particular to local direct-market agriculture. While the recent 2014 Farm Bill was moving through Congress, and still as of this writing, not one of the background papers or issue discussions on the AFBF website addresses the particular needs of local direct-market farmers.[26]

Agriculture's Focus on Privacy

Current agriculture industry policy firmly supports the protection of farmer confidentiality and privacy. This extends to preventing disclosure of such farm activities as conservation planning, test results for BSE (bovine spongiform encephalopathy, or "mad cow disease"), livestock identification, food safety reporting, and nutrient management.[27] The industry wants strong labeling on products used by farmers, products like livestock feed and pesticides. But there is a good deal of reticence about labeling that provides specifics for identifying where, how, and by whom farm products are gown that are sold to and used by non-farmers. The 2013 AFBF Policy Book expresses a good deal of concern with farm product labeling that would trace the origins of livestock, allow market discrimination based on biotechnology content, imply that organic foods are "in any way" superior to other farm products, identify animal waste as hazardous, or identify farm "production practices" that do not "affect... nutrition or food safety," presumably including labeling of products for their environmental responsibility. The activities of animal cruelty activists have led several states to pass or consider laws that prohibit the taking of pictures of agricultural activities on private farmland without the farmer's permission.[28]

It is certainly legitimate that a farmer would want to protect the confidentiality of his or her farm business activities from competitors. Product labeling can be expensive and burdensome. Too much information can encourage lawsuits. Pictures, taken out of context, can be misleading. So there are some legitimate concerns here.

But one really can't expect to help the public understand agriculture while at the same time either ignoring or closing off the sources of information that might enlighten that understanding and strengthen connections between farmers and their ultimate consumers.

Agriculture's insulation from public inquiry, influence, and liability comes at a price. Farmers also pay for protection from products liability with lower wholesale prices and by making themselves yet more dependent on monopolization by large, often multinational corporate food processing and distribution firms. Partly because the farmers are anonymous, these large firms have little need to be loyal to local farmers or to their communities. These firms' investors expect them to go anywhere on the planet, to buy from whomever has product to sell, to secure the largest market share, and to do so at the lowest possible price. Little else matters to them, so little else can be allowed to matter for the farmer who supplies them.

New standards universally applied at the food processor and distribution level could help change that. But it would also help if commercial farmers would embrace their direct-market colleagues and if they were to moderate their notorious preference for privacy.

Public Perception of Farmer Privacy

While farmers love their privacy, most are also very sensitive that they be seen as responsible members of their community. And, like most of us, farmers are typically quite proud of the work they do; they like to feel good about the value and the quality of the crops they grow. So there is another consequence of market isolation that is not so positive. The anonymity of the farm products marketplace also tends to drive farming to a low level of expected quality and responsibility.

Most farmers care a good deal about the natural environment. It affects the quality of their daily life and their sense of fulfillment. It affects their own health and that of their families and communities. And, not least, their success at growing crops or livestock depends heavily on their ability to integrate their production with the demands of the natural world around them. So it isn't surprising that farmers might take pride in protecting the natural environment on their own farms.

When a farmer-colleague behaves badly, it is frustrating because it makes one's own scruples seem pointless. One neighbor's negligence can reflect badly on all farmers in the community. It degrades the environment on which all farmers depend. It devalues agriculture, generally, in the public eye. And it increases the likelihood that all farmers will face increased environmental regulation.

An anonymous marketplace for farm products may insulate some farmers from social pressures or liability exposures. But it definitely throws all farmers together into the same pot when it comes to public perceptions of agriculture.

It is understandable that most farmers wouldn't want some litigious citizen digging through their Natural Resources Conservation Service files and looking over their shoulders to make sure everything they're doing on their own farm measures up to some unclear standard. It is also understandable if most farmers wouldn't spend much time worrying about the tiny percentage of their direct-market colleagues who sell their crops by explaining agriculture to the food-consuming public.

But the less the public knows about what you're doing, the more mysterious it becomes, and the more likely it is that they'll suspect that if they did know, they wouldn't like it. And the more likely it is they will paint you with your sloppy and irresponsible neighbor's brush.

For Environmentalists Only

[FARMERS, DO NOT READ!]

Creating Consumer Pressure

Consumer demand can be a powerful tool in protecting the environment. But it doesn't work if there's no pressure. The burgeoning local food phenomenon and the sensitivity of food processors to "green" market pressures are opportunities for environmentalists to exert some of that pressure.

Many people think of "eat local" as an environmental movement. And, in some ways, it is. But the reasons for eating local are quite diverse. Local food advocates care about the freshness, quality, taste, and healthfulness of food. They see access to fresh local food in community friendly venues like farmers' markets as a quality-of-life issue. And they are searching for food systems that assure that food is made available across society with fairness and reliability. Concerns are sometimes expressed about food transportation impacts on the environment. Human health would seem to be an environmental issue. And perhaps "quality of life" is too. But the local food movement appears to have only limited focus on how the actual growing of that food affects the environment.

For all the reasons discussed in this chapter, however, there are strong reasons why local consumers should connect local food with the local environment. All working farms have environmental impacts. Their continued existence is critical to future environmental health. They represent a big opportunity to mitigate for the current and future environmental damage done by others. And the proximity of local farms to the urban communities that are generating some of our most serious environmental problems (sprawl, water pollution, flooding, habitat loss, etc.) heightens their relevance.

These connections have not been completely missed by local food activists. But environmentalists could have a good deal of influence by getting involved in the many local food movements. Environmentalists can help make sure the environment is a part of the local food system.

Environmentalists and Farmer Privacy

There are some environmental advantages to farmer anonymity. It helps, for example, when it comes to enlisting farmers to participate voluntarily in environmental conservation on their farms. Before you conclude that farmers should just be compelled to provide more public disclosure about their operations, the impact of doing that deserves some careful thought.

One of the places this competition between privacy and public disclosure plays out is in farmer conservation stewardship and under state[29] and federal[30] Freedom of Information Acts.

Suppose you are a farmer who has come to the local conservation district office to get help. You'd like to adopt some new practices to keep pollution on your farm from running off into a local creek prized for its fish and wildlife. Let's call this Wilbur Creek. You have the district technical advisor come out to your place and you show her your operation—its strengths and its warts and weaknesses. She takes a lot of notes. Some of her recommendations seem a bit too expensive and maybe not that helpful. You're not ready to do them yet. But there are some other suggestions you feel you can afford, especially if you can get a bit of NRCS assistance with the cost. You'll see how the initial work goes and save her less appealing recommendations for later.

The NRCS office is co-located with the conservation district, so you and the district expert go back and have a conversation with the NRCS agent as well. He takes more notes and agrees to write up your proposal and see if he can get you the cost-share help you need. At some point you sign an application for this assistance, maybe with both the conservation district and with NRCS.

After several weeks your cost-share request is approved. NRCS and district staff experts work with you to implement the desired improvements to your property. You're happy with the outcome. The stream has benefited. You feel good about having taken action. And you're inclined to do more when the opportunity presents itself.

Meanwhile, in the town a few miles downstream from your farm, there is a local environmental activist group known as "Citizens to Restore Wilbur Creek." They've helped complete a number of riparian restoration projects in the past, but the water quality in the creek is still unsatisfactory. A more aggressive segment of the group's membership has recently begun to drive its agenda. They come to the local conservation district and NRCS office and file state and federal Freedom of Information Act requests to see the files on these agencies' projects affecting Wilbur Creek. Since you're a sizable landowner along the creek, they definitely want to see any records pertaining to your property. And, since you were so good as to make the effort to improve your property, there are some records there for them to see.

How do you, as the farmer, feel about their request?

You have, after all, received a good deal of free technical assistance at public expense. And you have received outright cost-share payments for improvements to your private land. This help and these payments were funded by local and federal taxpayers, people who would seem to have a legitimate right to know if their money has been wisely spent. That is going to require that they understand the need for those expenditures. And that's going to involve the disclosure of everything you revealed to these conservation district and NRCS staffers about all the problems you're having with controlling pollution. It's also likely to involve revealing your decision not to follow the district technical expert's advice on some of her recommendations—the ones you didn't agree with, couldn't afford, or weren't yet ready to adopt.

You agree that taxpaying citizens should have a right to see how their government spends their money. But it feels to you like these people with Citizens to Restore Wilbur Creek are actually on an information fishing expedition. They want to see if you or any of your neighbors may be potentially liable under the Clean Water Act. They're not interested in government accountability. They're looking for someone to sue!

Federal NRCS policy protects landowner confidentiality. The agency knows that without confidentiality, a great many farmers would never come near their offices no matter how much help they needed or how much they might be willing to do to protect the environment. The conservation district doubtless has the same view, but they may have a different policy, depending on the state's freedom of information laws. It could easily turn out that the district is required to turn over their records, while NRCS is not. Knowing this, some districts have been known to work out a deal with NRCS whereby their district records are actually retained in NRCS custody and can potentially be covered by NRCS confidentiality protections. This entire legal arena is, frankly, quite unsettled.[31]

Of course Citizens to Restore Wilbur Creek could probably get a court subpoena for these records if they and you were already engaged in litigation. But at the time of a Freedom of Information Act request, they are probably still just fishing. And this is what has you, the farmer, concerned. Who knows how they might interpret all those quickly taken notes from the relaxed conversations between you and the conservation district staffer. Your farm is better than most, but it is probably less than perfect. All this has you worried.

You also have a neighbor whom you know strongly resists making conservation improvements. He hasn't set foot in a conservation district office in his life and he never will. And it hasn't escaped your notice that, for that very reason, he has little to worry about.

There is one thing that will happen for sure if NRCS or the district does give them your records. You'd never go back into that office again either, and neither will any of your neighbors.

NRCS and the conservation district know the future success of their programs is at stake, so Citizens to Restore Wilbur Creek may have a fight on their hands.

Now, as an environmentalist again, how do you feel about this? Clearly the success of the nation's voluntary incentive programs depends on there being at least some level of confidentiality for such records. But, as a potential member of groups very much like Citizens to Preserve Wilbur Creek, you'd probably like to see them. This is an area where the farm and environmental communities need to come to a mutual understanding. Anything environmentalists can do to show good faith, to generate mutual trust and respect, is going to help. Issues like this need to be sorted out through negotiation and agreement, not in court.

CHAPTER 11

Choosing Between Zoning and Conservation Easements

Protecting farmland seems as though it could be an area of agreement between farmers and environmentalists. But, here especially, the challenge is not so much in recognizing the problem as in settling on a solution.

Let's take a look at the two most powerful tools we have to combat farm-land loss: managing growth and purchasing development rights. These are not, by any means, the only ways we have to address this issue. Of course increasing farm profitability will help, as will some assistance with environmental incentives and some moderation in environmental regulation. But given the overwhelming power of the market for land and the land-extensive nature of farming, some use of both of these two more direct approaches will be indispensable if we're serious about protecting farmland.

These two tools represent the regulatory and incentive-based alternatives in the land use arena. And, as we might expect, farmers and environmentalists have very different opinions about them.

Growth Management Laws

The Available Tools

Growth management typically involves a planning and a regulatory stage. First we map out what we believe our community should look like. Then we implement our plan by setting aside zones in which the most appropriate land uses are encouraged and where inconsistent ones may be restricted. We do this because we know it will help our community flourish economically and make it efficient, workable, livable, and safe. It will also help reduce our collective impacts on the environment.

Land use decisions in a capitalist economy are mostly driven by business considerations. So effective zoning must definitely consider business profitability. If our manufacturers, commercial office landlords, retail mall outlets, residential contractors, or our farms can't make a profit, they're either going to go somewhere else, or they're not going to be in business at all. The places where they conduct business must be designed so their businesses flourish.

Zoning laws can take many forms, but most typically they restrict or encourage subdivision and/or prohibit inconsistent uses within the protected zone. So, for example, if we want to retain a vigorous manufacturing industry in an urban area, we might create an industrial zone in which we require somewhat larger minimum parcel sizes appropriate to the kind of manufacturing we want to encourage. It should have access to highways and other supply and shipping routes, and it should allow the kinds of activities necessary to manufacturing. We might limit other uses in this zone that would be inconsistent with manufacturing/industrial activity. Uses like mixed offices, single or multifamily residences, or mixed retail sales might be prohibited. If we don't do this, the land will be fragmented up into parcels that are too small for a profitable manufacturing operation, the area will be flooded with offices, retail stores, and disruptive traffic, and the presence of residences will create nuisance and other community complaints about nearby industrial activities. Without protection, manufacturing will no longer be profitable in this area and we won't have a manufacturing sector at all.

Healthy commercial and retail businesses need good customer access. So we'll locate these activities in areas with good public roads and other transportation. We will want to allow office space for a strong financial, legal, business, and professional sector. We will try to locate these so they can be close to one another and where there is good public transportation for their commuting workforce. If we want to encourage the building of economically viable residential apartments, we're probably going to site them near public transportation, close to residential support businesses like grocers, restaurants, and other local retail services, and near parks, schools, and public accommodations. Without the insulation provided by zoning, most of these activities would be in trouble.

Similar protections can be necessary to preserve healthy agriculture. For example:

Parcel Size

Where agricultural zoning does exist, the first, most common approach is to simply designate minimum parcel sizes. These need to be large enough to protect the potential for genuine, financially independent, family farming. This will depend on the nature of the land and of local agriculture. But with the current average U.S. farm size at 418 acres,[1] with a typical financially independent irrigated potato farm at perhaps 500 acres, a non-irrigated wheat farm in the area of 5,000 acres, and a commercial ranching operation requiring perhaps 10,000 acres,[2] zoning for adequate parcel sizes can be a challenge.[3] And given the apparent ability and willingness of many residential landowners to purchase large parcels simply for the purpose of building a home, it can take very large parcel zoning to seriously discourage non-farm buyers.

Use Restrictions

The second common approach to zoning for agriculture is to prevent inconsistent activities within the agricultural zone. This can be complicated if we want to allow farmers to engage in direct-market retail sales and limited value-added processing, for example, while not allowing the farm to transform itself into a major food processing plant or a 40,000-square-foot supermarket. Avoiding incursion of non-farm residences is also a challenge because farmers and their families (at least in this country) typically prefer to reside on the land they farm, so residential use is usually permitted. Some growth management laws require that the agricultural property owner actually be engaged in working agriculture, perhaps by requiring a demonstrated level of ongoing agricultural income from the property as a precondition to approval of a residential building permit.[4]

With these laws, properties in these agriculture zones end up protected, regardless of the preferences of their individual owners, so the full benefits of the zone can be assured to all. Each farmer in that zone has some assurance that they won't wake up one morning to discover construction starting on a new condominium, small lot residential subdivision, or open-pit mine going in on the former farm next door. And the farm industry has some assurance that the land needed to sustain their local farm economy will not slowly disappear, choking out the support businesses, farm suppliers, processors, and other agricultural service infrastructure needed to make local farming profitable.

The Political Backdrop

With these kinds of tools available, it seems as though solving the problem of farmland loss should be easy: Just pass strong land use laws. In theory, this should be politically possible. Every state has laws that, at least, authorize its local communities to manage growth. The ever-increasing majority of voters are urban—their self-interests would generally seem better served by stronger, not weaker growth management. And surely the farm industry would want to protect the land it needs to stay in business.

But using effective growth management to help agriculture has proven difficult. Such laws are initially hard to get and then hard to keep in place over time. Most sizable cities and towns adopt some form of urban zoning. But this is of zero help outside the city limits, and it certainly doesn't diminish the traditional push to expand the town's boundaries. There are many county and township land use control efforts around the country, but little is typically accomplished in the rural counties where there is the most farmland to lose.

Rural residents also tend to have stronger feelings about private property rights. Farmers and other rural landowners don't like the idea of zoning—its operative impact is to restrict their freedom to subdivide or sell their land for higher-intensity uses. So it reduces property values.[5] It's hard to see the upside of that. So those counties where most of our farming is located, including many counties that are adjacent to highly populous ones, are often also the very communities that offer the strongest political resistance to growth management.[6]

Statewide land use laws could address agricultural zoning. But only thirteen states have actually adopted them. And nine of those provide only a state framework, still leaving major decisions up to local communities, setting the stage for resistance. Land use laws are a political minefield in the United States. Even in the states that have managed to adopt them, the parcel sizes they require in farm zones are often inadequate to protect agriculture.[7]

There is also little public appetite for increasing land use protections once initial zoning is in place. The public expectation seems to be that permitted uses will increase in intensity over time, but never that allowable uses will be further constrained. It can be all but impossible for elected officials to reduce zoning intensities later on.

A powerful American ethic prefers that communities be allowed to make their own local decisions. Most urban voters find it hard to see rural land fragmentation and farmland loss as a threat. When measures to protect farmland do appear on the public ballot or when they arise in election campaigns or in the legislative arena, rural farm landowners frequently oppose them, leaving many urban voters asking themselves: "If the farmers don't want to protect their farmland, why should I care?"

As difficult as they are to obtain, growth management laws, once in place, can be even more difficult to keep. Several states (including Oregon, which has one of the strongest and earliest statewide growth management laws in the country) have faced serious ballot measure challenges to those laws in recent years.[8] Perhaps it seems tempting for urban residents to dismiss landowner protests about property rights and takings as legally and constitutionally unreasonable. But when these issues come before the *voters,* those property rights arguments are not so easy to dismiss.

Thus, even where growth management laws are succeeding quite nicely in assuring the workability and efficiency of urban areas, our farmlands have, in effect, been relegated to a land use protection wasteland. The "smart growth" movement focuses mostly on just that—on allowing growth but making it smart—mostly in urban areas. Meanwhile, our society gives very little thought to the operational needs of the rural communities that lie outside the city. That leaves a gaping hole that assures we will have little protection for rural landscapes or for the long-term land needs of agriculture.

Landowner opposition to growth management quite often results in opposition by agriculture trade associations.[9] This, perhaps ironically, places these associations in the position of supporting the continued loss of agricultural lands in order to protect the short-term financial interests of the current members of their organizations. There are, however, communities where growth management laws have been in place long enough and with enough stability that most of the current landowners either acquired their property since the laws were adopted and have never had to face devaluation of their land or they can easily see the benefits and the need for protection.[10]

Purchasing Development Rights

The second powerful tool for the protection of agricultural lands involves the use of agricultural conservation easements. This is typically accomplished through state or local government "purchase of development rights" (PDR) programs.[11] Like growth management, PDR programs usually work by preventing inconsistent non-farm development on larger parcels, thereby reducing the land's market value to a point where farm businesses can afford to own it. But the difference is that the landowner agrees to these restrictions voluntarily, usually in exchange for payment of the lost market value.

Let's take a look at how a PDR program might work for our hypothetical farmer, Farmer Jones. He owns one hundred acres on which he grows a variety of crops. You may recall that farm businesses like his are usually able to afford to own land of this kind at a cost of about $3,000 per acre. As it happens, however, there is some urban sprawl affecting this community. If Jones's farm could be subdivided, it would actually be worth a great deal more.

Let's suppose that Jones would prefer to keep his farm in agriculture. Perhaps he could also use some cash to pay off debt. He decides to apply to the local PDR program. He agrees to have an easement recorded against his property that will permanently restrict its subdivision and prevent future non-farm development of his land. It currently appraises at $600,000. But once that easement has been signed and recorded, future subdivision and development won't be possible. At that point, the only likely buyers for this land will be other farmers. So, by signing the easement, he will have reduced its market value to the $300,000 a farmer would be able to pay.

Based on that appraisal, therefore, the PDR program managers agree to pay Jones the $300,000 difference in value in exchange for his agreeing to this easement. He will continue to own the land in fee, as the complete and absolute owner of the property. He can continue to live on and farm the property as he always has. And he can sell it, if he wishes. The only thing that has changed is that it will no longer be eligible for development and, thus, no developer will be interested in buying it. If he sells, the buyer will almost certainly be another farmer, and its value is likely to be limited to what a farmer would be able to pay—currently $300,000.

This easement transaction with the local PDR program will, therefore, not affect Jones's net worth. Going into this deal, he owned a $600,000 piece of real property. After the deal is completed, he will still own that property though it will have been devalued to $300,000. But he will also have received a $300,000 payment for the difference.

There are a many reasons a farmer like Jones might want to use a program of this type. For example:

1. *Business conversion/capital need:* A farmer who wants to stay in agriculture may need capital now. He may wish to make business improvements like buying a new tractor, building a new barn, or paying down debt.

2. *Semi-retirement:* An older farmer may want to retire or semi-retire and reduce her workload but doesn't yet want to move off the farm. A PDR program can provide the cash needed to do this without selling or breaking up the farm.

3. *Personal conviction:* A farmer may feel strongly that he doesn't want to see his life's work end up broken into small pieces for development.

4. *Estate liquidity:* A farmer may need cash liquidity in her estate to pay taxes. Or perhaps one child wants to farm, but others have gone on to other occupations, so the farmer needs cash in her estate to be able to treat all of her children fairly. The PDR payment and easement will allow her to accomplish this while still keeping the farm intact.

5. *Land expansion:* A successful farmer may wish to buy more farmland and expand his operation. But much of his net worth is tied up in development value on the land, value to which he can't get access without quitting farming and selling the land. The PDR payment will thus allow his landholding and his business to grow.

6. *Farm acquisition:* A young farmer who is just starting out may want to buy a farm but can't afford to pay the development value with what she will be able to earn from farming the land. Or a neighbor would like to expand, but the land is too expensive. If they can find a farm that has been (or can be) protected by an easement, they will only need to pay its agricultural business value.[12]

There are several broad advantages to PDR programs. Participation is voluntary. The programs protect farmland without destroying what may be very reasonable expectations for the value of privately owned land. They provide farmers with a variety of useful options for reinvesting without selling out. And the protection they offer is generally permanent, not subject to transitory local political winds, thus making sure there will be farmland available for future generations.[13]

Combining Growth Management and PDR

PDR programs can work quite nicely in conjunction with growth management. Suppose, for example, a community lacks the requisite political will to adopt zoning restrictions that are rigorous enough to fully protect their farmland. But they are able to get part of the way there. Perhaps, in this locale, it would actually take one-hundred-acre-minimum parcel sizes to truly protect their local agriculture. But the county commission faces too much opposition to make that happen. They settle, instead, on thirty-acre zoning and, at that level, they are able to muster the votes to get it passed.

Perhaps if they'd gotten the zoning they really wanted, they could have largely eliminated the need for a PDR program. But the zoning they did get has helped. Before they acted, local farmland was selling for six or eight times what it was worth for farming. At those prices, many farmers were selling out. Now, with thirty-acre zoning, that has cooled off. The farms are now only worth maybe two to three times their agricultural value. Farmers are still tempted. But sales to non-farmers and fragmentation of the community's farming land base have slowed down.

With this much accomplished, suppose they now decide to also adopt a PDR program. Because of the zoning law they were able to pass, the cost to the PDR program to buy easements is a good deal lower than it would have been. Their money will go much further. As a result, they are able to fund the program at a level that will allow them to buy development rights slowly over time, perhaps over the next twenty-five years. Since they are paying full market value for these easements, most of their farmers are interested. Also because of the zoning law they did pass, the rate at which farms are coming on the market has slowed. So they have enough money in the program to be able to buy the most strategically important easements as they become available on the market.

With these two programs in place, this community has, for the most part, stopped the sale of local farmland to non-farmers, protected agriculture's long-term future, and helped local farmers convert otherwise wasted investments in real estate into cash that can be shifted to more productive farm business and other needs.

An Unexpected Benefit of Using PDR and Growth Management Together

A growth management law, even one that is less than perfect, can help support a local PDR program so that, together, they can get the job done. Rich Doenges, the former manager for the Skagit County Farmland Legacy Program located in northwestern Washington State,[14] tells an interesting story about how this can also work the other way around, how a PDR program can also support growth management.

Skagit County is a rural, largely agricultural community about an hour north of Seattle. The county has growth management, but, prior to 1998, the county commission had been habitually easy-going about handing out rezones, variances, and exceptions under their zoning ordinance. Not long after they adopted their Farmland Legacy (PDR) Program, however, a subtle change began to occur. They still had farmers asking for their land to be rezoned, making all the usual arguments. But the commissioners' thinking about those requests began to shift.

As Rich tells it, after the PDR program was adopted, when you went to a commission meeting where such a rezone was on the table, you could watch the commissioners and see their wheels beginning to turn. The political character of the commission hadn't changed—these were still the same conservative Republicans that are almost always elected in Skagit County. But now, when they got such zone requests, they were looking at that landowner-petitioner and asking themselves: "Wait a minute. Didn't we, just last month, approve spending several hundred thousand dollars of hard-earned taxpayer money to buy development rights? And now, here's this landowner asking us to give them away to him for free."

Suddenly the commission had become a great deal tougher about giving away rezones on agricultural land. Development rights had acquired an actual, measurable value. The politics of zoning had changed.

Cost of Purchasing Development Rights

The disadvantage to PDR programs, of course, is their public cost. And because of their cost, these programs are typically underfunded, or funded over time, so it may take many decades before the needed large blocks of agricultural land can be fully protected. In the meantime, some of the unprotected properties may still become vulnerable to development.[15]

Thus people often fear that a PDR program will be prohibitively costly. But carefully applied, these programs can be made quite affordable. A number of circumstances can add up to help:

- *Spending is spread out over time:* Everything doesn't have to be done immediately. Most programs of this kind map out a twenty-five to forty-year time frame within which they hope to achieve their specified goals—usually a specific number of easement-protected acres.

- *Spending is strategic:* Not all farms need to be protected. The community will set priorities and decide which ones are most important.

- *Conjunction with growth management:* The cost of easement purchases can be diminished, as discussed above, if the local government exercises some discipline in also creating and maintaining a local growth management program—which they may be more inclined to do once the PDR program is in place.

- *Capital investment:* Keep in mind that these programs also make a capital investment in the community; the easements they buy are perpetual. So each purchase represents a one-time cost that should never need to be repeated.

- *Match with outside money:* The money provided locally can often be matched with money available in a state level program. It can be matched again with federal dollars through the Agricultural Conservation Easement Program (ACEP) (formerly FRPP).[16] So the local program will bring money into the community from outside. It is also possible to secure added funding from private sources (land trusts, charitable donors, agriculture industry businesses, etc.).

- *Combine with TDR:* It may be possible, at times, to secure added funding through a local transfer of development rights (TDR) program.[17]

- *Combine with environmental markets:* Payment for some agricultural easements may come from the kind of environmental market transactions discussed in Chapter 9.

- *Combine with environmental restoration projects:* Easement protection for a working farm can sometimes be joined together in an environmental restoration project on another part of the land, or for the protection of some other environmental value. Financial support may be secured from an environmental funder for the combined benefit.

- *Bargain sales:* Many farmers are also willing to accept discounted prices in order to sell an easement, potentially reducing the average cost of acquisitions by as much as 50 percent.[18]

- *Donations:* There will continue to be a few farmers who are able to donate easements outright; an organized PDR program in the community will have a plan into which such donations can be nicely fit, perhaps in cooperation with a local land trust.

Sometimes, PDR programs are bonded out, with the full extended dollar commitment spent in a short period up front and the money paid back over time. But easement acquisitions will more often be spread out over a long period of time, say twenty-five, thirty, or forty years, with the cost paid by the community as they go. This approach, of course, requires future political discipline to avoid gaps if anticipated revenue is diverted to some other purpose when political fashions shift.

Whichever approach is decided upon, once all of the potential contributions and considerations are taken into account, the actual local cost of such a program can become quite manageable.[19]

Using Community Process to Protect Farmland for the Environment—Wisconsin Farming and Conservation Together (FACT) and Florida Green Swamp Land Authority

Zoning is often seen as mostly an urban land use management tool. So when large natural and semi-natural rural areas need protection, communities face a different choice—usually between the outright purchase of land and its protection through environmental management regulation and conservation easement.

South central Wisconsin, for example, faced this dilemma. In 1999, the U.S. Fish & Wildlife Service (USFWS) proposed an Aldo Leopold National Wildlife Refuge for the Lower Baraboo River area of the state. The region contains remnant natural habitats, dry prairies, sedge meadows, oak forests, flood plain forests, and tamarack swamps. It is home to a variety of important local species as well as serving as an important stopover for sandhill cranes and other migratory birds. At the same time, the area also supports many private multigenerational family farms including dairies and other livestock operations as well as growers of corn, soybeans, alfalfa, potatoes, and mint.[20]

When the USFWS first proposed the refuge, there was immediate local opposition. Farmers and landowners saw this as a federal effort to intrude into their community and to publicly manage their private lands. They feared it would result in increased regulation on land use and land management. Blessed with insight, USFWS responded by encouraging the local community to develop an alternative to the proposed refuge. With this motivation, the Wisconsin Farming and Conservation Together (FACT) committee, comprised of landowners, conservation organizations, local government officials, and other interested community members, was formed.

Organizers say that local farmers came to the initial USFWS meeting on the refuge proposal carrying guns and that they left it discussing who would bring what for the potluck at the next meeting. Once they began to cooperate, the group came up with several strategies for protecting the targeted area, including:

- Purchasing development rights and other conservation easements on private lands to protect key habitats as well as working farms;

- Protecting riparian buffers, grasslands, wetlands, and woodlands needed for wildlife and doing so, where possible, without removing farmland from agriculture and while deed restricting restored or existing wetlands; and

- Identifying alternative management tools for farms (like changes in cultivation methods, delayed harvests to improve nesting cover, etc.) to provide improved habitat.

In a similar way, Florida's Green Swamp area also received protections through the work of a cooperative farmer–environmental community process.[21] The Green Swamp area contains some 560,000 acres of mixed cypress swamps, cattle ranches, and citrus orchards as well as the largest remaining wilderness areas in the state. It provides habitat for many threatened and endangered species, includes the headwaters of several rivers, and is a major source of drinking water from an aquifer that is, due to the local geology, especially vulnerable to pollution.

With increasing development pressure in the area, the 1974 Florida Legislature designated 295,000 acres of this region, in Polk and Lake Counties, as an area of "critical state concern." The counties were directed to develop comprehensive plans to protect critical natural resource values. But the landowner community was strongly against proposed land use restrictions that seemed likely to reduce property values. This opposition crystalized in 1991 when, in an effort to redirect accelerating development pressures, the counties offered a new plan that would have rezoned minimum lot sizes on many properties from five acres to twenty acres.

A vigorous response from farm and other landowners convinced the legislature to look for alternative solutions. A new Green Swamp Land Authority was created and funded with $30 million over three years to buy development rights as an alternative to the regulatory approach. The stated goal of this new law was to balance protection of ecological values with landowner property rights concerns.

The community process which followed overcame much of the community mistrust and strengthened local support for the effort, while encouraging a preference of conservation easements over outright acquisitions wherever possible.

Florida Green Swamp agricultural land, Don Frasier Family Farm, Polk County, Florida. *Photo by and courtesy of Marian Ryan*

For Farmers Only

[ENVIRONMENTALISTS, DO NOT READ!]

Why Farms Need Zoning

Farmers often rebel against the idea that there should be any need for zoning, easements, or any other government measures to protect farmland. They feel farm businesses ought to be profitable enough to fend for themselves in a free private land marketplace.

Zoning isn't, however, a matter of farms somehow being more "needy" than other businesses or land-use activities. Some kind of zoning is essential for most of our nation's industries. Consider manufacturing, for example. We know that if it becomes too hard for manufacturers to find larger spaces in logical, industrially zoned locations upon which to site their operations, they will go elsewhere. If the manufacturers move too far away, the workers will be forced to follow. If we don't provide this industry and their workers with protection, they will either be pushed further and further out to the urban edge with other land uses disrupted, or we will lose it entirely in our local community.[22]

Similarly, many of our cities grew up around naturally protected coastal harbors. Their economies were historically rooted in the maritime trades (shipping, commercial fisheries, etc.). These cities have universally seen the need to reserve the precious waterfront properties located on those natural harbors for maritime use. Without that protection, those rare properties would soon be overrun by condominiums, tourism, restaurants, offices, and a host of other, more intensive urban land uses. The result would be the rapid eradication of critical marine industries, the existence of which may still be essential to the cities' continued economic success.

Zoning for agriculture involves precisely the same calculus. We know that building houses, schools, and grocery stores around and in between our farms will make it impossible for those farms to operate. We know if we don't protect larger parcels for agricultural use, soon there won't be any of those parcels for a farmer to buy. And, even before the houses are actually built there, if the land gets too expensive, farmers aren't going to be able to afford it anyway. We also need to preserve a critical mass of agriculture to support the processors, suppliers, and farm service businesses farmers need to flourish. If we want to have farmers in our communities then we need to do something definitive about this, just as we have done for our manufacturers, retail stores, warehouses, commercial offices, condominiums, apartments, and single family homes.

None of these choices has anything whatsoever to do with subsidizing these industries, or with any sense that they somehow require special treatment. No one has argued that if these other businesses were left to their own devices the free economy would somehow address these problems. Quite the contrary, left to their own devices, the free economy seems certain to destroy them. We make these regulatory decisions because, without them, we'll lose these activities and all of us will be worse off.

Note also that these zoning decisions are not always going to be in the best short-term interests of the current owners of the land involved. The owner of any of the properties affected (along the waterfront, in a manufacturing zone, in a single-family residence zone) may very likely prefer having the option to sell without restriction. But, then, most everything we do collectively—from rules against jaywalking, to anti-trust laws, to the universal draft—inconveniences someone.

Land-use decisions can, of course, sometimes create special hardships that run counter to legitimate expectations by landowners in the stability of land use. We need to do our best to avoid that. But also keep in mind that this may run both ways. Failing to provide protections may be as painful as providing them. Consider what happens when a neighboring farm sells out and resulting development brings residences in close contact with the remaining farms. This can result in nuisance claims against the remaining farmers for the sights, smells, late hours, noise, dust, and other normal consequences of farming, activities that may have been going on in that community for hundreds of years.[23]

The Need for Zoning Certainty and Discipline

In those locales where agricultural zoning does exist, it is commonplace for farm landowners to petition their local governments for exceptions, variances, or rezoning for their property so they can subdivide and sell for development. The land may represent a landowner's total life savings. He or she may want to retire. The farm may be worth a great deal more money if it can be subdivided and sold to a developer than if it can only be sold at its agricultural value to another farmer.

The argument one hears in support of these petitions is almost always the same: "This land should be removed from agricultural zoning because it is *no longer profitable for agriculture*." Planning commissioners and elected officials can be quite attentive to this argument. It seems foolish to require that land be sold for less than what it is worth or that it be limited to a land use activity that is not its "highest and best use" if farming is no longer economically viable there.[24]

Most rural county or township elected commissioners are community boosters who want to encourage local growth and development and who see a new strip mall or housing development as desirable civic improvements. They may also feel (often incorrectly) that such growth will expand the tax base and help the public purse.[25]

When a local county commission or township approves such an exception or rezone on a farm property in an agricultural zone and allows that property to be sold for development, that action will almost certainly fuel speculation that other, similar properties in that community might also expect the same favorable treatment. This, in turn, drives up the price of land for everyone in that zone.

The result can be bitterly ironic for the remaining farmers.

As we've discussed, investments in farmland have a carrying cost. When the current market value of that land investment increases, its annual carrying cost also increases. And that increases the annual operating expense of the farm business that owns that land. So when a county commission approves one farmer's petition for a rezone, it has, in effect, increased the cost of doing business for every other farm business in that area. The commissioners have widened the inconsistency each of those farmers will face, in the years to come, between the operating costs of their farm business and the value of their land investment.

The Deceptiveness of "Profitability"

Also ironically, the "my land isn't profitable for agriculture" argument that causes all this to happen is probably flawed in the first place. The chances are that when Jones's neighbor told the commissioners that her farmland couldn't earn a profit, nobody asked her how she was figuring her expenses. Suppose she had a $1.8 million purchase offer staring her in the face. At, say, 6 percent, just the interest income alone on that money would amount to $108,000 a year. A person could invest that money and live comfortably off that income without having to till the fields, milk the cows, and worry about the weather and the price of corn.

That $108,000 per year might be as much as (or more than) this neighbor was actually earning from farming her property. If the land had only been worth $300,000, the neighbor's farm income would have been plenty to support the $18,000 annual land investment carrying cost and have a good deal left over to live on. But if someone is ready to throw $1.8 million in her direction, of course her farm "couldn't earn a profit." The unprofitability of her farm was a self-fulfilling prophesy.

Jones's neighbor behaved rationally. And when Jones also sells to a non-farmer, he will be acting rationally as well. The people who behaved foolishly in this scenario were not the farmers. They were the county commissioners who lacked faith in the long-term economic sustainability of their local farm community. Their political weakness probably torpedoed a growth management law that was beginning to succeed.

They may have believed they were helping out a few individual farmers. But what they really did was guarantee the long-term failure of the rest of their local agriculture industry.

"Givings" and "Takings"

Many farmers have come to believe that zoning laws are unfair and that financial investments in land should be treated differently from other investments. Of course government actions can affect the value of many kinds of investments, not just land. A favorable or unfavorable decision on approval of a new drug, on a patent application, on a business merger, or on interest rates set by the Federal Reserve can produce an instantaneous response in the stock market. An unanticipated new highway, bridge, school, commuter rail line, or urban boundary expansion might create great value for some landowners in the same way that value can be lost because of increased zoning restrictions on a rural farm or new height restrictions on a commercial office building.

Some of these events may be seen as "takings." Some can be thought of as "givings."[26]

Society needs sound and stable legal rules and rights of ownership for all investments, including for real property. Without some stability and predictability in rights of ownership, no one could earn, save, and invest in their future. Lending and borrowing would be impossible. Investment and economic activity would come to a halt.

But no investment, in land or of any other kind, comes with a guarantee. Government actions that give and take value are a part of the world we live in and are among the uncertainties we face with every investment we make. If the public was required to reimburse everyone who lost money whenever a government decision was made, governance would come to a halt. We, as taxpayers, would no more want this than we would want to have to reimburse the government every time it took some action that worked to our personal financial benefit.

Farm and other landowners will no doubt continue to use "unconstitutional takings" as a rallying cry to enlist public sympathy when property ownership turns out to be less stable than had been hoped or anticipated. The argument has validity; we all have an interest in stability, and we should do our best to make land ownership as stable as we can. But let's, at least among ourselves, recognize some of the "takings" claims we see as the political rhetoric that they are. If we are interested in working together to create and share a better future, it is important that we look at the actual interests we all have in common and avoid getting wrapped around the axle over some artificial and unrealistic moral absolute.

PDR Programs

A note of explanation is also needed about the impact of purchase of development rights programs in response to concerns farmers sometimes express about them:

Borrowing and Collateral

Farmers sometimes worry that selling an easement on their land will limit their capacity to borrow. Because the farm will have less value, they feel they will have less to offer to a lender as security. Since farmers frequently need ready access to credit, often annually just to plant their crop, limiting their lending capacity can be a significant issue for them.

Fortunately, this should not be a concern for a normal PDR transaction. The total net worth of a farmer who sells an easement should not be affected by such a sale at all. The land may have less value. But the farmer will have received the difference in cash. This cash will, presumably, have been invested in other assets which can themselves be used as security for future loans. Or this cash may have been used to enhance the farm's profitability, making it a better lending risk. Or the farmer may simply use the cash to reduce or eliminate the need to borrow. In any case, the outcome is the same. If anything, the farmer's position in securing a future loan may actually have improved.

A second answer to this concern is that commercial business lenders cannot usually consider non-farm business value when making these loans. There may be exceptions, but commercial business lenders will generally only consider the business value of the security they are offered. They expect business loans to be paid off out of the revenue generated by the business enterprise. They do not make what are referred to as "collateral loans" on which they might anticipate having to foreclose. Since the agricultural business value of land is driven by the profitability of the farm business that owns it, the land's value in excess of that sum is essentially irrelevant to a business lender.[27]

Unwise Financial Management

There is an old joke in farm country in which the farmer is asked what he'd do if he won the lottery. "I'd use the money to keep on farmin' till it was all gone," he says. Along these same lines, I have heard the concern expressed that a farmer who sells an easement is likely to simply spend away the cash and end up in a worse position just a few years down the road. The implicit assumption is that real-world farmers (just like joke ones) somehow aren't smart enough to properly shepherd their own cash and investments.

Agriculture is one of the most challenging businesses on the planet. Farmers are among the most competitive, tough-minded, and sensible people I know. If there is anyone who understands land and real estate deals, it has to be farmers. Clearly PDR programs need to do a good job of making sure participating landowners fully understand their transactions. (In my experience they do a very good job of this.) But to worry that farmers can't be trusted with their own money seems, to me, both arrogant and thoroughly misplaced.

For Environmentalists Only

[FARMERS, DO NOT READ!]

"Property Rights" and the Political Will

For most of us, real estate is the largest single investment we will make in life. This is truer yet for most farmers, whose land is not just a residence but also a livelihood.[28] So farm landowners are understandably sensitive to government actions that affect the value of their land.

But it isn't just farmers who are sensitive to this. Anything that might affect real property values will also be of interest to other voters, urban and rural. While property rights takings lawsuits may, in practice, be quite difficult to win, the property rights concerns expressed by farm landowners are an honest reaction to what can be genuine abuse. The potential political impact of abusing land-use regulatory authority can be quite real.

When one is truly and deeply worried about the sad state of the environment and its forlorn future, it is easy to contemplate how very nice it would be if we could simply regulate land uses so people are forced to manage their properties in ways that protect the future. But there are countervailing and legitimate social considerations as well. We also need to weigh in our special social expectations for stability when it comes to real estate.

There may be good reason for differences in perspective between rural and urban residents. City dwellers exist in constant close quarters with their neighbors. Everywhere they go—at work, at home, and in between—they have to be prepared for daily compromise on a host of personal wishes and preferences in exchange for the advantages of city life. This is apparent whether one is walking down a busy sidewalk, checking out at the grocery, waiting for a traffic light, or just refraining from cranking up the power mower early on a Sunday morning. Rural reactions to property rights are heavily influenced by their different life experiences and the resulting perspectives on the world. Those perspectives are just as valid as are the urban ones.

So the distinction between a taking and a community responsibility is a matter of balance, not "either-or." We don't all see that balance in the same way. Of course it isn't helpful for a farm landowner to assert property rights and government takings as a general war cry in response to all efforts to regulate land use. But it also isn't helpful for environmentalists to dismiss property rights claims as legally ignorant or somehow anti-social.

The Inherent Uncertainties of Growth Management Laws

Perhaps the greatest disadvantage of growth management as a tool for farmland preservation is its vulnerability to the vicissitudes of politics. Even in communities that have adopted serious zoning, things can change. One year the county commission is quite determined about protecting agricultural lands. Three or four years later, the commissioners have changed and suddenly the prospects for rezones, exceptions, or variances seem a lot better. Some of the land is rezoned and ends up falling to development. Then the political winds shift again and a more protective commission takes power.

Of course, when that happens, we can't go back and reverse the zoning or "un-develop" the farms that were lost. Property prices may settle down a bit, for a while. But land developers and speculators also know that things could shift back again in the next election cycle. So, undeveloped land prices don't really drop all that much. The system slowly but steadily ratchets away the undeveloped agricultural land base. Also, as we've seen, growth management laws face the same uncertainties at the state level, including through periodic ballot measure challenges.[29]

Removing these risks is one of the very big advantages of PDR programs.

The Expectation of Stability in Real Estate Investments

Of course, as argued above, there are no guarantees in any investment, including in investments in land. But we do need to think about real property differently.

Our laws already recognize those differences. For example, real estate contracts must be in writing while most other contracts can be oral. Land ownership documents are publicly recorded. Boundary encroachments must continue openly and visibly for (typically) seven to ten years before ownership is secured by adverse possession. One can sue a noisy or smelly neighbor for nuisance. Trespass is prosecuted as a crime. Breaking and entering is a felony. We have constitutional protections against unreasonable government searches of our homes and against the quartering of troops there. There is a legal "expectation of privacy" for conversations on one's private property or for items kept there. In some states there are special legal allowances for the use of violence in repelling intruders from a home.

We don't see special protections like these for personal property or for other financial investments.

For most of us (including for farmers), our real estate is most often our home and our castle, the retreat to which we return after each day's labors, our place of refuge where we hope to secure our possessions and protect our loved ones from the surrounding uncertain world.

So even if there were no actual legal protections against "constitutional takings" under U.S. law, even if all we're thinking about is politics, we can be sure most voters will tend to side with at least some level of certainty for interests in real estate. There may be only so far one can go with zoning before we run into the strong public sense that ownership of real estate deserves to be treated differently.

Conservation Advantage of Farmland Stability

Investments in conservation are quite often the longest term investments a farmer can make. Consider, for example, a farmer's investment in soil stewardship. Stable soils are very good for the environment. They are also, obviously, good for the farm—but usually only over the very long term. Most on-farm conservation investments are like this. They will often produce a financial return. But it may take decades or even generations. And, at the same time, such improvements are usually worthless to a developer.

As we've seen, this creates one of the big advantages to protecting farmland. If the land is protected, the farmer who owns it is much more able and likely to make these investments.[30] So the more certain and stable the protection, the more certain it is that those investments in conservation will be made.

CHAPTER 12

Climate Change

Our planet faces dramatic climate change. Human activity is a primary cause. The United States is a major contributor. Even if we change course quickly and decisively, we face dramatic harm to the environment and to human society. The more we do, the better off we will be. The longer we delay, the greater the damage.[1]

Today, there is no legitimate room for debate about any of these basic scientific conclusions.[2]

So let's take a look at the impact of climate change on agriculture, the impact of agriculture on climate change, and the potential for farmers to help deal with both in ways that provide the greatest benefit for both agriculture and the environment.

Climate Impacts on Agriculture

There are many anticipated impacts of climate change on agriculture.[3] To name a few:

- A warmer climate will further tax overdrawn sources of fresh water, which is already in short supply for irrigation in many parts of the country.[4]

- Severe weather events like downpours, windstorms, flooding, and droughts are likely to increase in frequency and severity.

- Weed populations, plant and animal diseases, and insect pests will change and proliferate, and current methods of control will become less effective.

- The quality of forage for livestock is likely to diminish, straining the capacity of the land to support grazing.

These impacts and others will differ from place to place, and from crop to crop. Some of the most serious impacts are expected on crops grown in already marginal climates, such as non-irrigated grains. And all these climate impacts are likely to interact with other, already extant, environmental and social problems, including those affecting agriculture, making them generally worse as well.[5]

Agriculture's Impacts on Climate

Agriculture also contributes to climate change and has been estimated to be responsible for about 8.6 percent of U.S. human-generated greenhouse gasses.[6] A few examples:

- Tillage releases carbon stored in the soil.

- Chemical fertilizers release nitrous oxide (to which agriculture contributes 69 percent of U.S. emissions). Nitrous oxide is an extremely potent greenhouse gas said to be 310 times as powerful as carbon dioxide (CO_2).[7]

- Rice cultivation and the fermentation of livestock waste produce methane (to which agriculture contributes 31 percent of U.S. emissions). Methane is also a powerful greenhouse gas, said to be over twenty times as potent as CO_2.[8]

There are, however, strategies through which agriculture can contribute solutions in addressing climate change. For example:

- Increasing sequestration of carbon in the soil by using farming systems that limit the tilling of the soil (and potentially through the addition of carbon-rich soil amendments);

- Planting trees in uncultivated areas or protecting existing forested or naturally vegetated areas on farms;

- Conservation management of livestock on rangeland;

- Reducing application of chemical fertilizers through precision farming or by substituting other more natural fertilizers;

- Capturing methane from waste in concentrated livestock operations and/or using anaerobic waste digestion to generate "green" electricity; and

- Reducing on-farm fossil fuel energy use and generating marketable, renewable wind energy.[9]

Increased agricultural production will be required to supply the food needs of a growing population.[10] So the wholesale loss of farmland is not an option. Fortunately, most of the strategies listed above, and others like them, can contribute substantially in addressing climate issues while keeping land in productive farming.[11] Most can be adopted by farmers using any of the wide variety of already well-known and thoroughly-studied conservation management practices.[12] And, most importantly, they can be applied in a way that is fully consistent with continued, successful, and profitable agriculture.

Agriculture can contribute to mitigating climate impacts in other ways as well. For example, it has been estimated that biofuels grown on farms could replace almost 20 percent of our country's consumption of fossil energy, potentially reducing U.S. greenhouse gas emissions by between 9 percent and 24 percent, and that they could do so without significantly raising food prices.[13]

Agriculture can also reduce society's climate impacts by helping to curb sprawl.[14] Urban sprawl can permanently destroy large areas of carbon storage in soils, farm crops, forests, and other vegetation. Sprawl also greatly increases commuter mileage, and therefore, the use of climate-damaging fossil energy. A vibrant, economically healthy agriculture industry that has broad community political support could serve as a bulwark against urban sprawl.

Agriculture's Climate Action Opportunities and Risks

Efforts to address climate change could generate substantial funding for many of the on-farm conservation practices discussed in this book. This might be provided through stronger appropriations for federal farm bill conservation programs. It might come from local and state-level efforts to address climate. It might result from a stronger U.S. market for carbon offsets. However it is provided, the outcome would be a considerable increase in outside funding flowing into and through agriculture. While increased use of biofuels is not expected to dramatically increase food prices, nonetheless, some increases might be expected, which may help some farmers.[15]

Public efforts to address climate also pose some risks for agriculture. Even if a cap on greenhouse gas emissions wouldn't affect the farm economy in other ways, it would probably result in higher energy costs, an important expense item for farmers.

Would climate legislation, therefore, end up an economic wash for agriculture, with losses to higher energy costs and gains resulting from a strong carbon market?

Strong provisions for carbon trading were included in the Waxman-Markey Climate Bill, which failed in 2009.[16] Following passage of Waxman-Markey through the House, several studies were undertaken to assess its net impacts on agriculture. Small increases in production costs (in the range of

2 to 4 percent) were projected for some crops, like corn, soybeans, and soft red wheat.[17] And some minimal land use changes were anticipated.[18] But the weight of the research strongly indicated that the likely gains for agriculture resulting from offset trading, increased funding for conservation stewardship, higher crop prices, biofuel opportunities, and potential methane energy generation opportunities, would outweigh any losses. The proposed climate legislation would have been a *net gain* for the agriculture industry[19] in the range of 1 percent to 4 percent.[20]

With new federal legislation out of the picture, at least for now, we are left with the current provisions of the Clean Air Act (CAA). This is the tool that President Barak Obama plans to use to take action on the climate with limits on emissions by U.S. power plants.[21]

It is important to be clear that the Clean Air Act does not include provisions for offset trading. So EPA regulations under the CAA will almost certainly not include an ag-friendly, USDA-run offset program like what was proposed in Waxman-Markey. The outcome of such CAA regulation would be primarily to cap emissions, with the same impacts on energy and fertilizer costs that worried the industry about the climate bill. It would also directly affect some larger dairy, beef, and swine operations and much of the poultry industry. But there would be none of the potential benefits for agriculture from the trading in offsets that might be allowed in a sensible climate bill.

The Current Farm Industry Position on Climate

Concerned about the potential for higher fuel and fertilizer costs,[22] much of the agriculture industry vigorously opposed the 2009 climate bill.[23] The official position of the American Farm Bureau Federation (AFBF), currently reflected in policy #503 in its 2013 Policy Book, is to support, in theory, carbon credit trading. But that same policy specifically opposes any legislation that would impose cap and trade.[24] Since the United States already has a voluntary carbon offset market, opposition to a carbon cap essentially closes the door on a meaningful climate market.

AFBF policy #503 specifically opposes: "any law or regulation requiring reporting of any GHG emissions by an agriculture entity," "any climate change legislation that would make America less competitive," "any climate change legislation until other countries meet or exceed U.S. requirements," "taxes on carbon uses or emissions," and "imposition of standards on farm and ranch equipment," among others.

This doesn't leave much room for any policy action to address climate change.

While opposing new climate regulation, the agriculture industry also vigorously opposes EPA regulation of greenhouse gasses through the authority of the existing Clean Air Act (CAA).[25]

CONSERVATION ECONOMICS

How a New Power Plant is Helping Dairies While Removing Greenhouse Gasses

In about 2001, a group of farmers in the lower Snoqualmie Valley near Monroe, Washington, sat down with an environmental group and the local Tulalip Indian Tribes in an effort to find a way for the farmers to deal with their dairy waste while also protecting the salmon runs in the Snoqualmie River. From that meeting, Qualco Energy was born.[26]

Today, Qualco operates an anaerobic digester that processes the manure from 1,300 cows as well as fish waste, cattle and chicken blood, trap grease, pulp, whey, and expired beer, wine, and soda. These waste products might otherwise find their way into surface and ground water. They would, almost certainly, otherwise decompose and release methane into the atmosphere. Instead, that methane is generating 450 kilowatts of renewable energy (soon to increase to 1.2 megawatts) as well as bedding for cattle and environmentally safe, Grade-A compost.

How do the cattle rancher and the five dairy farmers who contribute manure to this facility feel about it? For them, the project is a way to economically deal with their animal waste without expensive waste lagoons and stringent regulation. For the salmon restoration group and the Tulalip Tribes, the project also protects fish habitat and water quality.

Because the State of Washington is one of several states with a renewable energy requirement, Qualco can sell energy into the grid at a small but important premium. And because methane is a significant greenhouse gas, they are also arranging to sell credits into the current voluntary carbon market. These climate-driven financial benefits represent a significant addition to their bottom line that helps make the operation profitable.

For Farmers Only

[ENVIRONMENTALISTS, DO NOT READ!]

The Farm Industry's Interest in Climate Legislation

On balance, the evidence seems clear that agriculture would have been better off with a climate bill than without. One wonders what drove much of the industry's decision to oppose it.[27]

There are, of course, many progressive leaders and opinions within agriculture on climate change (as there are on most of the other issues mentioned in this book). And there were credible agriculture industry voices that supported the Waxman-Markey climate bill. But the American Farm Bureau Federation (AFBF)—the self-proclaimed "voice of agriculture"—took strong leadership in opposing it. The Farm Bureau has also placed the farm industry in the forefront of groups questioning the existence of, and human responsibility for, climate change.[28] Not only could the right climate legislation be beneficial for farmers, but leaving this issue in the hands of EPA to regulate under the Clean Air Act probably eliminates the benefits to farmers of a meaningful carbon market while retaining the downsides of higher energy costs.[29] Agriculture is a major U.S. industry that should legitimately take positions on national industrial policy. But in developing its policy for climate legislation,[30] it still seems like the Farm Bureau's skepticism about climate change, its inclination to oppose government programs generally, and its desire to weigh in on broad economic issues may have gotten the upper hand over what is best for actual farmers.

There will always be stress between what is in an industry's best short-term versus its long-term interest; survival next year can seem a lot more important than a brighter future thirty years from now. But in the case of climate legislation, it also seems clear that a good bill, which would include both cap and trade, could work quite well for agriculture, and would do so right away. By opposing this legislation, the Farm Bureau and several other agriculture groups chose, instead, to deliver the farm industry and the country into the hands of an Environmental Protection Agency that must now deal with climate using the Clean Air Act (CAA). Much of the CAA was written forty years ago, long before most people were worrying about climate issues. Now it must be enforced in a way which almost certainly will not benefit agriculture.[31]

The AFBF denies that EPA has authority under the Clean Air Act to regulate greenhouse gasses,[32] even though the U.S. Supreme Court—as recently as 2007—specifically directed that EPA exercise just this authority.[33] In 2011, the court reaffirmed EPA's exclusive authority in the matter and recently did so again in 2014.[34]

Currently, it appears that the Farm Bureau is relying on the hope that there will be new legislation to repeal EPA's climate authority.[35] A bill to accomplish this did pass the House but died in the U.S. Senate.[36]

The Politics of a "Farmer-friendly" Climate Bill

The Farm Bureau was obviously not alone in resisting climate legislation. But many major players in other U.S. industries support taking action on climate and many specifically supported the 2009 climate bill. For example, the membership of the U.S. Climate Action Partnership that supports such legislation includes Fortune 500 names such as: Alcoa, Chrysler, Dow Chemical, Duke Energy, Ford, GE, Honeywell, Johnson & Johnson, Pepsi, PG&E, Shell, Siemens, and Weyerhaeuser.[37] The list of climate bill supporters also included companies like Hewlett-Packard, Conoco-Phillips, BP America, and even the farm community's own highly respected John Deere.[38]

As friendly as it was for agriculture, Waxman-Markey could have been a great deal more favorable had most of the agriculture industry not opposed it. When a group positions itself in general opposition to a bill, the motivation for the bill's proponents (and writers) to listen to what that group might prefer that it contain should it pass generally evaporates. If you're going to oppose the bill anyway, why should the proponents care about your opinion? They're going to pay attention to the views of someone who might be willing to support the bill. So, with a somewhat more flexible policy approach from agriculture, there is a good chance Waxman-Markey could have been made even better for American farmers that it was.

A shift in agriculture's position could, in other words, greatly enhance its influence on the shape of any such future legislation.

And that stronger influence may be needed. Keep in mind that the whole idea of passing a "climate" bill is to reduce greenhouse gas emissions. So some kind of limit or cap on emissions is essentially certain if such a bill should pass. That such legislation would also provide a place for trade—for the purchase of mitigating carbon offsets, including offsets provided and sold by agriculture—is far less certain. Many people prefer a straight regulatory cap without any trade. And some prefer a "cap and tax" approach that requires polluters to pay graduated taxes for higher levels of greenhouse gas emissions as a disincentive to pollute.[39] The initial proposal from the Administration was for such a cap and tax approach.[40] And for a time, it seemed likely that the revenue from "cap and tax" would be spent on general government, not on carbon mitigation. With either a straight cap or a cap and tax of that kind, there would have been no market for potential agriculture carbon sequestration services.

With all the negative rhetoric that has surfaced about the entire concept of "cap and trade" in the period since Waxman-Markey failed, one wonders if including "trade" of any kind in a future bill might now prove quite difficult.[41]

The Future

To be clear, the AFBF is beginning to weakly acknowledge the existence of a climate problem. The current official published policy does not actually deny climate change nor its human causes. Note the wording as follows:

> Environmental organizations and some scientists contend that green-house gas (GHG) emissions from human activities (anthropogenic GHGs) are the principal cause for an increase in average global temperatures. They argue that unless measures are taken to reduce these emissions, the cumulative effect over coming decades will result in adverse changes in the world's climate and weather. GHGs include carbon dioxide, nitrous oxide and methane.[42]

But let's be real. The evidence of, and broad scientific community agreement on, climate change and its human origins is thoroughly credible and overwhelming.[43] If, as one might anticipate, climate legislation is inevitable in the not-too-distant future, making sure such a bill includes a way for farmers to be paid for improving the climate would seem to be very much in the interests of the agriculture industry. Positioning the industry to be able to get provisions of this kind seems quite important.

For Environmentalists Only
[FARMERS, DO NOT READ!]

Mistrust of Environmentalists

Yes, farmers tend to be conservative. And maybe that's mostly why the Farm Bureau still opposes climate legislation that could be good for agriculture. But a significant part of the reason many farmers find it difficult to accept the overwhelming science of climate change may also be because they deeply mistrust environmentalists, whom they believe are behind it.

Reversing that mistrust could be pivotal to reversing organized farm community opposition to climate legislation.

Concern about Solutions

Agriculture industry climate change denial may also be a product of farmer concerns that (despite the trade provisions in Waxman-Markey) other likely policy solutions to climate change will still end up ones that are unfriendly to agriculture. It must be admitted that environmentalists were less than enthusiastic about the Waxman-Markey trade provisions. And unless farmers can feel confident that acknowledging climate change will not just guarantee costly new regulations on farming, there's a reasonable chance they may remain in denial to the bitter end.

Opportunities for Agriculture—Support for Offset Trading

By this point, I hope you are convinced that successful, economically viable, well-managed working farms present much greater environmental opportunities than threats. In some parts of the country, notably in the West, sprawl and motor vehicle transportation represent our greatest climate impacts. Preserving our working farmlands will slow the fragmentation of our landscapes that leads to that sprawl and will enhance the huge potential for agricultural sequestration of carbon.[44]

One helpful starting point would be for major environmental organizations to decisively acknowledge offset trading, and other market-based mechanisms, as valid and useful tools for lowering the cost of environmental services. Right now, offset trading is vilified from both the left,[45] and the right.[46] Getting offsets to work properly is going to take some effort. Environmentalists, like everyone else, need to keep a close eye to make sure trading regimes do what they're supposed to. But we also need environmentalist leadership in supporting the underlying concept. Sound offset/mitigation regimes would help both agriculture and the environment. And they could shift the farmer perspective on climate change.

Keep in mind that straight offset trading isn't the only option. We could try the more traditional approach of properly funding USDA conservation incentives. We might enhance that funding so these programs could also sometimes offer an actual, meaningful market price for carbon mitigation services provided by farmers in excess of a settled baseline.

Money generated by a carbon tax should be used for conservation activities by farmers and others who sequester carbon and reduce emissions. If carbon tax revenue is used to fund general government services, we will have done only half the job and will have greatly increased the cost of the ultimate fix.

Given the widespread disparagement of "cap and trade" since Waxman-Markey,[47] it may be even more difficult to get it passed today than it was in 2009. Environmental support for trade or market-based regimes that help farmers could earn a lot of farm-community respect. That, in turn, would go a long way toward getting serious climate legislation passed in the foreseeable future.

CHAPTER 13

Livestock, the Public Lands, and the Environment

Globally, the raising of livestock employs some 1.3 billion people and provides about one-third of humanity's protein intake.[1] Livestock grazing occupies 26 percent of the ice-free land surface of the planet.[2] Since most of the United States is in a temperate climate, the numbers here are yet higher. The USDA estimates that 783 million acres, or nearly 35 percent of the nation's total land area, were available for livestock grazing in 2002.[3] The U.S. total annual farm-gate value of livestock sales is $154 billion (52 percent of total U.S. agricultural market value). Of this, cattle account for $61 billion.[4]

This is a truly massive industry. It has substantial impacts on the environment, and it provides a major part of the nation's (and the world's) supply

Cattle on the public lands. *Courtesy of the United States Bureau of Land Management*

of food. It is one of the major areas of confrontation between farmers and environmentalists, but offers great opportunities for cooperation.

Land Cost Pressures on the Livestock Industry

The U.S. livestock industry is in swift and steady transition toward concentration. The number of animals per farm is rapidly growing while the acreage per farm is shrinking. This is partly in response to the advantages of scale and the availability of modern technologies that make it possible.[5] But it is also driven by rising land costs and by the land-extensive nature of traditional livestock operations.

This transition is clearly illustrated in the dairy industry. A traditional dairy, like the one mentioned in Chapter 3, had perhaps two hundred cows spending most of their day grazing two hundred acres of open, managed pasture. It was easy for a dairy of this kind to be environmentally friendly. With only one cow per acre, and with good management, animal waste was deposited on the land at an agronomic rate where it would be taken up by plants before it washed off into a nearby stream or leached beneath the plant root zone and into the ground water.

A good many dairies still run like this today. But modern dairies increasingly find it necessary to grow. Important among their economies of scale is the cost of land. For a dairy, the land-cost dilemma is simple: you can't earn enough income from the milk provided by a single cow to support the cost of owning an acre of land to feed it. This is especially true in areas surrounding our cities where there is significant pressure from growth and development.

Because milk is perishable, the traditional dairy farm was located near its urban markets. Modern refrigeration and transportation, however, make it possible for new dairies to locate at greater distances from their urban markets, where land is cheaper and the neighbors are more hospitable. A new dairy of two thousand cows will be more concentrated, mechanized, and investment-intensive on much less land—perhaps only fifty acres. Much of the time, the cows will be confined in areas that are paved so waste can be readily removed and pumped into large manure storage lagoons where it accumulates in the winter. Then, in the warm, dry months when plant growth is strong, the waste will be sprayed onto agricultural fields growing high nutrient uptake crops like hay or corn.

These same trends toward less land and more animals are occurring in other livestock sectors like beef cattle, poultry, and hogs. For example, between 1992 and 2007, the number of U.S. hog farms fell by over 70 percent while total hog production remained steady.[6] Dramatic increases of concentration in poultry are also underway.[7]

American livestock farmers purchase the vast majority (if not all) of their feed from other farmers, and they increasingly dispose of their animal waste on land belonging to other farmers. Unsurprisingly, it can be difficult for a livestock operator to find nearby land to dispose of manure. It must be transported, at considerable expense, longer and longer distances for disposal. Its value as fertilizer is not usually sufficient to cover these costs. There are, therefore, economic pressures to apply it at greater than a proper agronomic rate.

Similar trends also affect the beef cattle industry where land-cost pressure can also be acute. Of course, traditional cattle country is often quite some distance from urban populations. One might hope that price pressures on the rangelands needed for ranching wouldn't be such a problem. Unfortunately, grazing cattle on the open, lightly vegetated range can require a lot of land,[8] so the agricultural business value (what ranchers can afford to pay for each acre of rangeland) tends to be considerably lower than for other sectors of agriculture—currently perhaps only $75 or so per acre depending on its quality. With cattle producers able to pay as little as $75,000 for one thousand acres of rangeland, their exposure to land competition from developers interested in subdividing that land for recreational or other uses can be acute even in the absence of easily accessible, on-site water.

Many Western cattle operators depend on grazing permits on public lands that need to be located near property owned by the ranch. In fact to qualify for a permit, a rancher is usually required to own a "base property" that is near or adjacent to the public land on which the permit will be issued.[9]

Unfortunately, such properties are especially appealing for recreational buyers who also like the access to public lands. So there is competition for these adjacent lands. As the public lands have become ringed by small, recreational parcels, access to them by ranchers has been slowly blocked, and their eligibility for the public grazing permits is also threatened.

In several Western states, this has led to creation of land trusts that are specifically devoted to protecting private rangelands from being converted out of ranching. These rangeland trusts are usually directed by a board of ranchers. Most of them were created by or with the participation of the local cattle industry.[10] The fact that conservative cattle ranchers would resort to the use of conservation easements (which they have traditionally mistrusted) to restrict future nonfarm development of private lands is a measure of the desperation many ranchers feel about preserving their disappearing rangelands.[11]

Impacts of Livestock on the Environment

With trends and pressures of this kind affecting so much of our nation's land, one might expect that there would be environmental impacts. And there are.

For example, the raising of livestock is believed to contribute substantially to the nation's water quality problems. It is estimated that some 43 percent of U.S. drinking water sources suffer pollution from livestock pathogens.[12] Worldwide, livestock are believed to be a major source of the pollution that contributes to eutrophication or "dead zones," in many coastal areas.[13] The prophylactic use of antibiotics for livestock is linked to the emergence of antibiotic resistant infections in humans.[14] In the United States, livestock are believed to be responsible for an estimated 55 percent of the total erosion and sediment into freshwater resources from agriculture.[15]

Livestock are also believed responsible for a substantial portion of human-caused greenhouse gas emissions contributing to climate change. And livestock, like other human activities, displace wildlife. Livestock now constitute 20 percent of total terrestrial animal biomass, and raising them (including the cultivation of their feed) occupies 30 percent of the world's land surface, thus replacing much of the natural wildlife and biodiversity which might otherwise have existed there. The United Nations Food and Agriculture Organization concluded in 2006 that, globally, "the livestock sector has such deep and wide-ranging environmental impacts that it should rank as one of the leading focuses for environmental policy."[16]

The Public Lands Grazing Controversy

Among the more visible environmental controversies involving livestock is the one over the leases and permits that are issued by various government agencies for grazing on public lands.

In the United States, the public owns huge areas of land, particularly in the eleven most western states where the federal government alone owns 361 million acres (48 percent of the total land mass of these states), 258 million acres of which are owned by just two federal agencies—the Bureau of Land Management (BLM) and the U.S. Forest Service (USFS). Several other agencies also own land including the U.S. Fish and Wildlife Service, Bureau of Indian Affairs, National Park Service, and Department of Defense. The governments of the western states also own vast areas of land that were ceded to them at statehood and are generally dedicated to earning natural resource income to support public education, hospitals, prisons, or other public needs.[17] Much of this state and federally owned land is leased to farmers for grazing livestock.[18]

With such vast areas in public ownership and grazed by private livestock, it is not surprising that the nation's ranchers and environmentalists might be at odds about how that land should be managed and about what uses best serve the public interest.

Environmentalists feel that grazing displaces native plant and animal species and degrades the natural environmental services that these lands would otherwise provide, such as cleaner surface and ground water, wildlife habitat, pollinators, and more functional hydrologic systems.

By contrast, ranchers believe that, in addition to feeding the nation, grazing cattle contribute to the health of the public range and are needed for its sustainability. They argue that they actively manage their cattle for the environmental health of the land and that they do this, in part, to make their long-term leases sustainable. They also feel that ranching cattle on public lands is a critical part of the economic and cultural heritage of their communities.

It is standard practice to re-issue grazing permits to the previous holder where the permit requirements have been successfully met. In addition to motivating compliance with permit requirements, this practice also motivates the permit holder to invest in sound, long-term stewardship of the land and thus it enhances the permit's useful value both for the permit holder and for the agency.

But remember, to qualify for such a permit, one must buy or control a "base property" adjacent to the permitted area.[19] So the permit ends up, indirectly, tied to the ownership of the land. When a new rancher buys one of these base properties he or she will do so contingent on also securing a renewal of the current owner's federal grazing permit. Or if someone who already owns a nearby property wishes to secure a permit, they may be able to purchase it from a neighbor. In either case, the buyer will pay extra, or separately, to take over the seller's future interest in that permit.[20]

In this way, ranchers have been forced to capitalize their interest in a permit. This is common for many other, similar "limited entry" permits which allow use of common public resources—to secure such a permit, one must buy it from an existing holder.[21]

A focal point for this continuing dispute has been over the price charged for permitted grazing. Fees charged by the BLM and USFS, for example, are based on a formula set by statute.[22] In 2002, this price came to $1.43 per animal unit month (AUM),[23] only slightly above the statutory minimum price of $1.35 per AUM. This was well beneath an average market value that had been estimated at $13.10 per AUM.

Environmentalists have argued that these low charges represent a substantial and unnecessary subsidy and that they lead to abuse of the public range. This "subsidy" has been estimated to amount to anywhere from $128 million to as much as $1 billion annually, depending on what is included in the calculation.[24] Ranchers feel their permit fees are fair given their obligations to properly manage the land, higher costs of grazing cattle on public lands, the fact that they were required to make a capital investment to obtain the permit, and the benefits that accrue to the public range from properly-managed grazing. They also feel that if there is a subsidy, it is one that is needed and justified.

A Quick History of Western Grazing, Permits, and Practices

It is important to know some history. Cattle and other livestock followed on the heels of America's western migration into the massive lands acquired by the U.S. government through the Louisiana Purchase, settlement of California, and the Mexican-American War. But as available lands diminished under homestead acts, through federal sales, and settlement, and as the number of ranchers increased, free access to the public range resulted in its overuse and damage to the soil, plants, wildlife, and waters. These concerns led to passage of the Taylor Grazing Act in 1934, which launched the permit system that has been in place for the past eighty years.[25]

Over those years, the number of permits authorized has steadily declined.[26] But even today, when we recognize a multitude of appropriate uses of public lands, private grazing is still considered an important public benefit. Its continuation has been firmly authorized by Congress,[27] which has also seriously considered, but not yet acted on, a proposed buyout of the capital value of some of these permits.[28] It may be arguable whether ownership of such permits technically constitutes a "property right."[29] But ranchers have certainly been given legitimate grounds to rely on their permits' continuing value. Permit holders typically come to anticipate that, unless they fail to live up to their permit requirements, they will continue to be able to use those permits for some time to come.

Whether grazing takes place on public or on private lands, there is a set of best management practices that can assure environmental impacts are limited. On private lands, USDA helps ranchers implement the practices in USDA's Natural Resources Conservation Service Field Office Technical Guide.[30] On public lands, the agencies establish standards for landscape health. For example, the Bureau of Land Management manages its grazing permits under a set of Rangeland Health Standards and guidelines. These standards were developed with input from citizen advisory councils across the West.[31] They address such issues as:

- Soil quality and compaction;
- Aquatic resources, riparian and wetland function, stream morphology;
- Presence and protection for desired species—native, threatened, endangered, and other special status species; and
- Water quality.[32]

Guidelines for the management of grazing are then adopted to help assure that these standards are met.

In the face of pressure from other interested users, ranchers are conscious of the vulnerability of their grazing permits. This includes pressure both from environmentalists and from non-ranching private landowners who own properties affected by activities on the public lands.[33] And it includes a host of recreational interests like hunters, fishers, hikers, campers, dirt bikers, off-road-vehicle enthusiasts, horseback riders, and wildlife watchers. These activities may or may not be consistent with environmental health. But all of them together, along with their ancillary economic support businesses (sporting goods suppliers, restaurants, hotels/motels, etc.), add up to a significant potential challenge to any cattle industry "hegemony" that might be believed to exist on the use of public lands.

Coordinated Resource Management (CRM)

One healthy response to this political threat has been the growing movement among agriculture conservation professionals and western ranchers to engage the larger community in making decisions about how land—especially public lands—will be managed. This process is called coordinated resource management (CRM).[34] By providing public transparency and involvement, it decreases suspicion that permitting agencies are somehow in the pocket of the cattle industry, or of any particular interest group. By allowing everyone to participate, it encourages each to accommodate the interests of others and reduces destructive public controversies.

CRM encourages the coordinated management of public and private lands so that the entire landscape is more productive, both environmentally and commercially.

How Conserving Rangeland Grew Better Cattle

Some years ago I had the chance to visit a cattle ranch in the Okanogan area of eastern Washington State. The rancher led our group to a ridge overlooking a large, sloping bowl of land about three-quarters of a mile across. At the foot of the bowl was a spring-fed stream surrounded by thick vegetation. The upper slopes were publicly-owned mountain foothill rangeland, vegetated but relatively dry. The land at the bottom of the hill was privately owned by the rancher; it had been in his family for three generations. For much of that time, the family had also held a grazing lease (or permit) on the surrounding public uplands.

When we were there, grazing cattle were sprinkled thinly across the entire hillside. The rancher pointed out several locations where he had installed small watering tanks for his cattle. He explained how, in his father's and grandfather's time, their cattle had tended to accumulate at the foot of the hill where they had easy access to the water in the stream. Because they clustered there, the grasses higher on the hillside and further from the stream were seldom grazed. Instead, the cattle overgrazed the vegetation near the stream, damaged the stream banks, and fouled the water.

With cooperation from the public agency owning the uplands, the rancher installed several watering tanks around the upper hillside. Water is pumped there from the stream on his family's property below. He also fenced his cattle out of the stream and the area around it. The widely dispersed sources of drinking water allow the cattle to spread out across the landscape where they can find more forage. When the first snows fall, the grass is still tall enough to provide grazing above the snow, and the cattle can stay there a little later each year. He has increased his herd size while preserving a healthy landscape. His cattle are better fed; his yearlings are today 40 percent larger than in his father's time.

Meanwhile, the stream, which empties into a salmon-bearing stream further downhill, is cleaner and healthier for the fish. Coordinating the conservation management of the public and the private lands has clearly benefited both.

Cow using nose pump to drink water from stream, Iowa. *Courtesy of USDA-NRCS*

For Environmentalists Only

[FARMERS, DO NOT READ!]

Land Cost and the Impact of Cattle

It isn't just environmentalists who regret the industrialization of livestock agriculture. Many dairy farmers are sad to see the disappearance of small, local, land-extensive dairies and their emergence in a form that more resembles a factory than it does a farm. Many cattle operators would prefer to see their animals spend more time on the range and less in confined feeding operations.

These trends are not inevitable. They reflect, at least partly, a failure of society to protect agricultural lands. With enough land, livestock can easily be managed to be very friendly to the environment. If we could protect their land, many of those smaller, local dairies and other local livestock operations might well be expected to return.

Agriculture and the Human Footprint Continuum

One of the ironies of the cattle grazing–environmental dispute is that, with proper management, grazing cattle probably involve less environmental risk, and can assure a healthier landscape closer to its wild and natural state, than is possible for nearly any other human natural resource activity. Yes, poorly managed grazing can harm the environment.[35] And grazing livestock will, of course, never leave a landscape completely untouched.

But there is much that can be done to eliminate those impacts.

Every human activity has environmental impacts. One might imagine a sort of environmental continuum for common human land uses, best to worst, with the most environmentally friendly uses at the top and the least friendly at the bottom. The downtown business district or perhaps the industrial area in any major city might have to be placed near the bottom of such a list as among the least environmentally desirable and as having the greatest, or the most intensive, environmental impacts. Suburban residential areas might rank a little better and earn a place further up this list, but still, other than a few tame trees, a natural backyard or two, and an occasional park, they provide only a few environmental services and generate a good deal of damage. Growing agricultural crops would presumably be higher yet. It displaces larger areas of otherwise natural land but also sustains healthy vegetation and an open, undeveloped landscape in an essentially "green" activity. Somewhere, probably higher yet on this list, would be the harvest of timber, assuming it is carefully managed and especially if it is a selective harvest. Cutting timber does involve the removal of trees. But trees can be replanted and replaced in another fifty or sixty years or so.

Somewhere around here in our hypothetical continuum, perhaps higher yet, we'd place the well-managed grazing of cattle. Yes, these cattle do displace some of the natural wildlife and can affect the natural vegetation. But when compared with downtown Manhattan, industrial Detroit, or suburban Los Angeles, their impacts are minimal. At a higher level, and perhaps creating yet lighter impacts in this continuum of human land activities, might be carefully managed hiking and wilderness recreation. There is, of course, the risk of fire. But the other impacts can be quite limited. The only thing better would be a landscape that is entirely untouched—if that is even possible in the modern world.

The key thing to note about a list like this is that none of these human land use activities exists in a vacuum. Each depends on all of the others. The urban downtown, with its tall office buildings and concentrated industry, can't exist without the people who are employed there and who live in those suburbs. Suburban residents earn their living in urban buildings and manufacturing plants. They live in homes made from the timber taken from forests. They eat the crops produced on farms and the cattle grazed on the public range. And they hike and recreate in the public forests and parks. In turn, the lumber and agriculture industries exist because the people in those cities need them. Even the hiking and recreation—and the businesses that support them—arise out of the needs of this same human population base.

All these land uses are interdependent. Assuming they are all managed responsibly, their impacts on the land must be taken together as the necessary collective impacts of all human society.

Knowing how all these uses support each other makes it much harder to envision how we could make environmental gains by cutting back on or eliminating *any* of them. We seem to readily accept the inevitability of growth for our cities. Our approach for environmental protection there appears to be to just contain their sprawl. But why would we automatically think that our cities can continue to grow while our farms and forests remain static or shrink?

Certainly grazing cattle (and other livestock) displace natural wildlife and vegetation that could occupy that same landscape. But if we remove cattle from the public (or private) range, and return those lands to natural habitat, we just shift the demand for food to some other, more intensive food-producing activity elsewhere. It is entirely likely that other environmental values will be affected by that shift, perhaps more important ones.

So let's not fool ourselves into thinking that by eliminating grazing cattle on the public range we have necessarily reduced our human environmental impacts. The 258 million acres in USFS and BLM grazing permits alone represent a third of all the available grazing lands in the United States.[36] While these lands may not always be an intensive source of feed, they certainly make a significant contribution.[37] Were we to eliminate cattle grazing there, all we would have accomplished is to move that environmental footprint somewhere else, perhaps further down on our continuum of land use activities, all of which harm the environment.

In some circumstances, the removal of cattle from a particular public range may be necessary to protect an endangered species or to improve some other specific critical environmental value. If there is a situation like that, the case for it needs to be made, and we need to take appropriate action.

But to prove an environmental benefit from eliminating cattle, it isn't sufficient to argue that they have environmental impacts—that they displace other species, damage natural plant communities, degrade water quality, pollute the atmosphere, or cause other harmful environmental problems. For each human activity or land use, it is not a matter of whether this happens; it always does. It is a matter of degree, comparison, and balance.

Cost Impacts of Grazing Fees

Opponents of public lands grazing leases argue that low lease prices do not cover the social cost of lost environmental values that are displaced by grazing cattle.[38] These "indirect" costs are said to be between $500 million and $1 billion annually.

Those of us who have advocated for policy on environmental issues understand how hard it can be to make a strong case in the political arena for protecting intangible environmental values. Arguing the spiritual beauty and magic of nature seldom stands up well against the local jobs and documented economic impacts of established businesses. That is one reason the environmental markets discussed in Chapter 9 are so important.

It is useful to assign a price tag to lost environmental values. But it is also important to appreciate the limits of doing so.

We would all assume that cattle displace other environmental values. But it does not follow that the cost of those losses represents a subsidy. And eliminating cattle will not necessarily restore the balance. To credibly make that case, you'd need to also show that the economic and land use shifts which would result from eliminating cattle there would be better for the environment and would cost less in such indirect impacts than what we're doing now.

If we stop grazing on the public lands but replace that with more cattle in large commercial feedlots, is that going to be an environmental improvement? Does that eliminate the subsidy? If people shift their demand for meat from beef to pork or chicken, or if we import more beef from overseas, is that better for the environment? If the needed calories come instead from soy or corn, or if people eat more processed foods, have we then made environmental progress?

Of course, this sets a very high bar for the argument. Unfortunately, the world is a complicated place.

But while the dollar value of environmental impacts can't really (at least alone) justify the elimination of a human activity like grazing cattle, it can help make the economic case for improving its environmental management. Let's suppose we learned that water quality impacts from grazing resulted in, say, $200 million per year in negative environmental impacts. And let's also suppose we knew that the industry could eliminate most of those impacts using management practices that, with farmer and cost-share investment together, might cost only $4 million to implement. Spending the $4 million on those new practices could sound very much like a bargain.

But, viewed in this light, a $200 million loss doesn't sound much like a subsidy.

CONSERVATION ECONOMICS

How Prized Cattle Can Be Sustainably Produced on Rangeland

Fred Colvin is a cattle rancher who lives near Tenino, Washington. He is also a much-respected conservationist and former president of the Washington Association of Conservation Districts. He was the first rancher in the state to protect his land from development with a USDA Grasslands Reserve Program easement. And with help from NRCS and the local conservation district, he uses a management plan for his livestock that protects native birds and other wildlife.

Fred once explained to me why he disagrees with those who claim that beef is an irresponsible food product. Beef opponents argue that it requires too much in the way of natural resource inputs for the food value and calories it provides.[39] But Fred says that beef is one of very few human food products that can be extracted from natural resources generated on some of the least naturally productive lands on the planet. Rangelands are often rocky, windy, semi-arid uplands. These lands definitely do generate environmental benefits, and they may be vulnerable to abuse. But they also can support almost no other kind of useful human crop. The beef product that results from grazing cattle there, however, provides highly prized sustenance for humans almost everywhere on the planet.[40]

Grazing cattle do, of course, displace other wildlife. But, carefully managed, that same land can still sustainably support livestock and continue to produce nearly all of its natural environmental services.

This is one reason cattle generate nearly 21 percent of total U.S. agricultural farm-gate sales.

For Farmers Only

[ENVIRONMENTALISTS, DO NOT READ!]

The Job Loss and Economic Impacts Argument

When environmentalists argue for eliminating a productive human economic activity like grazing cattle, it is not enough for them to point only to the environmental values that it displaces. It is also not sufficient for ranchers to cite the job losses and damage to the local economy that would result from its elimination.

Direct economic impacts are highly relevant and an important starting point in the discussion, just as are displaced environmental values. But it is also important to know whether those jobs and business profits might simply end up being shifted elsewhere in the system. What, if any, economic benefits might be realized elsewhere if the proposed change were made? Just as all humans cause damage to the environment to one degree or another, we also all need jobs. And economic impacts, just like environmental ones, are a matter of degree, comparison, and balance. Nobody wants to lose their job or livelihood. So if we're concerned about a certain group of jobs or businesses—say the local ones in a particular community—then it may be quite relevant if those particular jobs and businesses are at risk.

But if we're arguing over broader impacts on the economy, we're going to need to know if one person's lost job will simply be replaced by someone else's gained one.

Arguing Economics and Environmental Impacts

In public debates of this kind, an industry or economic interest will typically argue lost jobs and economic impacts. The environmental groups focus on the environmental issues and the indirect environmental/economic costs. But who wins that debate can turn on the ability to soundly address both the economic and the environmental components of the argument.

In a statewide ballot measure in 1995, Washington State voters were asked to prohibit certain types of commercial fishing gear. Initiative 640 would have eliminated types of gear that were less able to select for fish species deemed appropriate for harvest while leaving other protected species alive and unharmed. The initiative was presented as an environmental measure—as a way to save endangered salmon.

Unfortunately, I-640 was highly deceptive. It had not, as was implied, been written by environmentalists with a view to conserving troubled or endangered runs of salmon. Instead it had been written and was supported by sports fishing groups who were seeking to eliminate commercial fisheries so that sportsmen would be allowed to catch more salmon themselves. Commercial fishing gear itself was, generally, not as selective as sports gear. (Hook-and-line fishermen can often catch and release.) However, in practice, the commercial salmon fisheries were actually a great deal more selective than sports fisheries because commercial fishing was limited to geographic areas and specific times when the only salmon present were of the species and runs targeted for harvest. Commercial fishery impacts on non-targeted fish were actually very low—much lower, in fact, than sport fisheries. So the actual effect of I-640 would have been to eliminate most of these highly selective commercial fisheries and to increase the recreational fishing which actually had a considerably greater overall impact on non-targeted fish.

I was campaign manager for the "No on I-640" campaign. One of the first things we did was retain an economist to study the economic impacts and job losses that would result from passage of this ballot measure. Then I and my commercial fisheries colleagues sat down with our gifted campaign consultant, David Dix, to hammer out a public message that could win us the election. Our economist had estimated that 20,000 jobs would be lost if the measure passed. We explained this to David. We definitely wanted to use it.

I recall him saying: "Sure, that's good. That'll get you about 40 percent of the vote. But surely, if you eliminate the non-tribal commercial fishery, fewer fish will be caught. So doesn't this measure necessarily have to save some salmon?"

"No," I explained. "That's the irony. This doesn't work the way you might think. Salmon fishing is based on pre-season projections of how many fish are expected to return from the ocean. Using that projection, the Fisheries Department then sets a number of fish that can be caught, and that total catch number is allocated out and shared by several types of fisheries. If there is no Washington non-tribal commercial catch, all that will happen is that sports, tribal, Canadian, and Oregon fisheries will be allowed to catch more. Exactly the same number of fish will end up being caught either way."

"That's it, then," said David. "We'll say: '20,000 jobs lost—and not a salmon saved.' The jobs message will bring you the business-oriented voters.

And the environmental message will get you the rest of the votes you need to win."

That became our campaign slogan. We used it to create the framework for our argument in every presentation, editorial board interview, television debate, and public advertisement. And we turned around badly negative early polling numbers to decisively win the election by a nearly 58 percent vote.[41]

There were two memorable lessons from this campaign. The first is that the job loss and economic impact numbers we used did not account for jobs that might have been shifted to tribal or Oregon or Canadian fisheries or to sports fishing support businesses that might have benefited from the measure. We argued job losses without ever discussing potential job gains. But the question never came up. If we'd been challenged with the potential "shift" of jobs and impacts to others, we would have had to refine our economic argument and perhaps be more realistic about it.

The second lesson from this experience, and I believe the most powerful one, was how successfully our dual campaign theme reached out to both conservative and liberal voters, to those concerned about economics as well as to those worried about the environment.

In the final analysis, and in a democratic society, the choice in most natural resource disputes will end up being made by the voting public—whether that is through ballot measure or by elected officials paying attention to what they believe their constituents prefer. David Dix told us that 40 percent (more or less) of the public will always respond best to an economics/jobs-based message. And another 40 percent will always prefer an environmental message. In a natural resource dispute, you need to capture more than just your usual constituency. To win, you must make a case that will appeal to both the economic and the environmental voters.

If farmers want to make a stronger case and improve their success at convincing the public, they need to look for ways to make the environmental case for agriculture, just as environmentalists need to make the economic one for the environment.

CHAPTER 14

The Federal Farm Bill

The federal farm bill is the principal vehicle for American farm policy. Its periodic congressional reauthorization creates a national stage upon which the farmer–environmentalist drama plays out in public. It also provides major opportunities for farmers and environmentalists to work together.

More than three quarters of the total $400 billion or so spent in the most recent five-year farm bill authorization period (2008-2013) went to food stamps and nutrition. So it is the other quarter that actually provides programs that help farmers directly. Commodity programs (price supports and crop insurance programs) make up about 15 percent of total farm bill spending. Conservation programs make up about 6 percent. Other programs like research, rural economic development, and marketing make up the balance. The "conservation title" portion of the bill includes the entire Natural Resources Conservation Service budget and most of the nation's farm-related conservation spending. Total federal spending on conservation title programs over the most recent five fiscal years was about $22.5 billion (averaging about $4.5 billion per year). By comparison, about $61 billion (or about $12 billion per year) was spent over the same period on commodity programs.[1]

The authorized spending levels have changed somewhat under the new farm bill, but this is still major legislation backed by big money. Communities all across the country have come to see the conservation title as an opportunity to address local environmental issues with federal dollars. As with most federal spending, farm bill appropriations compete with one another. So efforts to increase funding for conservation can naturally (and often correctly) be seen as a real or potential challenge to funding for commodity programs. And direct farm-related expenditures also compete, at least to a degree, against spending on nutrition programs for the needy. This is the unfortunate political and fiscal dynamic behind today's farmer–environmentalist interactions over the farm bill.

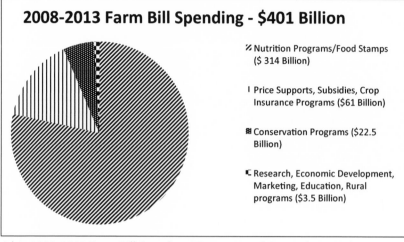

2008-2013 Farm Bill Spending - $401 Billion

⅄ Nutrition Programs/Food Stamps ($ 314 Billion)

Ι Price Supports, Subsidies, Crop Insurance Programs ($61 Billion)

▦ Conservation Programs ($22.5 Billion)

ᴎ Research, Economic Development, Marketing, Education, Rural programs ($3.5 Billion)

14.1 2008-2013 Farm Bill Spending (Congressional Research Service)

What Are Commodity Programs?

To understand agriculture–environmental competition over the farm bill, it is important to know some of the basics about commodity programs, including price supports and crop revenue insurance.

U.S. agricultural commodity support originated in the 1930s as a part of the New Deal.[2] It initially took the form of programs designed to increase farm prices by reducing the supply through payments to some farmers not to plant crops and by setting price minimums. These matured into programs that today:

1. Ensure that farmers receive at least a minimum price—set by Congress—for their crop by making up any deficiency between the set price and the actual price available on the open market. The new farm bill refers to this as the Price Loss Coverage (PLC) program.

2. Ensure that farmers receive at least the level of crop revenue (calculated as price times crop yield) that can be anticipated before planting. The program makes an advance projection of the total crop revenue expected to be received at the time of harvest based on the price it is expected the farmer will be paid and the likely crop yield the farmer will produce. The government then makes up any deficiency between this projection and the actual crop revenue available to the farmer on the open market at the time of harvest. Under the 2014 Farm Bill, this is called the Agricultural Risk Coverage (ARC) program.

3. Until it was eliminated in 2014, made payments to farmers based on their demonstrated history of crop production. This was referred to as the direct payments program. It disappeared under the 2014 Farm Bill.

Each of these programs provides a subsidy. The direct payments program was a direct subsidy. The Price Loss Coverage (PLC) program subsidizes farms to the extent that the price the farmer receives falls below the price set by Congress. Since that price has historically been set at a level significantly higher than one would anticipate from the normal market, it generally results in a payment to the farmer. (At times extraordinarily high grain prices have affected its level.) The ARC program is more like traditional crop insurance in that the price and the crop yield insured are actually projected ahead of the season based on historic norms and expected market and crop conditions. But losses paid under ARC are still not fully covered out of premiums paid by farmers. Farmers will pay a significant part of the cost, but the losses are mostly covered by the government.

With about $12 billion annually flowing into the agriculture industry, these programs represent a substantial source of revenue for many farmers.

For the most part, however, only those farmers who produce about one-third of the American crop value have been eligible to receive this assistance. These are the producers of so-called dry-bulk commodity crops. These include corn, wheat, soy, cotton, rice, oilseeds, peanuts, and sugar. (The dairy industry has its own separate program.) The other two-thirds of our farm industry receives no such assistance. Growers of fruits and vegetables, for example, are not included. Most of the farmers you as a consumer might deal with at a local farmers market, those who supply the produce section of your grocery store, or those who produce your poultry, eggs, or meats, are almost certainly not receiving these subsidies—at least not directly.

The Rationale for Commodity Support

The reason only some farm products have ended up eligible for farm bill subsidies mostly lies in their history. In the 1930s, there was grave depression-era concern about the collapse of international commodity prices. At the time, the only crops widely traded in larger national and international markets were the dry-bulk commodities—crops that could be easily shipped great distances and stored for long periods of time. Other more perishable crops that were mostly traded locally were not seen to need such protection.[3] Later on, when grain embargoes were adopted as a U.S. foreign policy sanction, price supports were a bulwark against resulting price impacts on U.S. grains. This, no doubt, further cemented their perceived necessity.[4]

Whether we're dealing with grapes from Chile, olives from Italy, beef from Argentina, or fruit juice from Thailand, modern food processing and preservation technology, refrigeration systems, speed of transit, and plentiful transportation energy, have placed nearly every food product on the international marketplace. So one is left to wonder why the principal farm bill risk management tools are still reserved for only about one-third of American farmers. What do the other two-thirds of our farmers think about this?

With the advent of broad international conventions and treaties on international trade, the rising influence of the World Trade Organization (WTO), the reduced threat of grain embargo, and the increasing maturity of the global economy, one might question whether these same concerns exist today. And the rationale for these programs has changed. The focus in the 2014 Farm Bill debate shifted to focus on risk management and insurance against the inherent risks in agriculture.[5] Farmers will, however, retain a significant subsidy.

Why These Programs Continue to Exist

Of course people always fight harder when they have something specific to lose than they do when there is only the promise that things might be better. But the answer is also that the U.S. agriculture industry has reshaped itself over the past eighty years to conform to the marketplace distortions created by these farm bill programs. Prices, practices, business plans, and expectations in the subsidized commodities, and in those businesses which deal with them, have come to count on these programs as a part of their operating landscape. Eliminating these subsidies would mean dramatic change and likely dislocations throughout the industry.

For example, there is a good deal of marginal land of limited productivity that has been devoted to growing some of our commodity crops, land that would have a good deal less commercial value were the commodity support programs to be eliminated. It is understandable that the owners of those lands might strongly resist farm program changes that could make their land uneconomic to farm and thereby dramatically reduce its value. Without some clear, well-funded alternative program (in conservation, for example) that offers similar financial prospects and certainties, it will be little consolation for them that their land might be better devoted to wildlife, native prairie, or other environmental uses for which they are highly unlikely to ever be paid.

Should these subsidies disappear, there is also land currently growing commodity crops that might be converted to the growing of other crops, like fruits and vegetables (referred to by USDA as "specialty crops"). The increases in production of fruits and vegetables that might result could reduce prices for specialty crops. This potential outcome worries current specialty crop producers. And, since 1996, commodity crop farmers have agreed to program conditions that legally restrict their right to convert their commodity crop land to the growing of specialty crops. With this protection from competition by their commodity crop counterparts, specialty crop producers have been willing to support the commodity crop programs even though the benefit they get is only indirect.

Grain subsidies also assure low market prices on livestock feed. The loss of government supports on grain prices would significantly increase production costs for beef, pork, chicken, milk, eggs, etc. So livestock producers also have something to lose from the loss of commodity programs.

Indirect farm bill impacts like this today ripple throughout the agriculture industry.[6]

The Arguments for Change

Historical opposition to farm bill commodity subsidy programs has been a great deal broader and more diverse than the agriculture industry support for them. But opponents have lacked the focus and immediate self-interest that one sees in the farm industry's support. The arguments against these programs are as varied as are the interests that offer them. Among the many arguments made against farm bill commodity subsidies are the following:

Commodity Subsidies Violate International Trade Standards

Government business subsidies discourage free trade. They artificially reduce the free market prices that must be charged by the subsidized producers for their crops, giving them unfair advantage over their competitors and artificially driving down prices for everyone. There have been legal challenges brought in the World Trade Organization (WTO) against U.S. farm subsidies, most notably by Brazil which claims that our cotton subsidy harms their cotton producers.[7] Complaints by Brazil and other countries are increasing the odds that the United States could experience extraordinarily costly, WTO-approved, international retaliation against both farm and other U.S. products (like our exports of aircraft parts and software, for example). To avoid that, the United States has provided payments directly to Brazil's farmers to hold off their case against us.[8]

Subsidies Encourage Growing Crops on Marginal Lands[9]

Much of the U.S. production of wheat, barley, and other grains comes from marginal, relatively dry, non-irrigated land. The argument is that this land could be converted back to native prairie grasses or other natural wildlife habitats. Some of these crops are also grown on steep hillsides or in dry windy areas that, under agricultural production, are vulnerable to erosion which creates special water quality and air quality problems. Without price subsidies, it is argued that many thousands of acres might be returned to their natural conditions.[10]

Subsidies Contribute to Global Poverty

The World Bank has estimated that eliminating farm subsidies worldwide would help raise 500 million people out of poverty.[11] Global poverty also has impacts on global political stability and terrorism, U.S. immigration pressure, U.S. export markets, and a variety of other issues of importance to all Americans.[12]

Subsidies are Unfair to Non-subsidized Sectors of Agriculture

Subsidizing some food products will make those products cheaper—bad news for those agriculture sectors not protected by subsidies. All food products, to some extent, compete with one another as consumers make choices about what to eat for dinner. This can create downward price pressure on unsubsidized products and can make it harder for non-commodity farmers to succeed in business and stay on their land. This adds to the challenges faced, for example, by fruit and vegetable producers whose farms are typically closer to urban areas and who therefore struggle to afford land in the face of pressure from urban sprawl.[13]

Subsidies Encourage Production of Unhealthy Foods

Much of the U.S. commodity crop production is exported. But at the same time, we would need 13 million more acres, nationwide, growing fruits and vegetables for everyone to meet our federal government's minimum dietary guidelines.[14] Subsidizing some crops but not others clearly increases the consumption of some foods over others, often not the healthiest ones. The most commonly cited example is the impact of low cost (subsidized) corn syrup on the American diet. Corn syrup is today used in a multitude of processed foods and drinks with resulting harmful impacts claimed on U.S. health and obesity.[15]

Subsidies Prevent Spending on Environmental Stewardship

High farm bill spending on commodity programs makes it difficult to secure new, much-needed spending increases on conservation programs. As we've seen, farmers see efforts to increase conservation spending as a threat to their commodity subsidies. Conversely, agriculture industry support for commodity subsidies also is seen by conservation groups as an obstacle to stronger conservation programs.[16] As long as the commodity programs continue, it may be difficult to make long strides in conservation.

While these are powerful arguments, they do not offer a unified prescription for change to subsidy programs.

Under the new farm bill the most obvious of these subsidies, direct payments, has disappeared. Conservation programs will also suffer cuts, as will other commodity programs. These losses are the product of our current budget deficit. The bulk of the several billion dollars saved through the elimination of direct payments will not shift to benefit agriculture in other ways. Mostly, savings from this and other cuts will fall out of agriculture entirely.[17]

The loss of direct payments and changes in the approach to price supports have paved the way for a simpler, more credible explanation to the public about why these programs are needed: farming is a risky business; we need these programs to ameliorate that risk.[18] The balance of the commodity programs can now be aptly described as risk management or insurance programs. They may also diminish the need to periodically seek relief from Congress when various regions of the country occasionally suffer very real climate-related and other disasters.

These remaining commodity programs still, however, represent a huge farm subsidy—one likely to continue to bother both Congressional budget hawks and much of the general public. And the shift to a risk management/insurance rationale still does not explain why only one-third of our farmers are eligible for these subsidies (or need this insurance). Surely all farmers face risks—not just those who grow commodity crops.

Shifting and Broadening Farm Bill Support

Farm conservation advocates have proposed alternative approaches by which the same levels of spending would continue to flow into U.S. agriculture, but in a way that avoids the problems with commodity programs. In broad outline, the thinking has been that we could eliminate existing subsidy payments that help just some farmers, and use the money instead to pay all farmers to adopt stronger environmental stewardship.

This approach is quite common in Europe. It would resolve U.S. vulnerability to challenges in WTO since government spending on environmental conservation is usually considered trade-neutral and not challenged as distorting the marketplace. It would presumably help protect marginal, environmentally sensitive lands while still keeping their owners in profitable farming. By paying farmers for environmental conservation rather than subsidizing lower prices, there should be reduced impacts (at least the direct ones) on farm prices and third world poverty. Such an approach would help all farmers stay in business rather than helping some at the expense of others. Preferential support for certain unhealthy food products would disappear since these conservation programs would be available to all farmers and all crops. The revenues saved from ending commodity programs would be converted for use in more socially responsible and politically sustainable conservation spending.

In practice, of course, such a change would not have equal impact throughout agriculture. Some farmers would lose; others would gain. The changes would need to be phased in slowly, over time, to give our farm industry an opportunity to adjust with minimum dislocation.[19]

It has been suggested that the existing Conservation Stewardship Program (CSP) could be used more extensively across agriculture and provide payments for farmers meeting certain minimum levels of conservation practice adoption.[20] The Conservation Reserve Program (CRP) might be used to assure that marginal land that falls out of production can still generate income for its owners as payment for the environmental benefits it provides. Or the current EQIP program could receive new funding that would allow it to purchase environmental services from farmers at full market value.

We could also look for specific ways to help the farmers who might suffer most from the loss of commodity subsidies and to assure that they would benefit from the increases in conservation spending. For example, a wheat farmer, some of whose marginal land becomes uneconomical for agriculture might instead find ways to earn money by protecting, restoring, and maintaining some of that same land as native prairie or as wildlife habitat. There might also be funding to pay for improved conservation practices on the land that remains in production. A dairy farmer or cattle rancher whose feed costs rise or who loses dairy price supports might make up the difference through increased cost assistance in installing a waste management system or storage lagoon, with investment and cost-share funding for an anaerobic digester, or with assistance in adopting a stronger rangeland management system.

Farmers could receive government assistance with managing risks. But with a significant portion of agriculture support paid in the form of conservation assistance, the public perception of the agriculture industry would become much more positive. Instead of pouring money into subsidies, which are seen as largely negative and economically dishonest, the public would actually be receiving something positive and important for its money. And agriculture's indispensability as an American environmental asset would assure it a continuing place as a beloved industry in the public mind.

For Environmentalists Only
[FARMERS, DO NOT READ!]

The Barriers to a Shift from Subsidies to Conservation

The agriculture industry might be a lot better off without commodity subsidies if current funding could be kept in agriculture and redirected into conservation programs. So, one might think that, over the years, ongoing farm bill reform efforts by environmental groups would have included many serious attempts to court mainstream agriculture groups as allies in securing such an outcome.

But they haven't. Aside from occasional attempts by one or another of the more centrist organizations, there has typically been little effort at farm–environmental dialogue.[21]

So, when environmentalists launch into the farm bill debate and begin making the arguments discussed above, what those farmers see is a crusade to take away their money. When it became apparent that the budget axe was likely to eliminate the direct payments commodity program in the 2014 Farm Bill, some commentators were positively gleeful, suggesting that this was "good riddance!" and expressing distress at the prospect that some of the money might get redirected into other farm programs.[22]

For farmers to leave behind their conservative, business, rural, often anti-environmental alliances and climb into bed with the environmental community is a very big step. Many of their current friends, including many elected officials, aren't going to like it. Maybe such a move is in their best interest. But it definitely isn't going to happen unless both sides have talked about it a good deal first.

The Myth of a "Monolithic" Agriculture Industry

Non-farmers, especially ones who disagree with the farm lobby, think of U.S. agriculture as a huge, tightly unified industry with immense power. But agriculture is unlike aerospace, software, automobiles, or steel. There are 2.2 million separate farm businesses in the United States.[23] They grow hundreds of crops and are spread across the entire country in every state and nearly every county or township. They farm a huge variety of landscapes in communities all around the country. The vast majority are not nearly so large or corporate as most people believe.[24] Each farmer faces unique local and individual challenges.

This is, in short, an independent, self-reliant group. So it isn't surprising that farmers from different regions, commodities, and types of agriculture have different opinions. Each of the farm groups represents different crops and perspectives; each tends to go its own way. Even the local, county, and state farm bureaus that make up the American Farm Bureau Federation are each quite different.

So communicating with them need not be top down. Environmental organizations often find working with farmers and farm groups at the grass-roots level much more successful.[25] What the environmental community has to offer is, after all, in the farm industry's best long-term interests. So why not use this egalitarian organizational structure, and the farmer bias toward independence, to advantage by starting lower down in the hierarchy and working up?

Counterproductive Language

We all tend to use incautious language in advocacy. It happens frequently in discourse on the farm bill. A flagrant example is in how people often mischaracterize one of America's strongest agriculture–environmental conservation programs, the farm bill's Conservation Reserve Program (CRP). This is one of the few conservation programs that reliably gets support from both farmers and environmentalists. CRP leases working agricultural land at its farm rental rate for conversion to natural vegetation, landscapes, and wildlife habitat.

Opponents of CRP, however, seem particularly fond of describing it as a program that "pays farmers not to grow crops."[26]

Suppose a state social service agency leased a privately-owned warehouse for public indoor recreation for urban youth. Would we describe that as a government program that "pays warehouse owners not to store merchandise"? Suppose the city purchased a vacant property so it could be used as a park. Would we describe that as a government program that "pays landowners not to build buildings"?

Such descriptions are nonsense. CRP leases these lands for the explicit and important purpose of environmental restoration. They provide bird and other wildlife habitat, protect native plants, preserve wetlands, and protect water quality.[27] Farmers get paid for doing that, as they should, and they generally support the program.[28]

Both farmers and environmentalists need to encourage others to use language that enhances rather than degrades public understanding of programs like CRP. We need the public to appreciate the critical place for such tools in protecting both farming and the environment if they are to support them in the years to come.

For Farmers Only

[ENVIRONMENTALISTS, DO NOT READ!]

A Stronger Rationale for Farm Bill Support

Let's face a couple of hard truths about the farm bill:

First, the vast majority of the public views our commodity programs as subsidies.[29] It takes some real mental contortions to argue that they aren't—even as they evolved in the 2014 Farm Bill debate. The good news is that the public also still likes agriculture, and much of Congress, at least at this writing, still appears willing to fund those subsidies—at least at some level. But most people are troubled by subsidies. Tolerance for them is always likely to erode in tough budget times making them ever-vulnerable to the budget axe. The recent demise of the direct payments program is a case in point.

Second, U.S. agriculture needs the government support. This is not because it is somehow inadequate or flawed. Rather it is, at least in part, because we expect farmers to provide services like keeping their land in farming and protecting the environment. But we've done a very poor job of making that realistically possible for them.

What agriculture desperately needs is a strong, modern public-interest rationale for why the ordinary citizen should support agriculture. Recharacterizing the remaining price and revenue support programs as "risk management" and "insurance" will help. But while that may help convince some people, for a while, let's at least not fool ourselves. Unless farmers are covering the full cost of these programs through premiums (and they're not), they are still subsidies.[30]

In the end, that is always going to be obvious to anyone who really looks.

A Farm Bill Strategy for the Long Term

Farmers need a strategy designed to prevent future losses like the 2014 outright loss of the direct payments program—a strategy that will help them maintain and even increase federal expenditures in support of agriculture over the years to come.

What might be the hallmarks of such a strategy?

- It would provide real, identifiable value to the public in exchange for their money. It would be seen to be addressing specific public needs.

- It would continue to provide serious help for working agriculture.

- It would broaden the support it provides so it is accessible to essentially all farmers.

- It would not violate WTO standards for free and fair international trade.

- It would not distort the marketplace in ways that encourage consumption of unhealthy foods, motivate damage to environmentally vulnerable lands, or aggravate international poverty.

- It would engage robust political support from a broad coalition of interested groups, including both farmers and environmentalists.

- It would help farmers reshape public perceptions so agriculture comes to be universally viewed as a valued contributor to society.

A good deal of this spending could be productively shifted to payments to farmers for voluntarily producing important environmental services, services that most farmers could generate without seriously impairing their farm products productivity and without making significant conversions of their land out of traditional agriculture. There are other opportunities as well. While such a program would be available to all farmers, it would inevitably affect some more than others. So farmers need to be at the table making sure the transitions are as painless as possible.

In the years to come, agriculture's tenacious hold on a sinking commodity program ship must not be allowed to push the nation to a point where, in a flat-out Congressional battle between farmers and non-farmers, agriculture loses and even more agriculture industry support disappears down the black hole that is the federal budget deficit, never to be seen again (think: direct payments). If that happens, current opportunities to influence the direction of change will be lost. And the outcome could be disappointing for farmers all across America, as well as for the environment.

CHAPTER 15

Tools for Dialogue—
the Common Ground

At this point, you may agree that farmers and environmentalists would be better off if they'd work together. But perhaps you see the odds of that happening as very slim.

Yet throughout this book we've seen examples of communities where they did just that.

So let's now take a quick look at some of these largely successful community processes and see why they worked. Then let's consider some specific ways one might go about initiating discussion between farm and environmental groups in the future. And we will finish by identifying some of the topics on which such discussions might be productive.

What Some of the More Successful Community
Programs Have in Common

Numerous examples of farmer–environmentalist collaboration have been cited in this book. Among them: the New York City Watershed,[1] Washington State's Ruckelshaus process,[2] Michigan's MAEAP,[3] Wisconsin's FACT,[4] and Florida's Green Swamp Authority.[5] Successes like these actually happen fairly often, wherever there is a conservation district, watershed council, public agency, or other community group or leader with the vision and determination to bring farmers and environmentalists together. These success stories demonstrate different approaches to addressing farm–environmental disagreements. But they share some common attributes:[6]

- Each community had to overcome a history of mistrust and rocky relationships between farm landowners and the local environmental community.

- There was the threat of, and a credible case for, significantly increased environmental regulation. Its adoption was uncertain, and it had potential downsides for both agriculture and for the environment.

- There was an authoritative commitment to funding for incentive-based, non-regulatory approaches, either now or in the future, should an agreement be reached.

- The convening parties (government or nonprofit) were sufficiently invested in the success of the process to commit adequate resources to fully complete it.

- Key parties were sufficiently committed to participate long enough and intensively enough to fully air, fact-check, and ultimately reach agreement on the major critical issues.

- The leaders representing the relevant groups or caucuses had sufficient authority from their own organizations to make binding commitments on their behalf.

- There was a clear purpose for the dialogue: an immediate problem or set of problems needed to be addressed and a clear outcome for the discussion was in view.

These favorable conditions may not always exist at the same time, but, in each of these examples, a situation had arisen that was sufficiently serious that the parties had no choice but to begin talking.

After many years of conflict, both farmers and environmentalists might be forgiven for being skeptical that their usual opponents can be counted on as faithful partners in some new coalition of the future. The main lesson from each of these examples of cooperation is that reliable partnerships in the political world, as in the business world, come about when: 1) self-interests align, and 2) people come to know and trust each other.

Identifying mutual self-interests isn't rocket science. And bringing people together to build relationships is just common sense.

Stimulating New Local Farm–Environmental Dialogue

Clearly there is a lot for farmers and environmentalists to discuss. Unfortunately, there aren't many non-competitive venues where those discussions can be constructive. If the only times the two groups interact are in court or at legislative hearings, their prospects of finding agreement seem poor.

Suppose we set out, in an organized way, to actively identify opportunities for them to exchange ideas and then specifically stimulated their use. One can easily imagine an extensive menu of such opportunities. Most are obvious once one begins to think about them. Some may already be happening—just not often enough. Some may never have been tried. But any of these opportunities could be initiated by a single farmer or farm leader, by an environmentalist, by an interested nonprofit or agency, or by anyone with an interest, some credibility, and the time, energy, and motivation to make it happen.

Consider these possibilities:

- *Key figure one-on-one*: Key leaders in a community (whether they have official status or not) from groups representing agriculture and representing the environment could arrange small, casual meetings to discuss emerging issues. Over time, these meetings could become regular. Others could be invited as appropriate for new topics of conversation. From these meetings may come opportunities to cooperate on specific matters.

- *Internal newsletter article exchange*: Most farm and environmental organizations have a membership magazine or newsletter whose purpose is, at least in part, to share opinions about issues facing the group. Farm and environmental groups could agree to exchange written opinion articles for their respective newsletters on key mutual issues. The newsletter editors might use this as a chance to present "pro and con" pieces together, perhaps in publications of both parties.

- *Newsletter subscription exchange*: Farm and environmental leaders could mutually subscribe to each other's newsletters or magazines. They might write articles for each other's publications on issues of particular mutual interest. The exchanges could be made known to the writers and subscribers for these publications and the exchange could be mentioned in the publication. Everyone would be aware that both audiences would be reading these materials.

- *Exchanging speakers at key meetings*: Farm and environmental groups could create opportunities at their meetings, conferences, and conventions for presentations from respected leaders from the opposite side of the issues. These events could be billed specifically as an opportunity to hear alternative points of view and to engage in a public discourse about them.

- *Joint presentation teams*: A speaker duo composed of one farmer and one environmentalist could make itself available to present an exchange of perspectives on key issues at farmer or environmentalist events, or at general public venues. After repeated presentations, they would become familiar with each other's arguments. Areas of common understanding or of sharp disagreement could be usefully identified.

- *Speakers bureau*: A jointly managed agricultural–environmental speakers bureau could facilitate placement of speakers from each side (or from both jointly—perhaps including the duo mentioned above) at meetings of groups on either side of the issues or for interested groups outside the farm–environmental family.

- *Joint submissions for general media publication*: Recognized leaders from farm and environmental groups could co-author and submit joint opinion articles on key issues for placement in general or targeted publications. Or they could cooperate in submitting separate opinion commentary pieces providing their respective positions for publication as a pro-and-con package.

These suggestions are, of course, only a starting point. Once these relationships began to form, cooperating farmers and environmentalists could pursue a great many similar opportunities, such as:

- *Convention/trade show exchange:* At their respective trade shows or conventions their organizations might offer invitations/tickets to their counterparts, or perhaps exchange free exhibitor booths.

- *Use of contact lists:* They might agree to a one-use-only membership contact list exchange that each group could use to make their own case on some issue to the members and supporters of the other side.

- *Jointly sponsored conferences:* They might sponsor a joint workshop or conference on an agriculture–environmental topic, with each publicizing attendance to their own members and constituents.

- *Debates:* They could hold a debate on a timely issue, similarly publicized and with invitations to legislators, public officials, and the press.

- *Farm–environmental forum:* They could hold a facilitated forum at which key public figures, elected officials, and community leaders, along with farmers and environmentalists, would be participants in finding answers to key specific farm–environmental issues.

- *Educational tours:* Both groups frequently conduct educational tours for interested citizens. They could jointly sponsor one of these tours, with speakers from both sides, and mutually promote the tour to their own publicity lists.

- *Electronic exchange:* Both sides could team up to present and discuss their mutual positions on a joint website, blog, chat room, or with a mutually accessible listserv.

As they grew more comfortable with one another, farm and environmental groups might encourage and facilitate the other's participation in their respective internal organizational policy process to assure that issues are presented for discussion that might be of importance to their opposite numbers. For example:

- *Policy processes:* They could share, with one another, the details of their respective internal policy development processes so the other could potentially influence those processes.

- *Exchange of policy resolutions:* They might exchange policy resolutions and submit the others' resolution for discussion and a vote of their board or membership at the next meeting. A supporter of the resolution could be invited to attend the relevant portion of the business meeting and to present their position in support of the suggested policy.

- *Standing committees:* Respective groups might agree to each create a standing committee or a task force within their own group responsible for informing themselves and taking leadership on agriculture–environmental issues. These committees would be a point of contact for each other.

Of course, existing farm or environmental groups or leaders in a community may simply lack the will, the interest, or the wherewithal to undertake these kinds of activities. But they aren't the only ones who could initiate activities like this. Any group or agency with an interest and some credibility with both sides could do so. This includes land trusts, conservation districts, rural environmental organizations, government agencies, nonprofits, and other community organizations of all kinds.

Such a mutually respected third party might:

- Identify key farm and environmental leaders and make initial contact to interest them in some of these ideas;

- Research and share useful information with each side about the internal policy-making processes used by "opposing" groups and suggest opportunities to influence those processes;

- Serve as go-between and convener in organizing presentations, events, initial meetings, or joint projects;

- Suggest topics for exchanges of presentations or written newsletter commentary;
- Suggest topics for joint media commentary and help place such commentary in the press;
- Provide research, editorial, and writing assistance to both sides;
- Ghost write commentary for leaders in both groups;
- Attend, mediate, document, and provide follow-up or other staff support as needed and desired by participants; and
- Independently make presentations, write commentary, and advocate directly with both sides concerning how stronger interchange between them is in the interests of both.

The cost of these activities could realistically be covered by charitable or public grants. Grantors, public or private, would be deeply impressed with a project proposal that came to them from a partnership between respected farm and environmental organizations.

Even a well-placed and determined individual could single-handedly stimulate a lot of constructive progress with tools like these.

Why Would Efforts Like These Have Any Chance of Success?

Interactions like the ones described above work because when people communicate directly with one another, they have no choice but to consider the other person's point of view. It's that simple.

If communication is public, there is additional motivation to seem reasonable to the as-yet unconvinced. When a farmer or an environmentalist sits down to prepare a presentation or to write an editorial that will be seen by people with an opposing perspective, they adapt their message. Communications professionals refer to this as "audience analysis,"[7] but for most of us it just comes naturally. In that process, perspectives change—both for the writer and for the audience.

Communications like these also work best when there is actually an exchange; when everyone knows that this public expression of opinion will have a response. If these exchanges are made with mutual respect, the odds of a positive outcome greatly improve.

The Challenges of "Linkage" and the Power in Avoiding It

Some people find it conceptually difficult to cooperate with someone on one issue knowing that they strongly disagree about something else. They feel everything has to be linked; that agreeing about some things weakens their position on others. Since there may be some issues where groups are severely polarized, insisting on linkage can make it impossible for them to ever come together on anything.

Proponents of linkage tend to focus on the outright win for such issues, forgetting that, especially in a representative democracy, policy outcomes where one interest group succeeds in simply beating down and thoroughly defeating another are actually quite rare. Efforts to secure wins of that kind can go on for years—even for generations. These areas of serious discord are very often disputes neither side is ever likely to actually win outright.

These intractable disputes are especially frustrating for elected policymakers whose job it is to find agreeable solutions.

When long-standing political enemies, like farmers and environmentalists, actually reach agreement, even on something small, the power of that agreement can be astonishing. Elected officials often fall all over themselves in their rush to help make such agreements work. Anyone who has lobbied a legislative body has stories to tell about events of this kind (though, perhaps not often involving farmers and environmentalists). So reaching such an agreement can produce big changes in a hurry.

The potential in outcomes like this can be a powerful motivation for interest group advocates to set the issues aside that seem intractable while working on ones where cooperation is possible. If you can agree, the chances of getting new policy actually adopted are excellent. And the more you make actual progress on the easier problems, the more you'll find the harder ones have become much less challenging.

Areas of Potential Agreement

So, there are a great many opportunities for farmers and environmentalists to communicate. And there are powerful reasons why they ought to do so. But, in addition, there are also many specific substantive issues upon which it seems likely they could be reasonably expected to find early common ground. Consider just a few:

- *Environmental incentives:* Farmers and environmentalists might jointly support funding for environmental incentives. Environmentalists may need to temporarily set aside their general preference for regulations but could get something done for the environment. Farmers would need to relax their usual dislike of taxes and the conviction that the environment is "just fine" but could forestall potential threat of regulation.

- *Purchasing development rights*: Farmers and environmentalists might support government programs that purchase agricultural conservation easements on working farmland. The farm community would need to believe such protections are desirable and that they could help preserve local working farms. Environmentalists would need to see protecting farmland as a sufficient priority to merit use of scarce public funding and see the protected farms as helping to slow sprawl and to improve the environment.

- *Environmental markets*: Farmers and environmentalists might cooperate in creating a policy framework for environmental markets. Farmers would need to set aside their discomfort with the regulations on other industries (polluters, developers, energy suppliers, water users, etc.) that are needed to make such markets work. But they could find a new market for natural resource services they can generate on their farms. Environmentalists would need to come to see cost-saving offsets and mitigation as positive for the environment. But the existence of such a market could make environmental protection more affordable and politically realistic.

- *Cost of community services studies:* Farmers and environmentalists might jointly fund studies that demonstrate the tax and community service cost impacts of developing natural resource lands like farms and forests. Farmers could use these studies to demonstrate that they already pay plenty in taxes and that additional public service expenditures on their behalf are justified. Environmentalists could use these studies to help show the cost impacts of unchecked development sprawl.

- *Research environmental benefits of farmland:* Farmers and environmentalists might jointly support and fund research that identifies and documents the environmental services that are or can be provided on undeveloped agricultural lands, services that are possible only if that land remains in working, profitable, private agriculture. Farmers could use the results to argue the public benefits of privately owned agricultural lands. Environmentalists might use this to support constraints on growth—something the farmers would need to be prepared to accept.

- *Planning for agriculture*: Farmers and environmentalists might cooperate in planning for the future of agriculture. While most communities have economic development plans, few of them include agriculture. And few have created plans specifically aimed at guiding the agriculture industry into a prosperous and successful future. Such a plan would be of obvious value to farm groups in their efforts to secure public support and capital investments that encourage their industry. For environmentalists, such a plan would also include the anticipated ways the farm industry hoped to deal with environmental issues.

- *Integrated pest management (IPM):* Farmers and environmentalists might join forces in seeking grants to support research on, and actual use of, cost-effective techniques for managing agricultural pests while reducing or eliminating the use of environmentally harmful or dangerous chemical pesticides.[8] New techniques for IPM could save farmers money as well as reducing their environmental impacts and the pressure for unfriendly regulation. The environmental benefits would be obvious.

- *Redirecting farm bill subsidy programs:* Farmers and environmentalists might agree to shift some of the funding for the fiscally threatened farm bill commodity subsidy programs in the direction of environmental incentive/conservation programs. Farmers would secure dramatically improved political and public support for the resulting programs which would no longer be thought of as subsidies. Environmentalists would make significant gains on an entire array of valuable farm bill conservation programs.

- *Scorecard for community efforts to support agriculture:* Farmers and environmentalists might cooperate to rank local communities on their efforts at protecting agriculture and at helping farmers improve the environment. The two groups would need to agree on the criteria. But with farm and environmental support, such a scorecard could put serious pressure on local politicians to improve or maintain their "score."[9]

- *Local food labeling and marketing:* Farmers and environmentalists might work together to adopt a set of local environmental management standards that could be made a requirement for certification under a local food label that could increase consumer support for local farm products. The environmental community might unilaterally increase its support in local food marketing and labeling campaigns in a way that would make it more explicit that people should buy local because it is better for the environment.

- *Community education about farming and the environment:* Farmers and environmentalists might jointly sponsor community education projects that help citizens understand the relationship between farming and the environment. Projects of this kind could include sponsoring artists and art shows that highlight agriculture–environmental issues, curricula for public school classes, and other educational venues.

Collaborations like these could become commonplace. They must, however, begin somewhere, and that may require a politically courageous elected or agency leader, a thoughtful farm or environmental group, or simply some individual community leader willing to risk reaching across the farm–environmental divide.

For Farmers

As a farmer and an advocate for agriculture, you are probably quite confident of the reason, truth, and justice of your positions on farm–environmental issues. If so, you will have no hesitation about explaining your point of view to any environmentalist or group of environmentalists. So this chapter was written for you.

If you're *not* willing to do that, maybe it's time to rethink those positions.

For Environmentalists

As an environmentalist and an advocate for the environment, you are probably quite confident of the reason, truth, and justice of your positions on farm–environmental issues. If so, you will have no hesitation about explaining your point of view to any farmer or group of farmers. So this chapter was written for you.

If you're *not* willing to do that, maybe it's time to rethink those positions.

CHAPTER 16

Two Visions for the Future of Agriculture and the Environment

The future of farming in America depends on how we cope with environmental issues affecting agriculture. One can picture two visions for that future. In the first, the farmer–environmentalist feud continues, agriculture slowly strangles, and the environment suffers. In the second, we collectively save and strengthen our farm industry while drawing upon its natural resource benefits to create an environmentally healthy American landscape.

Vision 1: Agriculture Dies and the Environment Suffers

If things continue the way they're going, there is no reason to suppose that agriculture's challenges will suddenly accumulate, overwhelm the industry, and cause it to collapse with some great and audible bang. Instead, losses for both agriculture and the environment will incrementally grow. Possibilities for cooperation and mutual benefit will shrink. Remedies will move ever further out of reach.

At the Urban Edge

As urban centers inexorably sprawl out across surrounding landscapes, farms will continue to fragment and develop. This will happen everywhere, but somewhat more quickly at the urban edge.

Sprinkled amidst this sprawl will be many small, as yet undeveloped parcels of land that will be suitable for small-scale farming. And there will be direct-market farmers willing to farm them. These farmers will increasingly be renters whose lease payments cover only the farm-business value of the land. The landowners (the farmers' landlords) will consider their properties primarily as investments with farming as an interim use to generate a small income (and sometimes qualify the land for a farm tax break) while waiting for development value to appreciate. These farm businesses may, therefore, be temporarily profitable so long as they are prepared to move on short notice. When the farm property does sell, a farmer who wishes to continue in agriculture will need to find other land to farm for a few years more until that also sells. We will also see a proliferation of low-investment crops that require limited on-farm fixture infrastructure, crops like hay or the limited grazing of livestock. And we will see horse farms that provide boarding, training, and similar services to nearby urban residents.

None of these trends will be obvious to patrons at the local farmers market; the urban-edge local food movement may continue to prosper and grow. For those who are paying attention, however, these trends will slowly become apparent on the rural landscape.

Farmer investments in the environment will be increasingly impractical because the assured tenure of farming will be too short for them to produce a farm business benefit. Because these properties will be smaller and more numerous, incentive program managers will find them costly to deal with. And because they are so clearly destined for future non-farm uses, they will also be unproductive candidates for cost-share. With so many farms and with incentives impractical, environmental stewardship will increasingly require regulation. Some farms will find these new rules onerous and will leave the business; their land will be sold, subdivided, and developed. This will yet further accelerate the need for environmental regulation on the farms that remain.

Deeper in Traditional Farm Country

The vast bulk of agricultural production will continue to be wholesale, and commercial agriculture will continue in areas further away from cities. But many of the family farms in these rural communities will also be under price pressure from recreational, retirement, rural residential, long-distance commuter, and high-tech industrial land uses. The rural agricultural land base will steadily fragment into smaller and smaller parcels making it ever harder for commercial family farmers to find land to start anew or to expand an existing operation. When a farm does sell for continued agriculture, increasingly the buyer will be a large, absentee, corporate farming operation, not a traditional family farmer.

Traditional agricultural communities will see new, non-farmer landowners sprinkled among the remaining working farms. These new residents will bring with them dogs, traffic, children, recreational activities, and urban expectations, and will make normal commercial agriculture increasingly inconvenient. Their greater expectations for community services will create pressure for higher taxes which will be disproportionately paid by the remaining undeveloped farm properties. They will make nuisance complaints. They will run for office and will vote.

As land acquires non-farm value, its owners will be less willing to invest in farm business improvements and productivity will suffer. The diminishing farm land base will also drive away wholesale processors and other local farm-support businesses. The loss of educated youth and reduced farmer investment will steadily erode our U.S. farmer competitive advantages in technology, low cost credit, and an educated farm work force. The U.S. international farm products market share will shrink.

Commercial farmers will find it harder to invest in environmental improvements as land costs rise, so fewer farmers will undertake environmental stewardship. There will be fewer large undeveloped farm parcels to provide opportunities to make up for the environmental degradation from growth and development. This will intensify the need and public demand for regulation. And it will heighten the need for increasingly farm-disruptive environmental practices and complete conversions of farmland to environmental uses. Farms will be the favored location for restored wetlands and other types of complete land conversions required to mitigate for urban development.

Discouraged Farmers

These changes will also be deeply discouraging for the farmers who continue to struggle on. Many will become convinced that agriculture is dying. Their future business decisions will maximize their land investment to the detriment of the best interests of their farm business or of the future of agriculture. As the number of deeply committed farmers diminishes and as their average age increases, a sense of fatalism will grow. Farm support businesses and rural farm communities will also come to generally believe that farming has no future. This will fuel a broad perception among policy makers and the public that agriculture is an historical throwback and that farms are merely land awaiting development.

Agriculture industry groups will become more and more defensive about anything that might disrupt the short-term plan by many of their members to quit agriculture and sell out to non-farmers. They will increasingly rely on "just say no" in their legislative policy. It will be more difficult to find funding or political support for agriculture's needs on issues like economic development, scientific research, credit, conservation, work force education, regulation, taxes, and nuisance suits.

No one will see the point.

Frustrated Environmentalists

In the face of the farmers' disinclination to think long-term, and given the diminishing opportunities to restore natural habitat and a better-functioning landscape, environmentalists will also become frustrated. The favored option for environmental mitigation will increasingly be outright acquisition and full conversion of farms to natural wetlands and habitat. Funding for incentives will seem pointless and counter-productive. The drumbeat for stronger regulations will strengthen and it will fall on fertile ground among a growing non-farm, urban constituency that sees the farm industry as subsidized and self-interested.

These full conversions and new regulations will further discourage farmers, leading to further defensiveness, further frustration by environmentalists, a greater sense of futility by both, and yet more new rules. Both agriculture and the environment will be slowly, but inevitably, drawn into a death spiral from which there is no realistic return.

Does all this sound vaguely familiar? It should. It describes what we are seeing today.

Perhaps we needn't worry. Maybe one day soon we all will be eating various tasty and highly nutritious artificial products cleverly processed from soy slurry that is pumped hundreds of miles through pipelines to industrial food facilities from huge monocultures grown in what today are the world's deserts. Perhaps our food will come from massive greenhouses floating in the ocean, from terraced planters mounted to the south-facing walls of our tallest buildings, or from hydroponic gardens powered by geothermal energy or cold fusion.

It seems unwise, however, to count on such a future.

Or perhaps this dystopian perspective is unduly pessimistic. Certainly the rate at which today's trends will play themselves out in practice is up for debate. But the dynamic for these outcomes is underway. If we do not change how farmers and environmentalists relate to one another, we will not change agriculture's relationship with the environment and with the rest of society. The environment will suffer. And, while it won't happen overnight, sooner or later American agriculture as we know it will die, perhaps with hardly a whimper.[1]

Vision 2: Agriculture Prospers and the Environment Flourishes

There is, however, quite a different vision for the future, in which farmers and environmentalists both come to appreciate their respective stake in the success of the other. There is nothing particularly idealistic or utopian about such a vision. It, too, will not happen overnight. But it can happen.

How Does It Begin?

It could start with a few modest efforts by farmers and environmentalists to bridge the gap between them. These could slowly accelerate and collectively reach a "tipping point,"[2] achieve a public critical mass, or "go viral." It might come to be generally understood that farming and the environment are mutually interdependent. This will require public leadership by some of today's key farmers and environmentalists. Most likely, it will happen slowly with a gradual accumulation of evidence and a steady rise in public understanding.

Facing Some Hard Truths

There are some truths about our situation that need to become more generally accepted by farmers and by environmentalists.

For example, environmentalists would need to appreciate that the failure of farm businesses very often results in irreversible environmental harm and that a great deal of environmental benefit can be generated on working, privately-owned farms by farmers who are motivated by profits.

Farmers would need to accept that fair competition and profitable agriculture require more than some theoretically ideal unrestricted marketplace. They would need to begin supporting necessary rules that bring all farmers up to a modest but common social standard of environmental performance. They would need to recognize that without some regulation there can be no marketplace and that reasonable rules can actually enhance fair competition and can be good for private, entrepreneurial agriculture. Agriculture trade groups, in protecting the interests of the entire industry and its long-term future, would need to begin supporting moderate and consistent growth management laws.[3] In doing so, they would become a powerful voice for economically sustainable agricultural landscapes.

Farmer–Environmentalist Interdependence

An agriculture community that understands and supports growth management would become an ally for environmentalists seeking to curb sprawl.

An environmental community that sees advantages to continued profitable agriculture would moderate their pressure for new regulations and limit their regulatory efforts to only what is absolutely necessary and would be slower to support full conversion of farms to environmental uses.

An environmental community that appreciates environmental markets might support them and help generate a new profitable line of business for farmers producing environmental services. Environmentalist also might help farmers make known to consumers the environmental advantages of local agriculture and help farmers strengthen the marketing of local or American-grown products.

An agriculture community that is fully conscious of the public frustration with federal commodity subsidies, and their resulting political vulnerability, might support shifting this funding into programs that paid farmers for their environmental benefits rather than just for being a farmer or growing a crop. These benefits might be offered to all farmers rather than just a few. Such a shift would transform these payments from a federal subsidy to a compensation for something that is greatly valued by the American public.

Environmentalists desperately need ways they can demonstrate the affirmative economic value of our emerging green economy. They need the public to understand how our nation's economic prosperity is strengthened by investments in protecting and restoring environmental health and natural resources. A prosperous and environmentally responsible agriculture industry will be the ultimate proof of this concept.

Farmers desperately need the support of the American people if they are to redirect the public's environmental energies toward conservation incentives and environmental markets and away from onerous regulations. An understanding mainstream environmental community could all but guarantee such support.

Restored Farmer Confidence in the Future

Their alliance with environmentalists, and the policy gains it produces, will restore farmers' confidence in the future of agriculture. The new possibilities opened up by this alliance will drive farm groups to seek out new proactive public policies for encouraging, growing, and improving their industry. To secure these new policies, farm groups will also seek out further new alliances with other politically active citizen groups and economic interests. This will constrain their use of "just-say-no" lobbying to situations that are truly life or death for the agriculture industry.

Farmers' thinking about their role in the community will slowly shift. And so will public thinking about farmers' relationship with the rest of us and with the environment. We will still, of course, see our farmers as critically valuable providers of food. But farmers will also be increasingly appreciated for their important contributions to our nation's environmental health.

These new alliances and growing public support will lead to new policies that protect farmland, that provide conservation incentives, and that create environmental markets for agriculture. But it will also support measures that strengthen farmers' productivity and business success—measures like greater help with marketing for local and American farm products, community economic development, low interest farm business credit, research and development for farm industry products and issues, technical assistance, ag education and training, and help with marketing U.S. farm products in international trade.

Because farming is profitable and the land is secure, farms will be passed down intact to future generations and new farmers will happily enter the business to replace those that leave. These younger farmers will have greater hope for the future and a willingness to invest in it. Rural communities whose economic health depends on stable, flourishing agriculture will also flourish. And the culture of competence, hard work, independence, self-reliance, and individualism that Americans draw from our agricultural heritage will continue to leaven and steady American social values and our economy in the years to come.

A New Sense of the Possible for the Environment

A farm–environmental coalition will also transform what is possible for environmentalists. With farmers and environmentalists working together for a healthier environment, the public will newly appreciate the potential in conservation and restoration investments. Competition for limited current public resources will give way to the potential that those resources can grow. With the irrefutable example of a genuinely sustainable agriculture industry staring us all in the face, we will be forced to recognize the economic value of a healthy environment. This example will fuel stronger understanding of other critical environmental needs. A healthy environment will come to be seen as an investment in a prosperous future rather than as a drag on the economy. As the benefits become apparent, it will be very difficult to return to the old ways of thinking.

A Transformation in American Politics

A new farm–environmental alliance will generate attention and political clout simply by virtue of being so positive and so unexpected. When the presidents of the American Farm Bureau Federation and the Sierra Club suddenly sit down together at a Congressional hearing and testify in favor of the same legislation, whatever that legislation is, members of Congress will happily pass it.

As their alliance matures, these groups will come to wield remarkable power simply because they so dramatically cross today's left–right, blue state–red state, liberal–conservative political divide.[4] As farm–environmental divisions heal, we might move on to other, similarly contentious disputes. Farmers and environmentalists might find themselves leading by example, if not by design. The very existence and success of such a coalition could help weaken entrenched positions of similarly situated groups throughout our society. Moderate politicians might find new ways to reach deeply into their opposing party's political camp on crossover issues. We might begin eroding some of the divisions between cultures, classes, and urban versus rural landscapes that have grown up in recent years and are today stalling our political system.

The political, social, economic, and environmental worth of such an outcome would be incalculable.

Notes

Chapter 1: The Farm–Environmental Paradox

1. Any of the conservation professionals with the nation's 3,000 local conservation districts, or any of the several thousand local agents of the USDA Natural Resources Conservation Service, will have similar stories. The interested reader can simply search the Internet for "conservation district success stories" for examples of this kind from across the United States. Several of the stories in this book were partially funded through the Pioneers in Conservation grants program administered by my former employer, American Farmland Trust. www.farmland.org/programs/states/WA/PioneersinConservation.asp.

Chapter 2: Farmland—Why We Lose It and Where It Goes

1. Actually 52 percent according to "Major Uses of Land in the United States—Resources and Environment Report Summary," Ruben Lubowski, Shawn Buchholz, Alba Baez, and Michael Roberts, (USDA/Economic Research Service, Economic Information Bulletin #14, May 2006). www.ers.usda.gov/publications/EIB14/eib14_reportsummary.pdf. There were 922,095,840 acres in agriculture held by 2,204,792 farms reported in 2007. "Table 1, Historical Highlights," 2007 Census, Vol. 1, Chapter 1: U.S. National Level Data (USDA Census of Agriculture). www.agcensus.usda.gov/Publications/2007/Full_Report/Volume_1,_Chapter_1_US/st99_1_001_001.pdf. This acreage probably represents more like 75 percent of the nation's private lands. Also, keep in mind that Census of Agriculture data on land in agriculture does not include a substantial portion of the 258 million acres of public lands grazed by livestock producers under lease and permit with the U.S. Forest Service and the Bureau of Land Management. See the definition for "land in farms" in the 2007 U.S. Census of Agriculture, Appendix B at B-14. www.agcensus.usda.gov/Publications/2007/Full_Report/Volume_1,_Chapter_1_US/usv1.pdf.
2. There are about 2.2 million farm businesses (2007, Census of Agriculture). Total U.S. population in 2012 was 313,914,040 according to "Quick Facts: U.S. Census" (2012 Census Data, U.S. Census Bureau). quickfacts.census.gov/qfd/states/00000.html. Of course ownership of each of those farms is probably spread among multiple individuals so the actual percentage of the population with some kind of ownership interest in farm acreage is likely higher.
3. According to the 2007 USDA Census of Agriculture, total annual market value of agricultural products sold is over $297 billion. See "Table 1, Historical Highlights," Census of Agriculture 2007—U.S. National Data (USDA Census of Agriculture). www.agcensus.usda.gov/Publications/2007/Full_Report/Volume_1,_Chapter_1_US/st99_1_001_001.pdf. These are referred to as "farm gate" sales—or the

value received by the farmer for crops sold. Thus, these amounts do not reflect the massive value additions by processors and wholesalers nor the total economic and employment impact of American agriculture which is certainly many times greater.

4. This is so, despite what you may read in the popular press. "Want to Make More Than a Banker? Become a Farmer!," Stephen Gandel, *Time*, July 11, 2011, 38. www.time.com/time/magazine/article/0,9171,2080767,00.html. Our nation's farms are a great deal less "corporate" than most of us tend to believe. And our farmers are not usually wealthy people. The 2011 USDA–ERS projection was for total national net farm income to reach a record high of $94.7 billion. With 2.2 million farms in the U.S., this indicates an average net annual farm income of about $43,000 per farm. For intermediate and commercial farms, including non-family farms, the average projected net income was $81,200 for 2014. See projections in: "Average Farm Business Net Cash Income Expected to Decline in 2014" (USDA Economic Research Service. www.ers.usda.gov/topics/farm-economy/farm-sector-income-finances/farm-business-income.aspx).

5. The value of land and buildings represents, on average, 85 percent of a farm business's assets. "Trends in U.S. Farmland Values and Ownership," Cynthia Nickerson, Mitchell Morehart, Todd Kuethe, Jayson Beckmann, Jennifer Ifft, and Ryan Williams, Economic Information Bulletin #92 (USDA-Economic Research Service, February 2012) iii. www.ers.usda.gov/media/377487/eib92_2_.pdf.

6. Economists and real estate professionals use the term "highest and best use" to refer to that use of property that maximizes its economic return.

7. "Major Uses of Land in the United States, 2002," Resources & Environment–ERS Report, R. Lubowski, M Vesterby, S. Bucholz, A. Baez, M. Roberts (USDA Economic Research Service), www.ers.usda.gov/publications/eib-economic-information-bulletin/eib14.aspx.

8. Of course, if their purpose is to invest short-term and sell for development later, such a purchase might make perfect economic sense.

9. See Tables 2 and 8 of the 2007 Census of Agriculture (USDA Census of Agriculture 2007). www.agcensus.usda.gov/Publications/2007/Full_Report/Volume_1,_Chapter_1_US/usv1.pdf. This is obviously much less than one can expect for almost any other land use.

10. In 2007, the overall average farm size in the U.S. was 418 acres (ibid.).

11. "Table 8, Land," (ibid.).

12. Of course many are incorporated while remaining family owned and operated.

13. See "Structure and Finances of U.S. Family Farms: 2005 Family Farm Report," Robert Hoppe and David Banker, (USDA Economic Research Service, Economic Information Bulletin #12, May 2006). www.ers.usda.gov/publications/eib-economic-information-bulletin/eib12.aspx. In particular, see the chapter on "U.S. Farms: Numbers, Size, & Ownership." This varies over time. More recent incomes appear to have risen.

14. Ibid. See the chart on page 18.

15. In many parts of the country, farmland is taxed at its agricultural value rather than its fair market value.

16. Fixtures are improvements to the land that are sufficiently permanent that they must be sold with the land when the land sells.

17. See "Farmers by Age," Tables 49 and 63 (USDA Census of Agriculture 2007), www. agcensus.usda.gov/Publications/2007/Full_Report/usv1.pdf.

18. As of 2010, large-scale family farms and nonfamily farms account for 12 percent of U.S farms but 84 percent of the value of production. "Structure & Finances of U.S. Farms: Family Farm Report," Robert Hoppe and David Banker (USDA Economic Research Service, Economic Information Bulletin #66, July 2010). www.ers.usda. gov/media/184479/eib66_1_.pdf. In 2007, 38 percent of the nation's farmland was owned by non-farmer landlords. "Trends in U.S. Farmland Values and Ownership," Cynthia Nickerson, Mitchell Morehart, Todd Kuethe, Jason Beckman, Jennifer Ifft, and Ryan Williams (USDA Economic Research Service, Economic Information Bulletin # 92, Feb. 2012), 30, www.ers.usda.gov/media/377487/eib92_2_.pdf.

19. See "Hidden Costs of Industrial Agriculture," (Union of Concerned Scientists, August 24, 2008), www.ucsusa.org/food_and_agriculture/science_and_impacts/ impacts_industrial_agriculture/costs-and-benefits-of.html. Also see the substantial body of popular nonfiction that has been published recently, including: *The Omnivore's Dilemma: A Natural History of Four Meals*, Michael Pollan (Penguin, 2007); *What Matters?: Economics for a Renewed Commonwealth*, Wendell Berry (Counterpoint, 2010); *Food Inc.: A Participant Guide: How Industrial Food is Making Us Sicker, Fatter, and Poorer—And What You Can Do About It*, edited by Karl Weber (Public Affairs, 2009).

20. For a more complete description, See "Sustaining the Land for Sustainable Agriculture," Don Stuart, *American Farmland*, Winter 2004, 10 (American Farmland Trust).

21. While the U.S. still typically exports more food than it imports, trade surpluses are no longer certain. "Increasing Imports of Food Creating Trade Problems for U.S. Economy," *Wall Street Journal*, November 8, 2004, as republished by North Food Group, *Agribusiness Examiner*, 379, November 10, 2004. www.northfoodgroup.com/ index.php/market-news/87-us-food-imports-now-exceed-exports. This leaves us to contemplate the potential for a world in which the U.S. will become as dependent on international supplies of food as we are, today, for oil.

22. There is no known nationwide estimate of the farm value–market value differential. Non-agricultural factors do have significant impacts. And in some periods of time, nationwide industry earnings, on average, cannot support the market value of its land ownership. "Trends in U.S. Farmland Values and Ownership," Cynthia Nickerson, Mitchell Morehart, Todd Kuethe, Jason Beckman, Jennifer Ifft, and Ryan Williams (USDA Economic Research Service, Economic Information Bulletin # 92, Feb. 2012), 30. www.ers.usda.gov/media/377487/eib92_2_.pdf. The farm-rent to market value ratio had declined significantly over the years, with the impact more dramatic in some regions than in others (ibid. 5-6). Also see the discussion, ibid. 7-10. Estimates for my home state of Washington based on farmer participation in our state's current use tax system suggest that roughly 75 percent of the working farmland, statewide, may have a market value that exceeds its agricultural value. Compare Census of Agriculture farmland acreage with Washington State Department of Revenue current use property tax statistics: "Table 19: 2010 Valuation of Current Use Land by County Agricultural Timber, & Open Space Lands Ap-

proved for Current Use Assessment." dor.wa.gov/Content/AboutUs/StatisticsAnd Reports/2011/Property_Tax_Statistics_2011/default.aspx.

23. "The Burgeoning Backlog: A Report on the Maintenance Backlog in America's National Parks," (National Parks Conservation Association, May 2004). www.npca. org/assets/pdf/backlog.pdf.

24. See "Fact Sheet: Why Save Farmland," (American Farmland Trust, Farmland Information Center). www.farmlandinfo.org/why-save-farmland.

Chapter 3: Agriculture's Environmental Risks

1. "Irrigation and Water Use," (USDA Economic Research Service Briefing Room). webarchives.cdlib.org/sw1rf5mh0k/www.ers.usda.gov/Briefing/WaterUse.

2. About 18 percent. This includes about 3 percent that is grazed woodland. "2007 USDA Census of Agriculture," Tables 8, 9, 10, and 11 (USDA–updated December 2009). www.agcensus.usda.gov/Publications/2007/Full_Report/usv1.pdf.

3. "2008 Farm and Ranch Irrigation Survey," 2007 Census of Agriculture (USDA National Agriculture Statistics Service). www.agcensus.usda.gov/Publications/2007/Online_Highlights/Fact_Sheets/Practices/fris.pdf.

4. "2007 USDA Census of Agriculture–Farm Numbers, Demographics, Economics," (USDA National Agriculture Statistics Service). www.agcensus.usda.gov/Publications/2007/Online_Highlights/Custom_Summaries/Data_Comparison_Major_Crops.pdf.

5. "2007 USDA Census of Agriculture Fact Sheet–Fruit, Berries and Tree Nuts," (USDA). www.agcensus.usda.gov/Publications/2007/Online_Highlights/Fact_Sheets/Production/fbn.pdf.

6. See "General Information about the U.S. Wine Industry," (Winegrape Growers of America). www.winegrapegrowersofamerica.org/files/documents/Wine_Industry_Fact_Sheet_final.pdf. (Statistic is for 2008.)

7. "2007 Census of Agriculture, Specialty Crops," Vol. 2, Part 8, Table 3 (USDA, November 2009). www.agcensus.usda.gov/Publications/2007/Online_Highlights/Specialty_Crops/speccrop.pdf.

8. See "Data Sets, Organic Production," Table 3 (USDA Economic Research Service). www.ers.usda.gov/data-products/organic-production.aspx.

9. "Food Miles: Background and Marketing," (ATTRA, National Sustainable Agriculture Information Service, 2008). attra.ncat.org/attra-pub/summaries/summary.php?pub=281.

10. Food imports and exports are roughly equal in dollar value though not volume. "Food imports may force new food policies," Ken Meter, *Grist*, February 10, 2008. www.grist.org/article/us-about-to-become-net-food-importer.

11. The 2013 USDA—ERS projection was for average national net farm income of about $81,200. "Average Farm Business Net Cash Income Expected to Decline in 2014," (USDA Economic Research Service). www.ers.usda.gov/topics/farm-economy/farm-sector-income-finances/farm-business-income.aspx. Seventy percent of American farms have gross sales of under $250,000. "Structure and Finances of U.S. Family Farms: 2005 Family Farm Report," Robert Hoppe and David Banker (USDA Economic Research Service, Economic Information Bulletin #12, May

2006). www.ers.usda.gov/Publications/EIB12/. In particular, see chapter on "U.S. Farms: Numbers, Size, & Ownership."

12. USDA does also offer various forms of crop insurance, but none will ever remove the traditional uncertainties of farming. See the USDA Crop and Livestock and Insurance, tools and calculators webpage at: www.usda.gov/wps/portal/usda/usdahome?navid=CROP_LIVESTOCK_INSUR.

13. "Perspectives on U.S. Farm Debt," David Kohl, *Corn & Soybean Digest*, Road Warrior, May 21, 2013. cornandsoybeandigest.com/blog/perspectives-us-farm-debt.

14. E.g., in grass seed production.

15. Clean Water Act, 33 U.S.C. §1251 et seq. (1972). See the summary at the U.S. EPA website: www2.epa.gov/laws-regulations/summary-clean-water-act.

16. See "U.S. Vulnerable to E. Coli Outbreak Like the One in Europe," Richard Knox, (National Public Radio, Shots: Health News from NPR, June 7, 2011). www.npr.org/blogs/health/2011/06/07/137027459/u-s-vulnerable-to-e-coli-outbreak-like-the-one-in-europe.

17. U.S. Food Quality Protection Act of 1996 (FQPA): Public Law 104-170 (H.R. 1627). See the EPA summary www.epa.gov/pesticides/regulating/laws/fqpa.

18. Discussed at the EPA website www.epa.gov/opp00001/factsheets/ipm.htm. Also see the discussion at the American Farmland Trust website www.farmland.org/programs/environment/solutions/integrated-pest-management.asp.

19. The USDA/Natural Resources Conservation Service has developed and studied hundreds of highly-strategic conservation practices of this kind that can, when properly applied, essentially eliminate pollution. See the NRCS Field Office Technical Guide (FOTG) available at www.nrcs.usda.gov/wps/portal/nrcs/main/national/technical/fotg.

20. See "The Gulf of Mexico Dead Zone," Monica Bruckner, Microbial Life: Educational Resources (Montana State University), serc.carleton.edu/microbelife/topics/deadzone. "The Gulf's Growing Dead Zone," *Time*, Bryan Walsh, June 17, 2008. www.time.com/time/nation/article/0,8599,1815305,00.html.

21. See "Facing Facts in the Chesapeake Bay," Michelle Perez, September 2009, Environmental Working Group. www.ewg.org/news/news-releases/2009/09/08/facing-facts-chesapeake-bay.

22. See "Rearing Cattle Produces More Greenhouse Gasses than Driving Cars, UN Report Warns," UN News Centre, Nov. 29, 2006. www.un.org/apps/news/story.asp?newsID=20772&CR1=warning.

23. See "Wild Salmon Endangered by Pesticides," Vital Choice: Wild Seafood and Organics, Craig Weatherby, August 19, 2008. vitalchoice.com/shop/pc/articlesView.asp?id=750. See also note on: Washington Toxics Coalition v. E.P.A., 413 F.3d 1024 (9th Cir. 2005) by Lewis and Clark Law School. www.elawreview.org/summaries/environmental_quality/clean_water_act/washington_toxics_coalition_v.html.

24. See "WR-2 Agriculture's Impacts on Wetlands and Riparian Areas–A Farmer's Guide to Agriculture and Water Quality Issues: Fact Sheets," (USDA, US EPA, NC State University Cooperative Extension, January 2004). www.cals.ncsu.edu/wq/wqp/wetlands/factsheets/FactsheetWR2.pdf.

25. See the general discussion at the website of the Union of Concerned Scientists, "Food & Agriculture–Industrial Agriculture." www.ucsusa.org/food_and_agriculture/our-failing-food-system/industrial-agriculture.

26. Other than in Minnesota. "Trumpeter Swan, Basis for Listing," (Minnesota Department of Natural Resources). www.dnr.state.mn.us/rsg/profile.html?action=element Detail&selectedElement=ABNJB02030.

27. This according to Martha Jordan of the Washington Swan Working group, a respected swan advocate who is well-known locally as the "swan lady."

28. See the Trumpeter Swan Society's website: www.swansociety.org and the site of the Washington Swan Working Group: www.swansociety.org/wswg/washington.htm.

29. The National Parks Foundation had funds for mitigation resulting from the removal of old dams on the Elwha River near Port Angeles, WA—also along the swans' Pacific Flyway.

30. The easement is today held by Capitol Land Trust in Olympia, WA. American Farmland Trust helped the Trumpeter Swan Society in the development of the easement transaction. More about the Gordon Dairy project at: www.farmland. org/programs/campaign/voices/wildlife-conservation-washington-dairy.asp.

31. "Global Trends: The Trend Toward Urbanization Appears Unstoppable," Guiles Keating, Oct. 14, 2010 (Credit Suisse). www.credit-suisse.com/us/en/news-and-expertise/ news/economy/global-trends.article.html/article/pwp/news-and-expertise/2010/10/ en/the-trend-toward-urbanization-appears-unstoppable.html.

32. "Agriculture's Waning Influence in Washington Hinders Farmers," Amy Mayer (National Public Radio, June 27, 2013). www.npr.org/2013/06/27/196133577/ agricultures-weakening-influence-in-washington-frustrates-farmers.

33. See the excellent article on the breadth of the Fourteenth Amendment at: "Rights of the People: Individual Freedoms and the Bill of Rights," Chapter 11: Equal Protection of the Laws (U.S. Department of State—InfoUSA). usinfo.org/enus/ government/overview/equal.html. Also see the discussion of the constitutional meaning of "discrimination" in: "Equal Protection of Law: Classifications and Civil Rights," Mark Stevens, Lt. Col. USMC (Ret.), Assistant Professor of Criminology, CA State University (June 25, 2003).

34. See, e.g., *Baker v. Carr*, 396 U.S. 186, 217 (1962).

35. See Swift Boat Veterans for Truth 2004 advertisement "John Kerry–Sellout" (2004), YouTube. www.youtube.com/watch?v=phqOuEhg9yE.

36. E.g., Clean Water Act section 402(l)(1) (33 U.S.C. 1342(l)(1)), relating to discharges composed entirely of return flows from irrigated agriculture; section 404(f)(1)(A) (33 U.S.C.1344(f)(1)(A)), relating to discharges of dredged or fill materials from normal farming, silviculture, and ranching activities, such as plowing, seeding, cultivating, minor drainage, harvesting for the production of food, fiber, and forest products, or upland soil and water conservation practices; section 404(f)(1)(C) (33 U.S.C.2 1344(f)(1)(C)), relating to discharges of dredged or fill materials for the purpose of construction or maintenance of farm or stock ponds or irrigation ditches and maintenance of drainage ditches; section 404(f)(1)(E) (33 U.S.C.1344(f)(1)(E)), relating to discharges of dredged or fill materials for the purpose of construction or maintenance of farm roads or forest roads or temporary roads for moving mining

equipment in accordance with best management practices. See EPA website water. epa.gov/lawsregs/guidance/wetlands/cwaag.cfm.

37. CERCLA (section 103) exempts application or handling of agricultural pesticides. "Releases Excluded from CERCLA Reporting," (US EPA). www.epa.gov/osweroe1/content/reporting/faq_excl.htm#53.

38. See "Air Quality Issues and Animal Agriculture: A Primer," Claudia Copeland (Congressional Research Service, Report for Congress, July 20, 2012), 22ff, CRS 7-5700. www.nationalaglawcenter.org/wp-content/uploads/assets/crs/RL32948.pdf

39. A quick look at the nature and diversity of the issues upon which farm groups take a negative position in their annual Congressional or legislative efforts is enough to illustrate this point. See, e.g., the American Farm Bureau Federation's list of policy issues online at: www.fb.org/index.php?action=issues.home. Or take a look at similar legislative tracking lists for some state-level farm organizations. E.g., see the Washington State Farm Bureau's legislative tracking lists for the current (2011) Legislative session listed with their periodic "Legisletters" www.wsfb.com/issues/legisletter. This is further confirmed by scanning through the current American Farm Bureau Federation's "2013 AFBF Policy Book." www.texasfarmbureau.org/PolicyBook/AFBF%20Policy%202013.pdf.

40. As a former commercial salmon fisherman, I saw this in the fishing industry as well. As salmon runs collapsed and catches diminished, fishermen were forced to adapt by entering multiple fisheries, buying larger boats, increasing efficiency, taking greater risks, and by marketing direct—just like farmers. There are still a great many highly successful commercial salmon fishermen today. But many quit the industry in frustration.

41. Migratory Bird Treaty Act: 16 U.S.C. 703-712 (1918 as amended). www.fws.gov/le/USStatutes/MBTA.pdf.

42. The Puget Sound Gillnet Salmon Commission today is deeply involved in the marketing of local salmon. See their website www.soundcatch.org.

43. See generally: "Water: Non-point Success Stories–Changes in Irrigation Practices Reduce Turbidity in the Lower Yakima River" (U.S. Environmental Protection Agency, Office of Water, September 2005). water.epa.gov/polwaste/nps/success319/wa_yakima.cfm.

Chapter 4: Opportunities Lost When Farms Disappear

1. There are clearly also social, cultural, economic, and other losses when farms disappear. But, since this book deals mostly with environmental issues, we will focus on those.

2. See "The Suitability, Viability, Needs, and Economic Future of Pierce County Agriculture: Phase I Report Responding to Questions Posed by Pierce County Council Resolution R2004-105s," Don Stuart (American Farmland Trust, 2004) www.co.pierce.wa.us/DocumentCenter/View/2910.

3. 2007 National Resources Inventory, Table 13, Sources of Newly Developed Land (USDA/Natural Resources Conservation Service). www.nrcs.usda.gov/wps/portal/nrcs/detail/national/technical/?cid=stelprdb1083372.

4. See, for example, the "Puget Sound Salmon Recovery Plan" of the Puget Sound Partnership. www.psp.wa.gov/SR_map.php.

5. See "Mixed Effects of Landscape Structure and Farming Practice on Bird Diversity," Christina Fischer, Andreas Flohre, Lars Clement, Peter Batary, Wolfgang Weisser, Teja Tscharntke, Carston Thies (*Agriculture, Ecosystems and Environment*, No. 141, April 2011) 119-125. www.sciencedirect.com/science/article/pii/S0167880911000594. "The importance of agricultural landscapes as key nesting habitat for the American Black Duck in maritime Canada," David Lieske, Bruce Pollard, Mark Gloutney, Randy Milton, Kevin Connor, Randy Dibbee, Glen Parsons, and David Howerter, (Waterbird Society, August 12, 2012). www.bioone.org/doi/abs/10.1675/063.035.0403. "Biodiversity conservation and agricultural sustainability: Towards a new paradigm of 'ecoagriculture' landscapes," Sara J. Scherr and Jeffrey McNeely (*Philosophic Transactions of the Royal Society–Biological Sciences*, Vol. 363, No. 1491), 477-494. rstb.royalsocietypublishing.org/content/363/1491/477. full.

6. According to the USDA, in the period 1954 to 2002, 66 percent of wetland conversions in the U.S. were due to agriculture. See "Chapter 2.3: Wetlands Status and Trends," LeRoy Hansen, *Agriculture Resources and Environmental Indicators*, 2006 Edition (USDA Economic Research Service, Economic Information Bulletin #16, July 2006).

7. Ibid. Urban uses have, more recently, replaced agriculture as the chief cause of wetland losses—and agriculture has become the major source of conversion back to wetlands.

8. *Making Mitigation Work: The Report of the Mitigation that Works Forum* (WA Department of Ecology, Publication #08-06-018, December 2008), see especially Recommendation 2–Watershed Approach. www.ecy.wa.gov/pubs/0806018.pdf.

9. The average total distance traveled by food in the U.S. appears to be 6,760 km (4,200 miles). The production of food, however, has the much larger total climate impact. See "Food-Miles and the Relative Climate Impacts of Food Choices in the United States," Christopher Weber and H. Scott Matthews, *Environmental Science and Technology*, 2008, 42, 3508-3513 (Carnegie Mellon University, March 14, 2008). www.foodpolitics.com/wp-content/uploads/food_miles_climate_impacts. pdf.

10. In recent years the U.S. has moved between being a net importer and a net exporter of food. See "U.S. to Become Net Food Importer," Doug Pibel, *Yes! Magazine*, May 5, 2005. www.yesmagazine.org/issues/media-that-set-us-free/1238.

11. See "Local Food Movement: The Lure of the 100-Mile Diet," Margot Roosevelt, *Time,* June 11, 2006. www.time.com/time/magazine/article/0,9171,1200783-1,00. html.

12. Conservation districts are small, local, special purpose governments that help private landowners voluntarily implement good land conservation stewardship.

13. "Electronic Field Office Technical Guide (EFOTG)," (USDA Natural Resources Conservation Service). www.nrcs.usda.gov/technical/efotg/. Also see *The Farm as Natural Habitat: Reconnecting Food Systems with Ecosystems*, edited by Dana L. Jackson and Laura L. Jackson (Washington, DC: Island Press, 2002).

14. Safe Drinking Water Act, 88 Stat. 1660 (1974), 42 U.S.C. sec. 300 ff.
15. Watershed Agricultural Council, 33195 State Highway 10, Walton, NY 13856, (607) 865-7790. www.nycwatershed.org.
16. See "American Boondoggle: Fixing the 2012 Farm Bill," Betty Goodwin, Vincent Smith, Daniel Sumner, (Washington, DC: American Enterprise Institute). www. aei.org/files/2011/11/03/-americanboondoggle_174848782104.pdf. Also see "Want to Make More than a Banker? Become a Farmer!" *Time*, Stephen Gandel, July 10, 2011. See, e.g. "Overregulation Remains a Top Issue for Agriculture," *Western Farm Press*, April 15, 2011. westernfarmpress.com/government/overregulation-remains-top-issue-agriculture.

Chapter 5: Voluntary Incentives—Pro and Con

1. See the USDA/NRCS Farm Bill website at: www.nrcs.usda.gov/programs/farm-bill/2008/index.html. Also see the USDA/FSA website for CRP www.fsa.usda.gov/FSA/webapp?area=home&subject=copr&topic=crp and for CREP www.fsa.usda.gov/FSA/webapp?area=home&subject=copr&topic=cep.
2. The 2014 Farm Bill incorporated the old Wildlife Habitat Incentives Program (WHIP) into EQIP, which now also helps pay the cost of restoring habitat and managing for the protection of wildlife.
3. See, for example: "A Benefits Assessment of Water Pollution Control Programs Since 1972: Part 1—The Benefits of Point Source Controls for Conventional Pollutants in Rivers and Streams—Final Report," U.S. Environmental Protection Agency, January 2000, prepared for EPA by the Research Triangle Institute. water.epa.gov/lawsregs/lawsguidance/cwa/316b/upload/2000_04_17_economics_assessment.pdf.
4. NRCS tracks unmet demand, but only for those who unsuccessfully apply for program assistance. Even measured in this way, demand for EQIP funding, for example, is still three to four times supply. It is estimated that only about 10 percent of landowners have actually implemented practices on their land because the funding is inadequate. See "Improving America's Conservation Efforts," USDA Report, sec. 3 Expand Economic Incentives for Conservation, 62, 63. www.nrcs.usda.gov/Internet/FSE_DOCUMENTS/nrcs143_012459.pdf.
5. See "Reconsidering 'Crowding Out' of Intrinsic Motivation from Conservation Incentives," Stephanie Stern, *Critical Issues in Environmental Taxation* (Chicago-Kent College of Law, 2008). papers.ssrn.com/sol3/papers.cfm?abstract_id=1464982.
6. See "Use of Penalties and Rewards in Agri-Environmental Policy," Yuki Yano and David Blandford (Pennsylvania State University–Department of Agricultural Economics and Rural Sociology, 2008). ageconsearch.umn.edu/bitstream/36873/2/Yano_Blandford.pdf. That NRCS struggles with "conservation compliance" under farm bill commodity programs also suggests the problem, see "A Fair Farm Bill for Conservation," (Institute for Agricultural and Trade Policy, July 2007). www.iatp.org/files/258_2_99437.pdf. One symptom of this is also producers' inclination to "game" the system: "The Pursuit of Efficiency and Its Unintended Consequences: Contract Withdrawals in the Environmental Quality Incentives Program," Andrea Cattanao, *Applied Economic Perspectives and Policy*, Vol. 25, No. 2, 449–469 (Agricultural and Applied Economics Association). aepp.oxfordjournals.org/content/25/2/449.full.

7. See generally, ibid.

8. There has been a good deal of writing on the issue of incentives versus regulations—much of it driven by self-interested parties. But, for an interesting set of case study comparisons, See "Regulatory Policy vs. Economic Incentives," (Environmental Literary Council, 2008). www.enviroliteracy.org/article.php/1329.html.

9. See "What is Nonpoint Source Pollution?" U.S. Environmental Protection Agency. water.epa.gov/polwaste/nps/whatis.cfm.

Chapter 6: Regulations—Pro and Con

1. 33 U.S.C. §1251 et sec. (1972).

2. 42 U.S.C. § 7401 et sec. (1970).

3. 16 U.S.C. § 1531 et sec (1973).

4. 16 U.S.C. Ch. 31 (1972).

5. See, e.g., "The Clean Water Act after 37 Years: Recommitting to the Protection of the Nation's Waters," Statement of Wade T. Najjum, Assistant Inspector General for Program Evaluation, U.S. EPA Office of Inspector General, Testimony before the U.S. House Transportation Committee, Oct. 15, 2009. www.epa.gov/oig/reports/2010/FinalStatementofWadeNajjum-EPAOIG.pdf.

6. The 9th Circuit opinion in the case lays out an interesting model for how dairy farms might be regulated. *Community Association for Restoration of the Environment v. Henry Bosma Dairy*, 305 F.3d 943 (9th Cir. 2002). See the law review comment of the same title in *Environmental Law* online (Lewis and Clark Law School). www.elawreview.org/summaries/environmental_quality/clean_water_act/community_association_for_rest.html.

7. RCW 90.64 (1998). apps.leg.wa.gov/rcw/default.aspx?cite=90.64.

8. Most states, and the federal government, have Administrative Procedures Acts which require open public processes be used in the adoption of regulations. For example, See U.S. Administrative Procedures Act, 5 U.S.C. 500 et sec. and Washington Administrative Procedures Act, RCW Ch. 34.05. apps.leg.wa.gov/rcw/default.aspx?cite=34.05&full=true.

9. For a discussion of this distinction, See *Leocal v. Ashcroft*, 543 U.S. 1, (2004).

10. See "When is Strict Criminal Liability Just?" Kenneth Simons, *Journal of Criminal Law and Criminology*, Vol. 87, No. 4 (Northwestern University School of Law, 1997). scholarlycommons.law.northwestern.edu/cgi/viewcontent.cgi?article=6932&context=jclc.

11. Note that EPA's own website on preventing nonpoint pollution focuses almost entirely on voluntary measures. water.epa.gov/polwaste/nps/outreach/point1.cfm.

12. www.ruckelshauscenter.wsu.edu/projects/caop.html.

13. Washington SB 5248 (2007).

14. Washington SB 6520 (2007).

15. See Washington ESHB 1886, 2011 Regular Session. Also see "A Framework for Stewardship: Final Report of the William D. Ruckelshaus Center on the Work of the Agriculture and Critical Areas Committee," William D, Ruckelshaus Center, October 2010. ruckelshauscenter.wsu.edu/documents/Ag_CA_Final_Report_for_web.pdf.

16. Technically, "pollution" is only present when certain chemical constituents are present in amounts that are considered harmful—or in "excess." Hence the dictum: "The solution to pollution is dilution."
17. E.g., passage of the Clean Water Act, Clean Air Act, Endangered Species Act, and Marine Mammal Protection Act in the early 1970s.
18. "The Gulf of Mexico Dead Zone," Monica Bruckner, *Microbial Life* (Montana State University). See note 45, Ch. 3.
19. "Summary of Findings: Assessment of the Effects of Conservation Protection for Cultivated Crop Land in the Great Lakes Region" (USDA/Natural Resources Conservation Service, September 2011). www.nrcs.usda.gov/Internet/FSE_DOCUMENTS/stelprdb1045481.pdf.
20. Sweet Grass Farm. www.sgfbeef.com/contact.htm.
21. KWIAHT Center for the Historical Ecology of the Salish Sea. www.kwiaht.org.

Chapter 7: Choosing Between Incentives and Regulations

1. See the excellent text on metrics: *Metrics 2.0: Creating Scorecards for High-Performance Work Teams and Organizations*, Ruth A. Huwe (Santa Barbara: Praeger, 2010).
2. Michigan's Agricultural Environmental Assurance Program (MAEAP). www.maeap. org.
3. Some state agencies function somewhat like this. See, e.g., "The Joint Natural Resources Cabinet." www.rco.wa.gov/documents/gsro/1999StatewideStrategyRec oversalmon.pdf.
4. See Michigan Act No. 1, Public Acts of 2011, SB122, March 8, 2011. www. legislature.mi.gov/(S(qzlhso550xbrn1yewrddsa2c))/mileg.aspx?page=GetObject& objectname=2011-SB-0122.
5. See the MAEAP fact sheet: "MAEAP—Get the Facts," www.maeap.org/uploads/ files/Pubs/MAEAP-Fact%20Sheet-January2012.pdf.
6. "Financial Costs and Environmental Outcomes of the Michigan Agriculture Environmental Assurance Program (MAEAP)," Carrie Lynn Vollmer-Sanders, *Journal of Soil and Water Conservation*, March-April 2011, Vol. 66, No. 2., www.jswconline. org/content/66/2/122.full.pdf+html.
7. See *Swinomish Tribal Community and Washington Environmental Council v. Western Washington Growth Management Hearings Board*, et al. (2007). This was reported in: "Property owners prevail in Supreme Court–GMA does not require mandatory buffers," *Kitsap-Peninsula Business Journal*, Oct. 8, 2007. www.citizenreviewonline. org/oct_07/25/buffers2.html.
8. *Lucas v. South Carolina Coastal Council*, 505 U.S. 1003 (1992).
9. *Agins v. City of Tiburon*, 447 U.S. 255 (1980).
10. See the remarkable video: "Man-Made Disaster at Bird's Point Levee," www.youtube. com/watch?v=iT78JC9WBLQ.
11. E.g., "Missouri House Speaker Steve Tilley: Flood Cairo, Illinois to Save Farmland," *Huffington Post Chicago* updated June 28, 2011: www.huffingtonpost. com/2011/04/28/missouri-house-speaker-st_n_855139.html.
12. For the current evidence of salmon declines, see, e.g., the website of the Washington Department of Fish and Wildlife. For example, see the listings of threatened

or endangered Chinook at: fortress.wa.gov/dfw/score/score/species/chinook. jsp?species=Chinook.

13. The width of the needed buffers is a matter of intense debate. Is it acceptable to make any economic use of the vegetation that grows there (e.g., for managed grazing, selective harvest, etc.)? Do these buffers start at the water's edge or must they also include the entire natural flood plain? This would eliminate much of the region's agriculture and several cities. The NRCS Conservation Reserve Enhancement Program (CREP) will pay to lease streamside salmon buffers up to 150' wide (sometimes more) depending on the anticipated height of native trees in the area. Should there be a smaller minimum width or does it depend on the circumstances?

14. There has been considerable study of the environmental impacts of riparian salmon buffers. See, e.g., "Riparian Buffers: Function, Management and Economic Implications for Agriculture," Jon Johnson, James Dobrowolksi and Carolyn Henri (Washington State University Department of Natural Resources, June 2009). puyallup. wsu.edu/agbuffers/pdf/bufferposter.pdf. Also see the Washington State University website on this issue: www.puyallup.wsu.edu/agbuffers/index.html.

15. After a three-year stay on development of local "critical areas ordinances" required under Washington's Growth Management Act, in 2011 the Governor signed a bill to formalize a hard-fought agriculture–environmental negotiation and help resolve what is required. Washington ESHB 1886 (2011 Session). apps.leg.wa.gov/billinfo/ summary.aspx?year=2011&bill=1886.

16. See, generally, the Washington Department of Ecology's website on SEPA. www. ecy.wa.gov/programs/sea/sepa/lawandrule.htm.

17. See, generally, the Washington Department of Ecology's website on SMA. www. ecy.wa.gov/programs/sea/sma/st_guide/intro.html.

18. Pollution impacts of urbanization on salmon in Puget Sound, for example, include: copper from brake pads; PCBs still found in transformers, plastics, insulations, adhesives, paint; PBDEs from flame retardants in sofa cushions, computers, wire insulation and drapes; petroleum dripping from motor vehicles; and a host of other sources. "Pollution lower, risks remain for marine life," Craig Welch, *Seattle Times*, May 29, 2011. 1. seattletimes.com/html/localnews/2015176223_stormwater29m. html.

Chapter 8: Taxes and Government Spending

1. "Fact Sheet: Cost of Community Services" (American Farmland Trust). www. farmlandinfo.org/cost-community-services-studies. Also see "A Meta-Analysis of Cost of Community Services Studies," Matthew Kotchen and Stanley Schulte, July 25, 2008. www.farmlandinfo.org/documents/37969/Meta-analysis_COCS.pdf. This conference paper analyzed 125 such studies and provides citations.

2. The study method for COCS studies is laid out in detail in "Cost of Community Services Studies: Making the Case for Conservation," American Farmland Trust, 2002. This publication is available for sale at: secure2.convio.net/aft/site/ Ecommerce?VIEW_PRODUCT=true&product_id=1021&store_id=1081&JSer vSessionIdr004=f5jmbeq5h5.app246a.

3. "Fact Sheet: Cost of Community Services" (American Farmland Trust).

4. Agricultural support businesses like food processors, farm equipment dealers, farm supply stores, etc., are included among the commercial or industrial land uses in these studies.

5. In communities that are already "blessed" with a good deal of commercial, industrial, and residential development, agriculture's contribution to county revenue, in percentage terms, may be quite small.

6. "Fact Sheet: Cost of Community Services" (American Farmland Trust).

7. See "The Cost of Growth in Washington State," Eben Fodor, Fodor & Associates (Columbia Public Interest Policy Institute, October 2000). www.fodorandassociates. com/Reports/COG_WA_2000_Exec_Sum.pdf.

8. The conservative website www.usgovernmentrevenue.com estimates that of the roughly $5.4 trillion Americans pay in taxes in 2013, about half is paid to the federal government, about 30 percent goes to the states, and the final 20 percent is paid in local taxes.

9. Just for scale, the typical annual $11.4 billion paid out in federal farm subsidies represents about one fourth of one percent of the $3.5 trillion in current federal spending. It also compares in scale with U.S. oil and gas subsidies. See "As Oil Industry Fights a Tax, It Reaps Subsidies," David Kocieniewski, *New York Times*, July 3, 2010. www.nytimes.com/2010/07/04/business/04bptax.html.

10. Some significant state expenditures (such as on transportation) are much higher, on a per-capita basis, in rural areas.

11. "Agricultural Trade Multipliers" (USDA Economic Research Service). www.ers. usda.gov/data/trademultiplier/calculator.aspx. Also see "Using Multipliers to Measure Economic Impacts," (California Economic Strategy Panel, 2002). www.pdfio. com/k-1122796.html.

12. "As Oil Industry Fights a Tax, It Reaps Subsidies," David Kocieniewski, *New York Times*, July 3, 2010. Oil industry subsidies from the federal government have been estimated to average roughly $10 billion annually: "Fossil Fuel Subsidies in the U.S.," (Oil Change International). priceofoil.org/fossil-fuel-subsidies. Also see "Analytical Perspectives: Budget of the United States Government, Fiscal Year 2014," (U.S. Office of Management and Budget). www.whitehouse.gov/omb/budget/analytical_ perspectives. According to *Harpers* Index, "The estimated value of government subsidies that will go to the oil and gas industries between now [November 2011] and 2015: $78,155,000,000." From: "The Thom Hartman Program," (*Harpers* Index, November 27, 2011). www.thomhartmann.com/forum/2011/11/harpers-index. That amounts to $19.5 billion annually.

13. "Breaking News…Insurance Industry Report Says Its Billions in Medicare Subsidies Should be Continued," (National Committee to Preserve Social Security and Medicare, September 15, 2009). www.ncpssm.org/EntitledtoKnow/year/2009/ month/9#.Udni-r7n_IU.

14. "Boeing-Airbus WTO Dispute: The EU Challenge to U.S. Government Subsidies to Boeing," European Commission at Defense-Aerospace.com, March 22, 2007. www.defense-aerospace.com/article-view/feature/80524/eu-states-its-case-in-airbus_boeing-dispute.html.

15. See www.nature.org/ourinitiatives/regions/northamerica/unitedstates/washington/ explore/farming-for-wildlife.xml.

16. This is the rationale behind, for example, the Uniform Commercial Code. See "Uniform Commercial Code (UCC)," Duke University School of Law, 2013. www. law.duke.edu/lib/researchguides/ucc.

17. See generally: *Nothing Like it in the World: The Men Who Built the Transcontinental Railroad, 1863-1869,* Steven Ambrose (New York: Simon & Schuster, Touchstone Books, 2001).

18. See, e.g., the discussion of growth management laws in: "Policy 9: Promote Intellectually Honest Public Discussion of Growth Management Policy, Environmental Regulation, and Property Rights" (Citizens Alliance of Property Rights). www. proprights.org/capr_policy9.php.

19. See, generally, *The Big Sort: Why the Clustering of Like-Minded America is Tearing Us Apart*, Bill Bishop (Boston: Houghton Mifflin Company, 2008).

Chapter 9: Environmental Markets

1. Portions of this chapter were based on "How Ecosystem Markets Can Transform Agriculture and Protect the Environment," Don Stuart (American Farmland Trust). www.farmland.org/documents/HowEcosystemMarketsCanTransformAgriculture-NEW.pdf.

2. According to the U.S. Census Bureau, the U.S. population is expected to grow to between 423 million and 458 million by 2050. See "U.S. Population Projections 2000-2050," Jennifer Ortman and Christine Guarneri (U.S Census Bureau). www. census.gov/population/projections/files/analytical-document09.pdf. As of mid-2013 the nation's population was estimated to be approaching 315 million. The U.S. population was about 132 million in 1940. See table: "Historical national population estimates, July 1, 1900–1999" (U.S. Census Bureau). www.census.gov/population/estimates/nation/popclockest.txt.

3. About one-half of the total U.S. land base. The concept discussed, here, originated with the late Vim Wright, a University of Washington professor of environmental studies and respected environmentalist.

4. For a detailed explanation, see "Guide to Environmental Markets for Farmers & Ranchers," Don Stuart and Dennis Canty (American Farmland Trust, 2010). www. farmland.org/environmentalmarkets.

5. See the materials collected online at the USDA Office of Environmental Markets. www.fs.fed.us/environmentalservices/OEM/index.shtml.

6. Note that there are significant environmental markets that are not driven by regulation—e.g., the current U.S. market for carbon is almost entirely driven by voluntary demand from firms and institutions seeking to improve the "green" market appeal of their products, services, or stocks.

7. See the Environmental Protection Agency's websites on acid rain at: www.epa.gov/acidrain/reducing/index.html and at: www.epa.gov/airmarkets/progsregs/arp/index.html.

8. See Chapter 2, "Guide to Environmental Markets for Farmers & Ranchers," Don Stuart and Dennis Canty (American Farmland Trust). www.farmland.org/documents/GuidetoEnvironmentalMarketsforFarmersandRanchers.pdf.

9. Ibid. Also see www.farmland.org/environmentalmarkets.

10. See Chapter 9, note 1, this volume.

11. See "Issue Up Close: Sustaining our remaining wetlands for people, fish and wildlife" (Washington State Department of Ecology, November 2006). www.ecy.wa.gov/pubs/0601009.pdf.

12. "Protecting America's Wetlands: A Fair, Flexible, and Effective Approach" (White House Office on Environmental Policy, Aug. 24, 1993). www.wetlands.com/fed/aug93wet.htm. "Advance Notice of Proposed Rulemaking on the Clean Water Act Regulatory Definition of 'Waters of the United States,'" 68 Fed. Reg. 199 (Jan. 15, 2003). See "Reforms needed in wetlands regulatory policy" (The National Academies, June 26, 2001). www8.nationalacademies.org/onpinews/newsitem.aspx?recordid=10134.

13. 33 U.S.C. §1251 et seq. (1972).

14. "Reforms needed in wetlands regulatory policy" (Washington, DC: The National Academies, June 26, 2001). www8.nationalacademies.org/onpinews/newsitem.aspx?recordid=10134.

15. "Compensatory Mitigation—Wetlands" (U.S. Environmental Protection Agency). water.epa.gov/lawsregs/guidance/wetlands/wetlandsmitigation_index.cfm.

16. Ibid.

17. "Guide to Environmental Markets for Farmers & Ranchers," Don Stuart and Dennis Canty (American Farmland Trust, 2010). Link for this and other materials relevant to this chapter at: www.farmland.org/environmentalmarkets.

18. Evidenced by creation of the new USDA Office of Environmental Markets. www.fs.fed.us/environmentalservices/OEM/index.shtml. In the fall of 2010, American Farmland Trust did a series of workshops on environmental markets in the Northwest and there was a good deal of interest among farmers and agriculture conservation stewardship professionals in the region.

Chapter 10: Local Food, Consumer Influence, and Farmer Privacy

1. About 0.4 percent. There are $1.2 billion in direct sales versus $297 billion in total market value of agricultural products sold. USDA Census of Agriculture 2007, Table 1. www.agcensus.usda.gov/Publications/2007/Full_Report/Volume_1,_Chapter_1_US/st99_1_002_002.pdf.

2. See table "National Count of Farmers Market Directory Listing Graph: 1994-2013," USDA agricultural marketing service. www.ams.usda.gov/AMSv1.0/ams.fetchTemplateData.do?template=TemplateS&leftNav=WholesaleandFarmersMarkets&page=WFMFarmersMarketGrowth&description=Farmers%20Market%20Growth&acct=frmrdirmkt.

3. See generally "The increasing role of direct marketing and farmers markets for western U.S. producers," Dawn Thilmany and Phil Watson, *Western Economics Forum*, April 2004, 19. ageconsearch.umn.edu/bitstream/27982/1/03020019.pdf.

4. See "Table 2: Market Value of Agricultural Products Sold" (USDA Census of Agriculture). www.agcensus.usda.gov/Publications/2007/Full_Report/Volume_1,_Chapter_1_US/st99_1_002_002.pdf.

5. For example, the percentage of the total food budget spent by residents in the Puget Sound area of Washington State on food grown in the twelve counties that surround

Puget Sound is currently estimated by local food advocates to be under 1 percent. If that were to increase to 5 percent, the change would more than double gross farm sales in the area. Such a change, especially combined with green demand, could have a dramatic effect on the local agriculture industry and on its environmental performance. According to the U.S. Census Bureau (see table for WA counties at: quickfacts.census.gov/qfd/states/53000.html), the twelve Puget Sound counties had a total 2012 population of 4,645,000. Average spending on food per person in the U.S. is $6,458 annually. "Consumer Expenditures 2011" (U.S. Bureau of Labor Statistics). www.bls.gov/news.release/cesan.nr0.htm. Therefore, the annual Puget Sound area food budget is about $30 billion; 4 percent of this is about $1.2 billion. According to the 2007 Census of Agriculture, total market value of crops sold grown in these twelve counties was about $1.1 billion. See the county profiles for Washington at: www.agcensus.usda.gov/Publications/2007/Online_Highlights/County_Profiles/Washington/index.asp. In an area like San Francisco, with a local "foodshed" defined to be food grown in a 100-mile radius of the city, the outcome might be somewhat less dramatic but still significant. See "Think Globally—Eat Locally: San Francisco Foodshed Assessment," Ed Thompson, Aletha Marie Harper, and Sibella Kraus (American Farmland Trust, 2008). www.farmland.org/programs/states/ca/Feature%20Stories/documents/ThinkGloballyEatLocally-FinalReport8-23-08.pdf.

6. Urban food groups involved in the farm bill debate include: Brooklyn Food Coalition, brooklynfoodcoalition.org/about-the-coalition; Community Food Security Coalition (national), www.foodsecurity.org/policy.html; California Food & Justice Coalition, cafoodjustice.org; Indianapolis Food, Farm, & Family Coalition, www.indyfoodfarmfamily.org/getinvolved-farmbill.html; Food Systems Network NYC, www.foodsystemsnyc.org/articles/farm-bill-march-2011; Northwest Farm Bill Action Group, www.nwfoodfight.org/farmbill.

7. Robert Lackey, a fisheries biologist with Oregon State University and with the National Health and Environmental Effects Research Laboratory, argues that there is a direct connection between declines in salmon runs and growth in human populations. More on Lackey's research at: oregonstate.edu/dept/fw/lackey/CurrentResearch.htm.

8. See "How does eating locally grown food help the environment?" EarthTalk, *E/The Environmental Magazine*, republished on About.com. environment.about.com/od/greenlivingdesign/a/locally_grown.htm.

9. www.salmonsafe.org.

10. www.fishfriendlyfarming.org.

11. www.foodalliance.org.

12. www.localharvest.org.

13. foodalliance.org/client-search.

14. See the chart published with the article "Factory Food," Hanna Fairfield, *New York Times*, April 10, 2010 www.nytimes.com/imagepages/2010/04/04/business/04metrics_g.html?ref=business.

15. www.wilcoxfarms.com.

16. www.certifiedhumane.org.

17. Salmon-Safe is administered in the Northwest by Stewardship Partners. www.stewardshippartners.org/programs/salmon-safe-puget-sound.
18. NORPAC. www.norpac.com/about.php.
19. SYSCO. www.sysco.com.
20. Tillamook. www.tillamook.com.
21. "Insights by Goldie: Tillamook Bans rGBH," Goldie Caughlin (PCC Natural Markets, April 2005). www.pccnaturalmarkets.com/sc/0504/goldie.html.
22. "How Big Brands Can Help Save Biodiversity," Jason Clay, World Wildlife Fund (TED Talks, July 2010). www.ted.com/talks/jason_clay_how_big_brands_can_save_biodiversity.html.
23. This originated in U.S. law in *MacPherson v. Buick Motor Co.*, 217 N.Y. 382, 111 N.E. 1050 (1916).
24. From 41 percent in 1900 to under 2 percent today. "The 20th Century Transformation of U.S. Agriculture and Farm Policy," Carolyn Dimitri, Anne Effland, and Neilson Conklin (USDA Economic Research Service, Economic Information Bulletin #3, June 2005). www.ers.usda.gov/publications/eib-economic-information-bulletin/eib3.aspx#.U1acgVeN5mY.
25. About 0.4 percent. There are $1.2 billion in direct sales versus $297 billion in total market value of agricultural products sold. USDA Census of Agriculture 2007, Table 1.www.agcensus.usda.gov/Publications/2007/Full_Report/Volume_1,_Chapter_1_US/st99_1_002_002.pdf.
26. See the 2013 American Farm Bureau Federation Policy Book www.texasfarmbureau.org/PolicyBook/AFBF%20Policy%202013.pdf. See the current AFBF Background papers www.fb.org/index.php?action=issues.home.
27. Ibid.
28. "Ag-Gag Laws." (SourceWatch—Center for Media and Democracy). www.sourcewatch.org/index.php/Ag-gag_laws. "'Ag Gag': More States Move to Ban Hidden Cameras on Farms," Cindy Galli and Randy Kreider (ABC Nightline–The Blotter, 3/15/13).
29. See the materials collected at the University of Florida's Brechner Center for Freedom of Information where links are provided to federal and state laws across the country. www.brechner.org/resources.asp.
30. Freedom of Information Act (FOIA), adopted in 1996 (Public Law 89-554, 80 Stat. 383; Amended 1996, 2002, 2007).
31. In Washington State, for example, our Public Records Act (RCW Ch. 42.56) would seem to require that such information be revealed. This has been a source of continuing struggle between NRCS and local conservation districts over the years.

Chapter 11: Choosing Between Zoning and Conservation Easements

1. Calculated from "Table 8: Land 2007 and 2002," (USDA Census of Agriculture, 2007) www.agcensus.usda.gov/Publications/2007/Full_Report/Volume_1,_Chapter_1_US/st99_1_008_008.pdf.
2. These very approximate farm sizes are based on the author's conversations, over the years, with individual farmers. So they will vary considerably from location to location and for different types of crops. There are definitely many examples of

farm operators that make do with a good deal less land or where a great deal more may be needed.

3. Some communities approve five- and ten-acre minimums. Fresno County appears to have had 640-acre parcel size minimums. See memo: "Board Briefing Report," (County of Fresno, CA, September 15, 2013). www2.co.fresno.ca.us/0110a/Questys_Agenda/MG74451/AS74452/AS74456/AI74459/DO74457/DO_74457.PDF). Oregon, reputed to have the most rigorous agricultural zoning in the country, has a statewide minimum parcel size of eighty acres. See the Oregon Department of Land Conservation and Development website www.oregon.gov/LCD/farmprotprog.shtml.

4. Oregon (again, a national leader in this arena) requires that at least $80,000 gross farm income be earned in two of the past three years. See "The New Face of Farming: Shaping Policies that Support Today's Agricultural Practices," (1000 Friends of Oregon, March 2012), 11. www.friends.org/sites/friends.org/files/reports/1000Friends-NFOF-Report-FINAL.pdf.

5. Although this is not necessarily always the case. See "Downzoning: Does it Protect Working Landscapes and Maintain Equity for the Landowner?" Rob Etgen, John Bernstein, Sarah Taylor Rodgers, Robert Gray, Peter Caldwell, Elgin Perry, Johnathan Chapman, and H. Grant Dehart (Maryland Center for Agro-Ecology, December 2003). www.farmlandinfo.org/downzoning-does-it-protect-working-landscapes-and-maintain-equity-landowner.

6. Though not always. Skagit County, WA, would seem to be a reasonable exception.

7. In Washington State, for example, which has one of the stronger statewide land use laws in the country, the largest agricultural parcel sizes protected in agricultural zones is forty acres, and a great many are smaller. With an average Washington farm size at about 450 acres, this greatly limits meaningful protection for farming.

8. Oregon voters passed Initiative 37 in 2004 which dramatically undercut their powerful Statewide Growth Management Law. But then, in 2007, they passed Initiative 49 which restored much of the lost ground.

9. For example, among the several statewide property rights ballot measures offered across the country during the 2006 elections, one in Washington State was actually led and publicly sponsored by the Washington Farm Bureau. Initiative 933 www.secstate.wa.gov/elections/initiatives/text/i933.pdf.

10. The Oregon Farm Bureau, for example, actively supports Oregon's rigorous Statewide Growth Management Law. See "Argument in Favor: The Family Farmers and Ranchers of Oregon Farm Bureau Ask You to Vote Yes on Measure 49," Measure 49 Voters Guide (Oregon Secretary of State). www.oregonvotes.org/pages/history/archive/nov62007/guide/m49_fav.html.

11. For more detail about how these programs work, see the four complete reports that analyze forty-six of the PDR programs around the country: "A National View of Agricultural Easement Programs," Alvin Sokolow and Anita Zerbrugg (American Farmland Trust, September 1, 2003 to December 4, 2006). www.farmland.org/resources/national-view/default.asp.

12. The items on this list were heavily drawn from: "Why a Farmer Might be Interested in Participating in a PACE (PDR) Program," Don Stuart (American Farmland

Trust). donstuart.net/wp-content/uploads/2012/01/21-Why-a-farmer-would-be-interested-in-PDR.pdf.

13. "From the Field: What Farmers Have to Say about Vermont's Farmland Conservation Program," Kirsten Fergusen and Jeremiah Cosgrove (American Farmland Trust). www.farmlandinfo.org/sites/default/files/From_The_Field_1.pdf. "Investing in the Future of Agriculture: The Massachusetts Farmland Protection Program and the Permanence Syndrome," a survey of farmers participating in the Massachusetts PDR program (American Farmland Trust). www.farmlandinfo.org/documents/29253/Investing_in_the_Future_of_Agriculture.pdf.

14. Rich Doenges later went on to manage the nationally recognized PDR program in Lancaster County, PA.

15. Fortunately, only a few farmers are interested in selling out in the course of any given year. But it helps for these programs to have ongoing funding to acquire easements on properties as they become available.

16. ACEP is explained at: "Farm and Ranch Lands Protection Program" (USDA/Natural Resources Conservation Service). www.nrcs.usda.gov.

17. A TDR program, in effect, taxes development in high demand, heavily-populated areas to provide funding for land protections in areas of low population. For a full explanation, See "Fact Sheet: Transfer of Development Rights" (American Farmland Trust, Farmland Information Center). www.farmlandinfo.org/sites/default/files/TDR_04-2008_1.pdf.

18. The State of Delaware, for example, has averaged over 50 percent savings through discounted easements. For information, contact: Delaware Department of Agriculture, Farmland Preservation Program, 2320 South DuPont Highway, Dover, DE 19901. The program is described online at dda.delaware.gov/aglands/index.shtml and is in the Delaware Code Chapter 9, Delaware Agricultural Lands Preservation Act, delcode.delaware.gov/title3/c009/index.shtml.

19. For the status and more detail about many of the principal easement programs in the U.S., See "A National View of Agricultural Easement Programs," Alvin Sokolow and Anita Zerbrugg (American Farmland Trust, September 1, 2003 to December 5, 2006). www.farmland.org/resources/national-view/default.asp.

20. Some of the contents for this section are based upon conversations with Buddy Huffaker, Executive Director for the Aldo Leopold Foundation, Baraboo, WI, and on an American Farmland Trust report provided for the Farming and the Environment Project entitled: "Dialogues with Agriculture: A Review of Processes Engaging Farm Groups in Protecting the Environment by Protecting Farmland," Don Stuart (American Farmland Trust, October 16, 2000). The FACT proposal is described online at www.fws.gov/midwest/planning/FairfieldMarsh/fairfinalAppA.pdf.pdf. Subsequently, the project became the Fairfield Marsh Conservation Partnership, www.fws.gov/midwest/planning/FairfieldMarsh/index.html.

21. See the American Farmland Trust report provided for the Farming and the Environment Project entitled: "Dialogues with Agriculture: A Review of Processes Engaging Farm Groups in Protecting the Environment by Protecting Farmland," Don Stuart (American Farmland Trust, October 16, 2000). Also see the Sierra Club: florida.sierraclub.org/greenswamp.asp and Green Swamp: www.swfwmd.state.fl.us/education/interactive/greenswamp/greenswamp.html.

22. See the comments and materials at: "Doughnut Cities: Everybody connected with urban planning has known for decades that allowing suburbs to spread is not a good idea, yet suburban growth continues," (The Free Library, 2004). www.thefreelibrary.com/Doughnut+cities%3A+everybody+connected+with+urban+planning+has+known...-a0118377283.

23. Many farm communities adopt laws that attempt to limit such nuisance claims. But since nuisance law is grounded in the common law that the U.S. inherited from the British at the time our Constitution was written, there are constitutional limits on the extent to which such claims can be restricted by simple legislation.

24. Note that the concept of "highest and best use" takes into account current lawful zoning. This subtlety may not be apparent, however, to a public official whose next election is in doubt.

25. More than 150 independent cost of community services (COCS) studies around the country strongly suggest that the logic of this thinking is flawed. See "Fact Sheet: Cost of Community Services Studies," (American Farmland Trust, Farmland Information Center). www.farmlandinfo.org/cost-community-services-studies.

26. See "Agricultural Sustainability and Smart Growth: Saving Urban-Influenced Farmland," Ed Thompson Jr. (Funders Network for Smart Growth, April 2001). law.wustl.edu/landuselaw/Articles/Archived/agriculture_paper.pdf.

27. I've had several conversations about this with professional farm lenders at Farm Credit and other commercial bankers. They universally agree.

28. The value of land and buildings represents, on average, 85 percent of a farm businesses' assets. "Trends in U.S. Farmland Values and Ownership," Cynthia Nickerson, Mitchell Morehart, Todd Kuethe, Jayson Beckmann, Jennifer Ifft, and Ryan Williams (USDA-Economic Research Service—EIB#92, February 2012) iii. www.ers.usda.gov/media/377487/eib92_2_.pdf.

29. See "Eminent Threat," Denise Roth Barber (National Institute on Money in State Policy, June 22, 2007). www.followthemoney.org/press/PrintReportView.phtml?r=324.

30. See "Sustaining the Land for Sustainable Agriculture," Don Stuart, *American Farmland* (American Farmland Trust, Winter 2004), 10.

Chapter 12: Climate Change

1. My appreciation to the American Farmland Trust whose work on this topic was used in completing this chapter. See www.farmland.org/programs/environment/climate-change/default.asp.

2. "Fifth Assessment Report: Climate Change 2013" (Intergovernmental Panel on Climate Change, 2013). www.ipcc.ch/publications_and_data/publications_and_data_reports.shtml. Also: "Climate Change 2007: Synthesis Report" (Intergovernmental Panel on Climate Change, 2007). www.ipcc.ch/publications_and_data/ar4/syr/en/main.html. Also see "Global Climate Change Impacts in the United States (2009)" (United States Global Change Research Program). www.globalchange.gov/what-we-do/assessment/previous-assessments/global-climate-change-impacts-in-the-us-2009. See also: "Remarks by the President on Climate Change," Georgetown University (The White House, Office of the Press Secretary, June 25, 2013). www.whitehouse.gov/the-press-office/2013/06/25/remarks-president-climate-change.

3. "Global Climate Change Impacts in the United States–Agriculture (2009)" (United States Global Change Research Program, 2009), 71ff. downloads.globalchange.gov/usimpacts/pdfs/agriculture.pdf.

4. "Global Climate Change Impacts in the United States—Water Resources" 41ff. downloads.globalchange.gov/usimpacts/pdfs/water.pdf.

5. "Global Climate Change Impacts in the United States—Ecosystems" (United States Global Change Research Program, 2009), 79ff. downloads.globalchange.gov/usimpacts/pdfs/ecosystems.pdf.

6. "Global Climate Change Impacts in the United States—Agriculture (2009)" (United States Global Change Research Program, 2009), 71ff. downloads.globalchange.gov/usimpacts/pdfs/agriculture.pdf.

7. US EPA Climate Change, Nitrous Oxide. www.epa.gov/nitrousoxide/scientific.html.

8. US EPA Climate Change, Methane. www.epa.gov/methane/index.html.

9. The listed strategies are discussed in "Guide to Environmental Markets for Farmers & Ranchers," Don Stuart and Dennis Canty (American Farmland Trust, 2010). See also "Climate Friendly Farming," (Washington State University Center for Sustaining Agriculture and Natural Resources). csanr.wsu.edu/pages/CFF.

10. Ibid., note 239. "Global Climate Change Impacts in the United States–Agriculture (2009)."

11. As major policy initiatives for climate change, the U.S. has listed several USDA conservation programs including: Conservation Reserve Program (CRP), Environmental Quality Incentives Program (EQIP), Conservation Stewardship Program (CSP), Wetlands Reserve Program (WRP), and Wildlife Habitat Incentives Program (WHIP). "Fifth Climate Action Report to the U.N. Framework Convention on Climate Change" (U.S. Department of State), Chapter 4, Policies and Measures, 56-57. www.state.gov/e/oes/rls/rpts/car5. All of these programs mostly focus on other environmental objectives yet also provide considerable co-benefits for sequestering carbon and reducing greenhouse gas emissions.

12. These are the practices described in the USDA/Natural Resources Conservation Service Field Office Technical Guide (and discussed further in Chapters 5 and 7).

13. "Agriculture's Role in Greenhouse Gas Mitigation," Keith Paustian, John Antle, John Sheehan, and Eldor Paul (Pew Center on Global Climate Change, September 2006), 40-57 (42, 56). www.pewclimate.org/docUploads/Agriculture%27s%20Role%20in%20GHG%20Mitigation.pdf.

14. See, e.g., "California Sees Sprawl as Warming Culprit," John Ritter (*USA Today*, June 6, 2007). www.usatoday.com/weather/climate/globalwarming/2007-06-05-warming_N.htm. See also "The climate impacts of land surface changes and carbon management, and the implications for climate change mitigation policy," Gregg Morland et al., Climate Policy (Climate Policy.com), Vol. 3, 149-157. pielkeclimatesci.files.wordpress.com/2009/10/r-267.pdf.

15. H.R. 910, the Energy Tax Prevention Act, passed the House April 7, 2011.

16. American Clean Energy and Security Act of 2009, HR2454, also known as the Waxman-Markey Bill or the Climate Bill. www.govtrack.us/congress/bills/111/hr2454.

17. "The Effect of Higher Energy Prices from HR 2454 on Missouri Crop Production Costs" FAPRI-MU Report #5-09 (University of Missouri–Food and Agriculture Policy Research Institute, July 2009). www.fapri.missouri.edu/outreach/publications/2009/FAPRI_MU_Report_05_09.pdf. Also see "Costs and Benefits to Agriculture from Climate Change Policy," Bruce Babcock, *Iowa Ag Review Online*, Summer 2009, Vol. 15, No. 3 (Iowa State University–Center for Agricultural and Rural Development). www.card.iastate.edu/iowa_ag_review/summer_09/article1.aspx.

18. "Impacts of Climate Change Legislation on Agriculture in the Rocky Mountain States: Arizona, Colorado and New Mexico," Brian Hurd, Christopher Goemans, George Frisvold, and Janine Stone. (American Farmland Trust, April 2, 2010). www.farmland.org/documents/AFTRM-SWRegionSummaryReport.pdf.

19. Ibid. See also "The Effects of Climate Change on Agriculture, Land Resources, Water Resources, and Biodiversity in the United States," Report by the U.S. Climate Change Science Program and the Subcommittee on Global Change Science, Peter Backlund, Anthony Janetos, and David Schimel, et al. (U.S. Climate Change Program Office, 2009). www.amwa.net/galleries/climate-change/CCSP_Ag_Report.pdf. Also see "Costs and Benefits to Agriculture from Climate Change Policy," Bruce Babcock, *Iowa Ag Review Online*, and "A Preliminary Analysis of the Effects of HR 2454 on U.S. Agriculture" (U.S. Department of Agriculture–Office of the Chief Economist, July 22, 2009). www.usda.gov/documents/PreliminaryAnalysis_HR2454.pdf.

20. "Impacts of Climate Change Legislation on Agriculture in the Rocky Mountain States: Arizona, Colorado and New Mexico," Hurd et al.

21. In his address on climate on June 25, 2013, the President did mention state "market-based" programs as a model for federal action, so it is, at this moment, unclear whether some sort of trading could come out of proposed new EPA regulation. Ibid., note 235, "Remarks by the President on Climate Change."

22. The Waxman-Markey Bill did contain exemptions that would protect farmers from increased fertilizer prices. "A Preliminary Analysis of the Effects of HR 2454 on U.S. Agriculture" (U.S. Department of Agriculture–Office of the Chief Economist, July 22, 2009). www.usda.gov/documents/PreliminaryAnalysis_HR2454.pdf.

23. American Clean Energy and Security Act of 2009, HR2454, also known as the Waxman-Markey Bill. www.govtrack.us/congress/bills/111/hr2454. The correlative Senate Bill was the Clean Energy, Jobs and American Power Act of 2009, S.1733, known as the Kerry-Boxer Bill. www.govtrack.us/congress/bills/111/s1733. See the 2013 AFBF Policy Book, specifically the policy on Climate Change #503. www.texasfarmbureau.org/PolicyBook/AFBF%20Policy%202013.pdf. See the notice of the AFBF position "The Farm Bureau: Denying Climate Change, undermining Labor, and Losing Relevancy in 2010," Paula Crossfield, Huffpost Green (*Huffington Post*, January 13, 2010). www.huffingtonpost.com/paula-crossfield/the-farm-bureau-denying-c_b_421437.html. "Farm Bureau not a fan of climate change legislation or regulation," Kristy Foster Seacrest (*Farm and Dairy*, March 11, 2010). www.farmanddairy.com/news/farm-bureau-not-a-fan-of-climate-change-legislation-or-regulation/14407.html. Not all ag groups opposed the climate bill. The National Wheat Growers Association took a positive position in light of prospective benefits to agriculture. So did the National Farmers Union. The National Corn Growers

Association remained neutral. See "Farm Bureau Fires Back Against Climate Bill's 'Power Grab,'" Allison Winter, Climatewire, *New York Times*, January 11, 2010. www.nytimes.com/cwire/2010/01/11/11climatewire-farm-bureau-fires-back-against-climate-bills-93758.html.

24. "2013 AFBF Policy Book," policy on Climate Change–#503. www.texasfarmbureau. org/PolicyBook/AFBF%20Policy%202013.pdf.

25. Ibid. "Clean Air Act–Green House Gas Regulation," American Farm Bureau Federation, Issue Paper, July 2013. www.fb.org/issues/docs/cleanair13.pdf. The Clean Air Act is at: 42 USC Ch. 85.

26. See the Qualco Energy website qualco-energy.org.

27. See the notice of the AFBF position "AFBF: Vote No on Climate Bill," June 25, 2009. www.fb.org/index.php?fuseaction=newsroom.newsfocus&year=2009&file=nr0625. html.

28. "Scientists Request Meeting with Farm Bureau President to Discuss Group's 'Inaccurate' Stance on Climate Change" (Union of Concerned Scientists, January 7, 2010). www.commondreams.org/newswire/2010/01/07-2 The letter itself can be found at ucsusa.org/assets/documents/global_warming/climate-scientists-letter-to. pdf. The farm industry's denial of climate change is increasingly inviting scorn. See "Big Ag on Climate Change: 'What me worry?',", Tom Laskawy (*Grist*, September 28, 2009). www.grist.org/article/big-ag-on-climate-change-what-me-worry. The American Farm Bureau Federation's annual national meeting in 2010 presented a workshop entitled: "Global Warming: A Red Hot Lie?" See "At the *NY Times*, Elevating the Voice of Farmers on Climate Change," Matthew Nisbet (BigThink. com, November 22, 2010). bigthink.com/ideas/25196.

29. Note that the President did mention state "market-based" approaches as a model for federal action in a 2013 speech on this topic. Ibid., note 235 "Remarks by the President on Climate Change."

30. AFBF 2013 Policy Book, #503. www.texasfarmbureau.org/PolicyBook/AFBF%20 Policy%202013.pdf.

31. EPA regulation could apparently regulate some ag sectors directly. See "Clean Air Act/Green House Gas Regulation," American Farm Bureau Federation, Issue Paper, June 2011. www.fb.org/issues/docs/cleanair13.pdf.

32. "Clean Air Act/Green House Gas Regulation," American Farm Bureau Federation, Issue Paper, June 2011. www.fb.org/issues/docs/cleanair13.pdf.

33. *Massachusetts v. Environmental Protection Agency*, 549 U.S. 497 (2007).

34. *American Electric Power Co. v. Connecticut*, docket No. 10-174, decided June 20, 2011. *Utility Air Group v. EPA*, decision announced June 23, 2014.

35. Ibid., note 265, "Clean Air Act/Green House Gas Regulation."

36. H.R. 910, the Energy Tax Prevention Act, passed the House April 7, 2011.

37. See a complete list of members of the U.S. Climate Action Partnership at www.us-cap.org/about-us. See "A Call for Action: Consensus Principles and Recommendations from the Climate Action Partnership." us-cap.org/USCAPCallForAction.pdf. Other climate bill supporters included: Hewlett-Packard, John Deere, ConocoPhillips, and BP America as well as a number of major U.S. labor organizations. See "Myths and Facts Surrounding Climate Change Legislation" (American Farmland

Trust), 5. www.farmland.org/documents/ClimateChangeMythandFact-American FarmlandTrust_002.pdf.

38. Ibid. "Myths and Facts Surrounding Climate Change Legislation" (American Farmland Trust).

39. "Exxon Supports Carbon Tax", *Calgary Herald* (Canada.com, January 9, 2009). www.canada.com/calgaryherald/news/calgarybusiness/story.html?id=e8aecbbb-16c6-412d-8054-7e64e2b176ef. "On Carbon, Tax and Don't Spend," Monica Prasad *New York Times*, March 25, 2008. www.nytimes.com/2008/03/25/opinion/25prasad.html. For a complete listing of the business and other supporters of a carbon tax, see "Carbon Tax," Wikipedia. en.wikipedia.org/wiki/Carbon_tax.

40. "Cap and Tax Collapse," *Wall Street Journal*, Review & Outlook, April 3, 2009. online.wsj.com/article/SB123872261427685233.html.

41. "Who Pays for Cap and Trade? Hint: They were promised a tax cut during the Obama campaign." *Wall Street Journal*, Review & Outlook, March 9, 2009. online.wsj.com/article/SB123655590609066021.html. "Beware of Cap and Trade Bills," Ben Lieberman (The Heritage Foundation, December 6, 2007). www.heritage.org/research/reports/2007/12/beware-of-cap-and-trade-climate-bills.

42. American Farm Bureau Federation policy paper on "Climate Change." www.fb.org/issues/docs/climate14.pdf.

43. See Chapter 12, Note 2, this volume. "Fifth Assessment Report: Climate Change 2007," "Climate Change 2007: Synthesis Report," "Global Climate Change Impacts in the United States 2009."

44. "Agriculture's Role in Greenhouse Gas Mitigation" (Pew Center on Global Climate Change, September 2006), iii. www.pewclimate.org/docUploads/Agriculture%27s%20Role%20in%20GHG%20Mitigation.pdf.

45. "FTC Asks if Carbon-Offset Money is Well Spent," Louise Story, *New York Times*, Business, January 9, 2008. www.nytimes.com/2008/01/09/business/09offsets.html.

46. "Another Inconvenient Truth: Behind the feel-good hype of carbon offsets, some of the deals don't deliver," *Bloomberg Businessweek* (Bloomberg.com, March 26, 2007). www.businessweek.com/magazine/content/07_13/b4027057.htm. See "Farm Bureau Fires Back Against Climate Bill's 'Power Grab,'" Allison Winter, ClimateWire, *New York Times*, January 11, 2010. www.nytimes.com/cwire/2010/01/11/11climatewire-farm-bureau-fires-back-against-climate-bills-93758.html.

47. "'Cap and Trade' Loses Its Standing as Energy Policy of Choice," John M. Broder, *New York Times*, Environment, March 25, 2010. www.nytimes.com/2010/03/26/science/earth/26climate.html?_r=0.

Chapter 13: Livestock, the Public Lands, and the Environment

1. "Livestock's Long Shadow: Environmental Issues and Options," Henning Steinfeld, Pierre Gerber et al. (Food and Agriculture Organization of the United Nations, 2006). ftp://ftp.fao.org/docrep/fao/010/a0701e/a0701e00.pdf.

2. Ibid. This increases to 30 percent when one includes land devoted to raising feed.

3. This included 587 million acres of permanent grassland pasture and rangeland, 62 million acres of cropland pasture, and 134 million acres of forested rangeland.

Part of this land was private, part state and local government lands, part tribal lands, and part federally owned lands. "Environmental Interactions with Agricultural Production: Grazing Lands and Environmental Quality" (USDA Economic Research Service). webarchives.cdlib.org/sw1rf5mh0k/www.ers.usda.gov/Briefing/AgAndEnvironment/animalagriculture.htm.

4. "Table 2: Market Value of Agricultural Products Sold Including Landlord's Share and Direct Sales: 2007 and 2002" (USDA Census of Agriculture, 2007). www.agcensus.usda.gov/Publications/2007/Full_Report/Volume_1,_Chapter_1_US/st99_1_002_002.pdf.

5. "Low Costs Drive Production to Large Dairy Farms," James McDonald and William McBride, Amber Waves, Vol. 5, No. 4 (USDA Economic Research Service, September 2007). ageconsearch.umn.edu/bitstream/125326/2/DairyFarms.pdf. Also see "Changes in the Size and Location of U.S. Dairy Farms," James MacDonald, Erik O'Donoghue, et al. (USDA Economic Research Service, Economic Research Report #47, September 2007). www.ers.usda.gov/publications/err47/err47b.pdf.

6. "Changing Economics of U.S. Hog Production," Nigel Key and William McBride (USDA Economic Research Service, Economic Research Report #52, December 2007). www.ers.usda.gov/publications/err-economic-research-report/err52.aspx.

7. "Fact Sheet: Animal Agriculture and Water Pollution" (PEW Environment Group). www.pewenvironment.org/uploadedFiles/PEG/Publications/Fact_Sheet/Animal%20Agriculture%20and%20Water%20Pollution.pdf.

8. For example, the U.S. Bureau of Land Management estimates that, in FY 2010, it permitted 8.2 million animal unit months (AUMs) on the some 157 million acres of land it manages for livestock grazing—or some nineteen acres per AUM (which is, in turn, as little as only one-twelfth of the year, depending on seasonal conditions at a given location). See "Fact Sheet on the BLM's Management of Livestock Grazing" (U.S. Department of Interior, Bureau of Land Management, March 2014). www.blm.gov/wo/st/en/prog/grazing.html.

9. Ibid.

10. Cattlemen's associations in several states have created their own land trusts to help reduce the conversion of rangeland into recreational and other development. Notable among these is the Colorado Cattlemen's Agricultural Land Trust (www.ccalt.org); the Oregon Rangeland Trust (www.oregonrangelandtrust.com); the California Rangeland Trust (rangelandtrust.org); and the Klamath Basin Rangeland Trust (www.kbrt.org). The Washington Cattlemen's Association's recitation of the top challenges faced for the state's 2008 Future of Farming Report listed first the "ability to find (lease, buy, rent) grazing lands both public and private." See "Future of Farming: The Beef Industry Perspective," Jack Field, Washington Cattlemen's Association. agr.wa.gov/FoF/docs/Beef.pdf.

11. Environmentalists have asked me if a rangeland trust, whose board was entirely composed of cattle ranchers, could be relied upon to properly protect the land. If the purpose of the easements involved were limited to preserving fish or wildlife, perhaps that *might* be a legitimate question. But where the purpose is to preserve open, undeveloped private land that can be devoted to sustainable ranching, it seems to me cattle ranchers would constitute the very best and most dependable board of directors possible.

12. This and other concerns are listed in: "Fact Sheet: Animal Agriculture and Water Pollution" (PEW Environment Group). Ibid., note 287.

13. "Livestock and Environment," (Food and Agriculture Organization of the United Nations, Animal Production and Health, updated January 10, 2013). www.fao.org/ag/againfo/themes/en/Environment.html. Also see "Fact Sheet: Animal Agriculture and Water Pollution" (PEW Environment Group).

14. See "Antibiotics in Agriculture" (Organic Trade Association). www.ota.com/organic/benefits/antibiotics.html. These impacts may also be less substantial than has been generally claimed. "Limiting antibiotic use for livestock could raise food prices," Douglas Call, *Seattle Times*, January 10, 2014, A11. seattletimes.com/html/opinion/2022634923_dougcallopedantibioticsmeatxxxml.html.

15. "Livestock's Long Shadow: Environmental Issues and Options," Henning Steinfeld, Pierre Gerber, et al. (U.N. Food & Agriculture Organization, 2006), 162. ftp://ftp.fao.org/docrep/fao/010/a0701e/a0701e00.pdf.

16. Ibid., 18 percent. This is a greater share than transportation. Note that this U.N. report attributes a large share of these contributions to land use changes such as deforestation—something that may still be occurring to a limited degree in the U.S., but which is certainly much diminished here as compared with other parts of the world. See "Environmental Interactions with Agricultural Production: Grazing Lands and Environmental Quality" (USDA Economic Research Service). webarchives.cdlib.org/sw1rf5mh0k/www.ers.usda.gov/Briefing/AgAndEnvironment/animalagriculture.htm, See also: "Livestock a Major Threat to Environment" (U.N. Food & Agriculture Organization, November 29, 2006). www.fao.org/newsroom/en/news/2006/1000448/index.html.

17. See, generally, "Trust Lands in the American West: A Legal Overview and Policy Assessment," Peter Culp, Diane Conradi, and Cynthia Tuell, Lincoln Institute of Land Policy. (Sonoran Institute, 2005). www.lincolninst.edu/subcenters/managing-state-trust-lands/publications/trustlands-report.pdf.

18. "Assessing the Full Cost of the Federal Grazing Program," Karyn Moskowitz, Chuck Romaniello (Center for Biological Diversity, October 2002). www.biologicaldiversity.org/publications/papers/assessing_the_full_cost.pdf.

19. "Fact Sheet on the BLM's Management of Livestock Grazing" (U.S. Department of Interior, Bureau of Land Management, Feb. 5, 2013). www.blm.gov/wo/st/en/prog/grazing.html.

20. "Public Land Policy and the Value of Grazing Permits," L. Allen Torell and John Doll (Western Journal of Agricultural Economics, 174-184, 1991). ageconsearch.umn.edu/bitstream/32630/1/16010174.pdf.

21. Another example is the limited entry permits held by many U.S. commercial fishers. See, for example, the website of the Alaska Commercial Fisheries Entry Commission which manages that state's limited entry program. www.cfec.state.ak.us.

22. Public Rangeland Improvement Act of 1978, 43 USC Sec. 1901 ff. uscode.house.gov/download/pls/43C37.txt.

23. An animal unit month (AUM) is one month's use of an amount of land forage which can sustain a single animal (usually a cow).

24. "Assessing the Full Cost of the Federal Grazing Program," Moskowitz and Romaniello. (Center for Biological Diversity, October 2002).

25. 43 U.S.C. 315. See "The Taylor Grazing Act," U.S. Department of the Interior, Bureau of Land Management. www.blm.gov/wy/st/en/field_offices/Casper/range/taylor.1.html.
26. Permitted AUMs declined from 18.2 million issued in 1954 to 8.9 million in 2012. "Fact Sheet on the BLM's Management of Livestock Grazing," (U.S. Department of Interior, Bureau of Land Management, March 2014), ibid., note 288.
27. Federal Land Policy and Management Act of 1976, as amended, Public Law 94-579. www.blm.gov/flpma/FLPMA.pdf.
28. "Long-Awaited Federal Grazing Buy-Out Legislation Is Introduced in Washington, D.C.," press release (Western Watershed Project, October 20, 2003). www.westernwatersheds.org/news-media/online-messenger/long-awaited-federal-grazing-buy-out-legislation-introduced-washington-d.htm.
29. "The Multiple-Use Conflict Resolution Act Will *Not* Create New Rights in Grazing Permits" (National Public Lands Grazing Campaign). www.publiclandsranching.org/htmlres/fs_no_grazing_rights.htm. Also at www.publiclandsranching.org.
30. See Chapter 5 and the USDA/NRCS Electronic Field Office Technical Guide (EFOTG) www.nrcs.usda.gov/technical/efotg.
31. "Rangeland Health Standards Handbook" (Department of the Interior, Bureau of Land Management, January 19, 2001). www.blm.gov/pgdata/etc/medialib/blm/wo/Information_Resources_Management/policy/blm_handbook.Par.61484.File.dat/h4180-1.pdf. Also see "Fact Sheet on the BLM's Management of Livestock Grazing" (U.S. Department of Interior, Bureau of Land Management, March 2014). Ibid., note 288.
32. For example, see the BLM's: "Utah Rangeland Health Standards" (Department of Interior, Bureau of Land Management). www.blm.gov/ut/st/en/fo/vernal/grazing_/rangeland_health_standards.html.
33. For example, non-farm landowners whose properties border on public lands in open range areas are often frustrated by the need to personally undertake the expense to "fence out" cattle grazing on adjacent public range.
34. "Coordinated Resource Management: A Voluntary and Collaborative Problem-Solving Process for Resource Management Issues" (Society for Range Management). www.rangelands.org/education_crm.shtml. This site provides CRM contacts throughout the West.
35. "Issue Paper: Environmental Impacts of Livestock on U.S. Grazing Lands" (Council for Agricultural Science and Technology, November 2002). oregonstate.edu/dept/range/sites/default/files/l_Impacts_of_Livestock_on_U_S__Grazing_Lands.pdf.
36. Based on 2002 figures: "Environmental Interactions with Agricultural Production: Grazing Lands and Environmental Quality" (USDA, Economic Research Service). webarchives.cdlib.org/sw1rf5mh0k/www.ers.usda.gov/Briefing/AgAndEnvironment/animalagriculture.htm.
37. According to "Assessing the Full Cost of the Federal Grazing Program," Karyn Moskowitz, Chuck Romaniello (Center for Biological Diversity, October 2002), public lands may provide only about 4 percent of all cattle feed in the entire U.S. However, these lands provide a much larger percentage of that in the eleven western states where most public lands grazing occurs. And they probably provide a majority in many of the specific local communities that depend on them.

38. "Assessing the Full Cost of the Federal Grazing Program," Karyn Moskowitz, Chuck Romaniello (Center for Biological Diversity, October 2002).
39. "Is Meat Sustainable?" *Worldwatch Newsletter*, Vol. 17, No. 4 (Worldwatch Institute, July-August 2004). www.worldwatch.org/node/549.
40. Fred Colvin's view is supported by Allan Savory in his famous "TED talk "Allan Savory: How to green the world's deserts and reverse climate change," May 4, 2013, YouTube. www.youtube.com/watch?v=vpTHi7O66pI. There may, however, be limits on how far this concept can be carried. See "All Sizzle and No Steak: Why Allan Savory's TED talk about how cattle can reverse global warming is dead wrong," James McWilliams, *Slate,* April 22, 2013. www.slate.com/articles/life/food/2013/04/allan_savory_s_ted_talk_is_wrong_and_the_benefits_of_holistic_grazing_have.html.
41. See "Initiatives to the People," I-640 (Office of the Washington Secretary of State). www.sos.wa.gov/elections/initiatives/statistics_initiatives.aspx.

Chapter 14: The Federal Farm Bill

1. "Actual Farm Bill Spending and Cost Estimates," Jim Monke and Renee Johnson, CRS 7-5700–R41195 (Congressional Research Service, 12/13/10), Table 2. Actual Reported Expenditures and CBO Baseline Projections, 2008-2012. johanns.senate.gov/public/?a=Files.Serve&File_id=28fb61d1-f00d-4c8d-b9db-bf7 cef4002e0. See also "Budget issues shaping a farm bill in 2013," Jim Monke (Congressional Research Service, 10/24/13) Table 3, 14. www.fas.org/sgp/crs/misc/R42484.pdf.
2. Agricultural Adjustment Act of 1933 (Pub.L. 73-10, 48 Stat. 31, enacted May 12, 1933) and the later Agricultural Adjustment Act of 1938 (P.L. 75-430).
3. "Farm Subsidy Tradition and Modern Agricultural Realities," Daniel A. Sumner, *The 2007 Farm Bill and Beyond*, Bruce Gardner and Daniel Sumner (Washington, DC: American Enterprise Institute), 29. aic.ucdavis.edu/research/farmbill07/aeibriefs/20070516_Summary.pdf. There was also concern over foreign manipulation of international markets. U.S. farm producers were seen as vulnerable and at an unfair disadvantage in these open international markets. Unlike their foreign competitors, American farmers had to play by U.S. market rules. (The dairy industry is a more recent exception—it also has its own price support program justified by the particular variability of dairy prices.)
4. The existence of price supports may also have had the reverse effect—helped make grain embargos seem like a logical tool since U.S. producers would be insulated from their negative impacts.
5. "Video: Chairwoman Stabenow–2013 Farm Bill on the Senate Floor," FarmPolicy.com, farmpolicy.com/2013/05/20/video-chairwoman-stabenow-2013-farm-bill-on-senate-floor. On May 20, 2013, Senate Ag Committee Chair Debbie Stabenow was quoted in floor debate as stating: "That is why we have what we call the farm bill. We have a farm bill because farmers are in the riskiest business in the world." Note also the change in program names: the former price supports or Countercyclical Payments program is now called: "Price Loss Coverage." The Average Crop Revenue

Election (ACRE) has now become: "Agricultural Risk Coverage." These new names clearly imply a risk protection, insurance-like foundation for these programs.

6. Among these additional indirect impacts are those on many rural communities whose local economy depends on commodity agriculture.

7. "The Status of the WTO Brazil-US Cotton Case," Randy Schnepf (Congressional Research Service, CRS 7-5700, December 12, 2013). www.fas.org/sgp/crs/row/R43336.pdf.

8. "U.S. pushed to reform cotton subsidies in farm bill as Brazil watches," Paige Mc-Clanahan, *The Guardian*, Global Development, July 19, 2012). www.guardian.co.uk/global-development/2012/jul/19/us-cotton-subsidies-farm-bill-brazil. This is, in effect, a further subsidy.

9. For example: "The Case for Crop Insurance Reform" (Environmental Working Group). www.ewg.org/farmbill2013/the-case-for-crop-insurance-reform.

10. "Farm Program Payments are an Important Factor in Landowners' Decisions to Convert Grassland to Cropland," GAO Highlights, GAO-07-1054 (U.S. Government Accounting Office, September 2007). www.gao.gov/highlights/d071054high.pdf. Note that, in reality, a more likely short term fate for these lands might be their conversion to non-native invasive vegetation.

11. "Unilever Chief Attacks Farm Subsidies," William Surman (Farmers Guardian, Jan. 20, 2011). www.farmersguardian.com/home/business/unilever-chief-attacks-farm-subsidies/36647.article.

12. "You are what you grow," Michael Pollan, *New York Times Magazine*, April 22, 2007. michaelpollan.com/articles-archive/you-are-what-you-grow/; "Farm Bill Robs Poor to Pay Rich" (Center for American Progress, August 16, 2007). www.americanprogress.org/issues/2007/08/care.html.

13. Ninety-one percent of our nation's fruits and 78 percent of our vegetables (non-subsidized crops) are grown on the urban edge. See the chart at: "Food in the Path of Development," (American Farmland Trust, Farming on the Edge). www.farmland.org/programs/localfood/fresh-food-grown-on-the-urban-fringe.asp. This concern, of course, runs counter to the previously mentioned specialty crop restrictions on commodity farmers.

14. "United States Needs 13 Million More Acres of Fruits and Vegetables to Meet the RDA," Jennifer Morrill, Press Release (American Farmland Trust, July 7, 2010). www.farmland.org/news/pressreleases/13-Million-More-Acres.asp.

15. "U.S. Farm Bill: Dictator of the American Diet," Rosa Perr (Minnesota 20/20, April 29, 2011). www.mn2020.org/issues-that-matter/health-care/us-farm-bill-dictator-of-the-american-diet. Also see "You are what you grow," Michael Pollan, *New York Times Magazine*, April 22, 2007.

16. "New Polls in Five States Show Farm Subsidy Cuts and More Conservation Spending Would Improve Public's View of Congress" (Environmental Defense Fund, October 2, 2007). www.edf.org/pressrelease.cfm?contentID=7135.

17. See, generally, "Farm bill dairy deal emerges," Jacqui Fatka, *Feedstuffs*, January 17, 2014. feedstuffs.com/story-farm-bill-dairy-deal-emerges-45-107470. "Budget Deal Would Slash Farm Bill Direct Spending," (National Sustainable Agriculture Coalition, Dec. 11 2013). sustainableagriculture.net/blog/fy14-budget-deal.

18. "Video: Chairwoman Stabenow–2013 Farm Bill on the Senate Floor" (FarmPolicy. com).
19. Transition provisions have been included in most of the serious farm bill proposals of this kind.
20. See the description of the Conservation Stewardship Program at the NRCS website www.nrcs.usda.gov/wps/portal/nrcs/main/national/programs/financial/csp.
21. Such as the efforts of Environmental Defense and American Farmland Trust leading on the 2008 Farm Bill.
22. For example: "New Farm Bill Offers Up Some Old Failings," Editorial Board, *Washington Post,* WP Politics, June 20, 2012. articles.washingtonpost.com/2012-06-20/ opinions/35459082_1_crop-insurance-direct-payment-program-direct-payments. "Farmers, Lawmakers Braced for Cuts in Subsidies," Jim Abrams, *Washington Post,* WP Politics, June 4, 2012). articles.washingtonpost.com/2012-06-04/politics/ 35461541_1_direct-payments-crop-insurance-farm-programs. "The Downfall of Direct Payments," Sara Sciammacco (Environmental Working Group, May 1, 2013). www.ewg.org/downfall-direct-payments.
23. "Table 8: Farms, Land in Farms, Value of Land and Buildings, and Land Use: 2007 and 2002" 2007 Census of Agriculture (USDA Census of Agriculture). www. agcensus.usda.gov/Publications/2007/Full_Report/Volume_1,_Chapter_2_US_ State_Level/st99_2_008_008.pdf.
24. Of course many small family farms are "incorporated." But average *gross* receipts from crops sold averages about $135,000 per year and less than 10 percent of U.S. farms earn total gross income of over $250,000 annually (crops sold plus government payments). See "Table 3: Economic Class of Farms by Market Value of Agricultural Products Sold and Government Payments," 2007 Census of Agriculture (USDA Census of Agriculture). www.agcensus.usda.gov/Publications/2007/Full_Report/ Volume_1,_Chapter_1_US/st99_1_003_003.pdf.
25. E.g., Sage Grouse Initiative. www.sagegrouseinitiative.com.
26. For example: "The CRP: Paying Farmers Not to Farm," Special Series: Going Green in Agriculture, Dan Charles (National Public Radio, July 15, 2005). www.npr.org/ templates/story/story.php?storyId=4736044.
27. "Conservation Reserve Program" (USDA/Farm Service Agency). www.fsa.usda.gov/ FSA/webapp?area=home&subject=copr&topic=crp.
28. "2013 AFBF Policy Book," Policy # 235 (American Farm Bureau Federation). www. texasfarmbureau.org/PolicyBook/AFBF%20Policy%202013.pdf.
29. "You are what you grow," Michael Pollan, *New York Times Magazine,* April 22, 2007. "Farm Bill Robs Poor to Pay Rich" (Center for American Progress, August 16, 2007). www.americanprogress.org/issues/2007/08/care.html.
30. "Farmers belong on a tractor, not under the bus," Mark Gerdes (*Ames Tribune,* June 7, 2013). amestrib.com/sections/opinion/columns/mark-gerdes-farmers-belong-on-tractor-not-under-the-bus.html#small.

Chapter 15: Tools for Dialogue—the Common Ground

1. Chapter 4.
2. Chapter 6.

3. Chapter 7.
4. Chapter 11.
5. Chapter 11.
6. See also "Dialogues with Agriculture: A Review of Processes Engaging Farm Groups in Protecting the Environment by Protecting Farmland," Don Stuart for the Farming and the Environment Project (American Farmland Trust, October 16, 2000).
7. See, e.g., "Presentation Skills: Presentation Preparation, Audience Analysis," *The Total Communicator*, Vol. 1, Issue 4 (Executive Communications Group, Fall 2003). totalcommunicator.com/audience_article.html.
8. See the website of the Northwest Center for Alternatives to Pesticides, www.pesticide. org.
9. For example, "Losing Ground: Farmland Protection in the Puget Sound Region," Dennis Canty, Alex Martinsons, and Anshika Kumar (American Farmland Trust, January 2002). www.farmland.org/documents/AFTLosingGroundReportWeb.pdf.

Chapter 16: Two Visions for the Future of Agriculture and the Environment

1. My respects to T.S. Eliot, "The Hollow Men," 1925.
2. *The Tipping Point: How Little Things Can Make a Big Difference*, Malcolm Gladwell (New York: Little Brown & Co., 2000).
3. See "Argument in Favor: The Family Farmers and Ranchers of Oregon Farm Bureau Ask You to Vote Yes on Measure 49," Measure 49 Voters Guide (Oregon Secretary of State). www.oregonvotes.org/pages/history/archive/nov62007/guide/m49_fav. html.
4. *The Big Sort: Why the Clustering of Like-Minded America Is Tearing Us Apart*, Bill Bishop (Boston: Houghton Mifflin Co., 2008).

About the Author

Don Stuart is a principal with Stuart Consulting. He is the former Pacific Northwest regional director for American Farmland Trust (AFT), a national nonprofit working to protect farmland and assure its environmentally sound management. Previously, he served as executive director for the Washington Association of Conservation Districts (WACD), and executive director for Salmon for Washington, a trade association representing commercial salmon fishermen and fish processing firms.

In all of these positions, Don dealt with public policy and environmental issues and lobbied at the local, state, and federal levels. He also served as campaign manager in the successful defense of a Washington statewide ballot initiative (I-640). In 1996, he ran for the United States Congress in Washington's 1st District.

Don's website at www.donstuart.net provides a wealth of research and written materials on agriculture, natural resources, and the environment.

Index

Ag practices act, 87–88, 97
Agricultural Conservation Easement Programs, 62, 171
Agricultural Risk Coverage program, 212
Air quality, 34, 52, 107, 130, 216
Amazon.com, 2
American Farmland Trust, 49, 115, 150, 243ch1n1, 248n30, 257n18, 262n1, 272n21
American Rivers, 45
Army Corps of Engineers, 54, 55, 70, 103, 110, 139
Audubon Society, 44–45

Baselines, 134, 136, 141, 194. *See also* Environmental markets; Offsets, environmental
Beecher's Cheese, 1
Benefits to the environment from agriculture, 145, 200, 207, 218, 232, 240; from conservation practices, 128–29, 130–31, 186–87, 202, 233; cost effectiveness of, 8, 23, 63, 79; from environmental markets, 136–39, 263n11; loss of when farms are lost, 25, 49, 50–52, 58–59
Best available technology, 78
Best management practices (BMPs), conservation practices, 34–35, 59, 105, 143, 151, 156, 159, 237; benefits from, 21, 63, 66, 98, 102; climate and, 187; consumer influence on, 145, 147–53; Costs of, 67, 132–33, 141, 207; environmental markets and, 128–29, 130–31, 138, 141; EQIP cost support for, 62; Farm Bill and, 214, 218, 251n4; Field Office Technical Guide and, 36, 51, 52–53, 263n12; livestock and, 81–82, 200, 207; pollution prevention with, 106, 87–88, 247n19, 248n36
Best practicable technology, 77
Bird's Point, Illinois, 110
Boeing, 2
Buffers, environmental, 50, 133, 135–36; benefits of, 137, 149; conflict over, 107, 111–13, 254n13; pollution and, 52, 53, 79, 87; salmon and, 3, 56, 62, 63, 87, 88, 111–13, 149, 254n14; wildlife habitat and, 23, 52, 173
Bureau of Land Management (BLM), 198, 199, 200, 205, 243Ch2n1, 267n8
Business vulnerabilities of farms. *See* Economic pressures on farm businesses

Cairo, IL, 110
Cap and trade, 128, 187, 188, 190, 192, 193, 194. *See also* Offsets, environmental
Carrying cost of investments in land, 16, 17, 26, 177, 178
Cattle. *See* Livestock
Cherry Valley Dairy, 1, 2, 4
Clean Air Act (CAA), 41, 47, 77, 90; climate and, 72, 129, 188, 189, 190, 191
Clean Water Act (CWA), 41, 47, 72, 84, 85, 90, 129, 160; nonpoint pollution and, 69, 95, 96; strengths of, 77, 80; weaknesses of, 79, 85–86; wetlands and, 35, 138, 139
Climate change, 23, 51, 93, 185–94, 264n21; impacts on agriculture from, 185–86; opportunities for agriculture to improve, 52, 147, 187–88, 250n9, 263n11. *See also* Impacts on the environment from agriculture; Waxman-Markey climate bill
Cochran, Larry, 21
Colvin, Fred, 207, 270n40
Common ground, 231–234. *See also* Dialogue between farmers and environmentalists; Successes in reaching cooperation
Competition in business of agriculture, 30–33
Conservation Districts, 3, 62, 75, 99, 159–61, 229, 259n31; conservation economics and, 54, 70, 135, 207; cost share assistance from, 66; environmental markets and, 143; functions of, 52, 61, 73, 74, 250n12; successes by, 74, 225, 243ch1n1
Conservation easements, agricultural, 232, 267n11; choosing between zoning and conservation easements, 163–184; cost of, 171–72, 261n15; effects/benefits of, 128, 131, 167–69, 170, 175, 179, 180; environmental markets and, 141; examples

of, 1, 3, 38, 53, 54, 197, 207, 248n30; programs to purchase, 62, 111, 172, 173, 174, 261nn18–19. *See also* Agricultural Conservation Easement Program (ACEP); Development rights, purchase of

Conservation economics, 10, 14, 36, 63; examples/stories of, 21, 37, 47, 54, 70, 98, 120, 135, 149, 150, 152, 189, 202

Conservation Reserve Enhancement Program (CREP), 61, 62, 135, 254n13

Conservation Reserve Program (CRP), 61, 62, 218, 220, 263n11,

Conservation Stewardship Program (CSP), 62, 74, 218, 263n11, 272n20

Consumer influence, 13, 43, 105, 142, 145–53, 156; examples of, 36, 149, 150; tools and opportunities for, 9, 145–46, 147, 148, 153, 155, 158, 233, 240

Consumer Product Safety Administration, 84

Coordinated Resource Management (CRM), 201–202

Cost of community services studies, 115–16, 232, 262n25

Costs of environmental gains, 8, 25, 53, 84, 151; assistance with, 36, 53, 62, 66, 103, 193, 251n2; impact of on farmers, 3, 36, 57, 59, 105, 187–88, 193; relevance of, 62–66, 67–69, 92–93, 95–97, 99–100, 102. *See also* Effectiveness of environmental improvement; Environmental markets; Fairness in environmental improvement; Incentives for conservation

Cost of purchasing development rights, 171–172

Cost of regulation, 11, 22, 40, 77, 95

Cost of returning developed land to agriculture, 49

Cost share incentives assistance, 81, 105, 159, 160, 207, 218, 236; concerns about, 66, 67–69, 132–33; USDA programs, 36, 62, 103

Critical areas ordinances, 88, 254n15

Department of Ecology (DOE) (Washington State), 47, 80

Development rights, purchase of (PDR), 167–69, 179–83, 232, 260n11; cost of PDR, 119, 171–72; creditworthiness and

PDR, 179–180; environmental markets, utility in, 131, 141, 142; financial management and PDR, 180; growth management combined with PDR, 169–71; need for, 26, 27, 51; programs for purchase of, 10, 173, 174, 261n14. *See also* Environmental markets

Dialogue between farmers and environmentalists, 225–234; linkage and how to avoid it, 230–231; tools for, 226–230. *See also* Common ground; Successes in reaching cooperation

Diversity in agricultural lands and crops, 30

Dix, David, 209, 210

Duvall, WA, 2, 4

Easements, agricultural conservation, 1, 111, 175, 197, 232, 261n15, 261nn18–19, 267n11; choosing between zoning and, 167–72; effect on environmental improvement, 3, 21, 128, 131; environmental markets and, 141; examples of, 38, 53, 54, 62, 172, 172–74, 207, 248n30. *See also* Development rights, purchase of

Economic drivers for farmland loss, 15–20

Economic pressures on farm businesses, 30–33, 56–57, 201. *See also* Farmland loss, causes of

Ecosystem services markets. *See* Environmental markets

Effectiveness of environmental improvements, cost effectiveness; criteria in choice between incentives and regulations, 102–103, 104; environmental markets and, 127, 134, 144; environmental regulation and, 72, 77, 85, 87; funding and, 73–75; land use management, 10, 12, 163, 166; need for, 8; opportunities for on agricultural land, 39, 50, 51–52, 97, 105, 233; voluntary incentives and, 10, 63, 64, 66, 68. *See also* Cost of environmental gains

Endangered Species Act (ESA), 47, 70, 72, 77, 90, 129

Environmental markets, 10, 58, 127–44, 172, 206, 232, 240, 241, 256n6, 257n18; benefits for agriculture from, 141–42; benefits for the environment from, 137–39. *See also* Baselines; Offsets, environmental

Environmental Protection Agency (EPA), 35, 94, 103, 150; TMDL enforcement, 86, 90; examples of enforcement by, 80, 82, 151; nature of enforcement by, 90, 252n11; wetlands and, 139; environmental markets and, 188, 189, 190, 191, 264n21, 265n31

Environmental Quality Incentives Program (EQIP), 62, 218, 251n2, 251n4, 263n11

Fairness in environmental responsibility, 3, 12, 40, 46, 59, 93; criteria for choice between incentives and regulations, 100–102, 103, 104, 105; environmental markets and, 134, 142; farmland protection and, 26, 27; incentives and, 10, 66, 134; livestock grazing on public lands and, 200; political action and, 90, 91, 92, 93, 97, 178; regulations and, 9, 66, 80–83, 85, 134, 109

Farm Bill, 61, 155, 211–223; climate and, 187; coalitions needed for, 217–19, 219–21; commodity programs, 76, 212–17; conservation programs, 217–19; nutrition and, 146; rationale for public support of, 221–23; spending levels in, 211–12; subsidies under, 118, 119, 124

Farm Bureau, 97, 108, 135, 220, 242, 249n39; climate positions of, 188, 190–91, 193, 265n28; local food positions of, 155; property rights positions of, 260nn9–10

Farm Service Agency (FSA), 61

Farmers markets, 53, 145, 148, 155, 158

Farmland loss, 15–29, 163, 165, 166; causes of, 15–20, 142, 143, 166, 167, 177–78, 182, 245n22; conservation advantage of preventing, 183; consequences of, 25–26, 51–56, 57, 117, 141, 147, 177, 183, 186; reversibility of, 49. *See also* Benefits to the environment from agriculture; Development rights, purchase of (PDR); Zoning and farmland loss

Federal Aviation Administration, 84

Federal Emergency Management Agency (FEMA), 130

Federal Trade Commission, 84

Field Office Technical Guide (FOTG), 36, 52, 200

Fish Friendly Farming certification, 148

Florida Green Swamp Authority, 172–74, 225

Food Alliance, 148, 149

Food and Drug Administration (FDA), 35

Food Quality Protection Act (FQPA), 35

Gates, Bill, 112

Gordon, Jay, Gordon Dairy, 37–38

Growth management. *See* Zoning

Human health, 93, 216; consumer concerns about, 145, 147, 150, 155, 158; farm bill and, 216–17, 218, 222; farm family, impacts on, 33, 107, 151, 157; risks to, 35

Impacts on the environment from agriculture, 29, 158, 204–206, 208, 254n14, 268n14; climate, 186–88, 250n9; examples of, 36–37, 71, 95, 95, 98, 216; livestock, 195–96, 198, 200–201, 207; pesticides, 8, 34, 35–36, 95, 150, 233; potentials for damage, 7–8, 33–36, 58

Incentives for conservation, 12, 13, 59, 61–76, 77, 81, 241; advantages and disadvantages, 25, 62–66; choosing between incentives and regulations, 42, 99–114, 252ch5n8; difficulty to secure, 43, 69, 72–75, 76, 86–87, 97; environmental markets and incentives, 132, 133, 134, 138, 141, 142, 194; examples of, 53, 62, 88–89, 94, 226; funding for, 10, 12, 231, 233, 236, 238; limits to and disadvantages of, 58, 67–69, 75–76; taxes, spending, and incentives, 119, 121, 122–23, 124, 125. *See also* Regulation of farming

Infrastructure loss of farm support businesses, 25, 116, 165, 237, 255n4

Initiative 640, 44, 45, 208, 209

Inspection and licensing, 84

Integrated pest management (IPM), 36, 150, 233

Jordan, Martha, Trumpeter Swan Society, 38, 248n27

Just say no, 40–42, 46–47, 96, 108, 109, 143, 237, 240

King County, WA, 1–4

Lake Washington, WA, 111–113

Land uses in U.S., 15–16, 195
Livestock and the environment, 195–211; impacts on environment, 198; land cost pressures on livestock industry, 196–197; public lands grazing, 198–201, 206–207. *See also* Coordinated Resource Management CRM
Local food, 1, 11, 22, 26, 57, 233, 236; environmental significance of, 51, 147–48, 158, 250n9, 257n5; farmland loss and, 51; political significance of, 43, 142, 145–46, 154–55, 258n6; successes for, 53, 149, 150, 151. *See also* Human health; Consumer influence

Marine Mammal Protection Act (MMPA), 72, 77
Marketplace as solution for farmland loss, 26–27
Meyers, Scott, Sweet Grass Farm, 98
Michigan Agriculture Environmental Assurance Program (MAEAP), 105–106, 225
Microsoft, 2, 112
Migratory Bird Treaty Act, 44
Mitigation, environmental, 23, 64, 130, 232; cost of, 3; farmland loss and, 50, 128, 139–40, 237, 238; funding for, 133; benefits for environment from, 136–39, 187, 191–92; benefits for agriculture from, 141–42, 158; opportunities for, 9, 51, 158; need for, 5, 9, 10, 25, 127, 128–29. *See also* Baselines, Cap and trade; Environmental markets; Offsets, environmental

Natural Resources Conservation Service (NRCS), 36, 51, 61, 157, 200, 211, 243ch1n1, 247n19
Nature Conservancy, 121
Nelson, Eric, 1–5, 86
New Deal, 212
New York City Watershed Project, 52–53, 75, 225
Nisqually River, 149
Nonpoint pollution, 72; alternative approaches to, 79, 81; dairies and, 87; farmland loss and, 23, 50; incentives and, 69, 252n11; political strategy for, 94–96; regulatory limits in controlling, 72, 77, 85–87, 87–88;

urban development and, 50. *See also* Water quality; Air quality
Nooksack River, 54–55
Nooksack Indian Tribe, 54
Nordstrom, 2
NORPAC Foods, of Stayton, OR, 148, 150–151
Northwest Chinook Recovery, 135

Offset ratios, 138
Offsets, environmental, 232; benefits for agriculture from, 136–39, 187, 188, 193–94; benefits for environment from, 128–29; need for, 10, 191; opportunities for, 51, 130, 133. *See also* Baselines, Cap and trade; Environmental markets; Mitigation, environmental
Opportunities to improve environmental performance, 8, 9, 13, 36, 39; climate, 187–88; 193–94; environmental markets, 127–29, 130–31, 137–139, 141–44; farm bill, 211, 222; farmland loss and, 3, 8, 23, 51–52, 58–59, 237–38; growth management and, 124–125; local food, 148–53, 158; political, 107, 114; successes in making use of, 53; wetlands, 139–40. *See also* Benefits to the environment from agriculture; Consumer influence

PCC Natural Markets, 152
Permits, environmental, 2, 3, 4, 90; dairies and, 84; environmental markets and, 130, 138; growth management and, 112, 165, 166; mitigation conditions, 64; political issues and, 95–97; water quality (NPDES) permits, 78–80, 86. *See also* Environmental markets; Permits, grazing on public lands; Zoning;
Permits, lgrazing on public lands, 197–201, 202, 205, 243ch2n1, 267n8, 268n21, 269n26. *See also* Livestock and the environment; Permits, environmental, Public lands
Pierce County, WA, 2
Pike Place Market, 1
Price Loss Coverage program (PLC), 212, 213, 270n5
Privacy for farmers, 153–54, 155–57, 158–61

Public lands, 127, 195, 197, 198–201, 206, 243ch2n1, 269n33, 269n37. *See also* Livestock and the environment; Permits, grazing on public lands

Qualco Energy, 189

Regulation of farming, 13, 77–79, 84–85, 92, 231–33; choice between incentives and, 11–12, 59, 99–114, 134; climate and, 188–91, 193; constraints on, 83–84, 85–87; environmental markets and, 129, 130, 134,141–42; examples of, 47, 53, 88–89, 98, 105–109, 110–113,172–74, 225–26; farmland loss and, 22, 23, 25; free market and, 26–27, 121; growth management and, 163–167, 181; need for, 9, 10, 58, 76, 94–96, 157, 236–37; overregulation, risk of, 11, 53, 56–57; political strategy on, 96–97, 99, 107–109; practicality of, 87–88; strengths of, 66, 80–83; takings and, 107; weaknesses/limits of, 13, 64, 65, 66, 80–83, 134; wetlands and, 35, 50, 98. *See also* Inspection and licensing; Strict regulatory liability; Incentives for conservation
Reiner, Dale, cattle rancher, 135–36
Riparian areas, 79; benefit to environment, 79, 137; conflict over, 111–112, 159; cost share assistance for, 62; examples of protection for, 53, 54, 71, 88, 135, 137, 173; farmland loss and, 8, 23, 45; impact of agriculture on, 35, 37; impact on agriculture, 3, 111, 254n14; livestock and, 201; opportunities to improve, 52; takings and, 107. *See also* Buffers, environmental; Salmon
Ruckelshaus Process, Washington State, 88–89, 225

Salmon, 44, 82,132, 209; examples of projects to protect, 54–55, 70–71, 88, 98, 135, 149, 189, 202; impact of agriculture on, 2–4, 37. *See also* Buffers, environmental; Riparian areas
Salmon-Safe certification, 148, 149, 259n17
Seattle, WA, 1–2, 111–13, 149, 152, 170
Sierra Club, 45, 242
Skagit Valley, Skagit County, WA, 120–21, 170, 260n6

Snohomish County, WA, 2, 70, 135
Snoqualmie River, 2, 4, 189
Stability in real estate investment, 182–83
State Environmental Policy Act (SEPA), 112
Stewardship Partners of Seattle, 149
Strict regulatory liability, 85–87
Successes in cooperation, 75; balance and fairness, 12; common factors in, 225–26; examples of, 52–53, 88–89, 105–106, 172–74. *See also* Common ground; Conservation Economics; Dialogue between farmers and environmentalists
SYSCO Corporation, food supplier, 150–51

Takings as a grounds for regulatory relief, 40, 90, 107, 111, 167, 178–79, 181, 183; givings and takings, 178–79
Taxes, 115–27, 168, 231, 255n8; climate and, 188, 192, 194; cost of community services, 115–16, 124, 232; development rights and, 26, 171, 177, 261n17; growth management and, 117–119; incentives and, 76, 122; politics of, 76, 95–97, 108, 122–123; public responsibility for environmental harm and, 43, 101, 113
Tide gates, 70–71
Tillamook Creamery, 152
T-Mobile, 2
Total maximum daily load (TMDL), 47, 78, 86, 96, 105, 129
Transfer of development rights (TDR), 172, 261n17
Trumpeter swans, 37–38, 248n30
Tulalip Indian Tribes, 189

U.S. Fish & Wildlife Service (USFWS), 44, 103, 173, 198,
U.S. Forest Service (USFS), 198, 199, 205

Voluntary conservation. *See* Incentives for conservation
Vulnerability of farm businesses. *See* Economic pressures on farm businesses

Washington Association of Conservation Districts, 99, 207
Water quality, 206; environmental markets and, 128, 130; examples of success in

improving, 21, 47, 52–53, 105, 189; farm benefits for, 8, 50, 52; farm bill and, 216, 221; farm impacts on, 34, 94; livestock and, 198, 201; politics of, 41, 90, 94–96, 96–97; strategies for improving, 72, 77–79, 87, 131; wetlands and, 140. *See also*, Clean Water Act

Waxman-Markey climate bill; benefits for agriculture from, 93, 187–88; impacts on agriculture, 93,187–88, 264n22; opposition to, 190–91, 192; politics of, 192, 193, 194; support for, 191, 264n23, 265n37. *See also* Climate change

Wetlands; environmental markets, 128, 129, 130, 131, 133; examples of successes for, 37, 98, 121, 173; farmland loss and, 13, 22, 142–44, 237, 238; impacts of, 56; impacts on, 29, 35, 50–51, 250nn6–7, incentives and, 64, 102; livestock and, 201; mitigation system, 138, 139–40, opportunities for protection of, 8, 52, 62; politics of, 58, 221; social responsibility for, 45–46. *See also* Clean Water Act; Water quality

Wetlands Reserve Program (WRP), 74, 263n11

Whatcom County, WA, 54

Wilcox Family Farms, 149

Wildlife habitat, 13, 56; environmental markets and, 128, 129, 130–133, 136, 173, 189; examples of successes for, 37–38, 54, 70, 88, 98, 120, 135, 149; farm benefits for, 4, 23, 50, 144; farm bill programs and, 216, 218, 220, 221; impacts on, 2, 8, 34, 35, 37; Incentives and, 74, 102; livestock grazing and, 199, 205; local food and, 147, 148, 158; opportunities to improve, 51, 52, 63, 64, 137; salmon, 3, 88, 111; watershed approach to, 79, 139–40; *See also* Buffers, environmental; Riparian areas; Salmon

Wildlife Habitat Incentives Program (WHIP), 74, 251n2, 263n11

Willamette Valley, Oregon, 150–151

Wisconsin Farming and Conservation Together (FACT), 172–173, 225

World Trade Organization (WTO), 214, 215, 218, 222

Yakima River, 47–48\

Zoning, 7, 10, 26, 27, 51; combined with purchased development rights, 169–71; conservation easements and zoning compared, 163–83, 165n3, 262n24; growth management, tools for, 163–167; parcel size restrictions, 164; uncertainties of, 182; use restrictions, 165